1983 UPDATE

OF

SCRIPPS-HOWARD

HANDBOOK

Third Edition 1981

Poynter Institute for Media Studies
Library

AUG 1 7 '87

THE PURPOSE OF THIS SUPPLEMENT is to bring readers up to date on changes in the Scripps-Howard organization since publication of the last Scripps-Howard Handbook in 1981.

There are a host of new faces in important positions. Individual properties have expanded. There have been acquisitions, and there have been divestitures. The title of business manager at newspapers has become general manager to give a better description of duties, although the general manager and the editor remain co-managers of the local operation.

We have included a number of biographical profiles, but because of space limitations they are not as complete as those in the permanent Handbook.

In the area of personnel, five new positions were created in Scripps-Howard's central office in Cincinnati: Vice president, services/special publications; director of advertising; director of operations/metro newspapers; director of operations/city newspapers; and graphics director. A new director of circulation was named.

New editors were appointed at daily newspapers in El Paso and Birmingham, while new general managers were named in Pittsburgh, Fullerton, Stuart and Evansville. General managers also were appointed at non-daily publications in Southern California, Bardstown, Ky., and Jupiter, Fla., and the Scripps-Howard Web Press Co. in Louisville.

Scripps-Howard Broadcasting Co. announced a new officer with the title of senior vice president, a new vice president, a new president of its Cable Services Co., and a new director of engineering. New general managers were appointed at broadcast stations in West Palm Beach and Portland, Ore., and a third was reassigned to Cincinnati.

A new chairman of the board and a new president/chief executive officer stepped up at Cordovan Corp. and the Scripps-Howard legal team at Baker & Hostetler got a new captain.

The Scripps-Howard Foundation, in its desire to further excellence in journalism through education, announced a gift of $1.5 million to Ohio University, and the university renamed its journalism school for E. W. Scripps.

Among properties acquired or launched were a newspaper advertising art and copy service in California; three new business journals by Cordovan Corp.; an AM & FM radio station in Portland, Ore.; cable television service ventures in Knoxville and Pittsburgh and five cable franchises across the country. In Jupiter, Fla., another newspaper was acquired and merged with the Courier. Southern California Publishing Co. started five more weekly newspapers.

Divestitures included United Press International, WNOX-AM in Knoxville, Campbell County (Ky.) News and Scripps-Howard Press in Louisville.

CONTENTS

GENERAL MANAGEMENT and DAILY NEWSPAPERS
Highlights..4
Banks Leonard 6
Robert A. Eisenbraun.............................6
Gilles R. Champagne 7
Randy Cochran...................................8
Tony Delmonico 8
David W. Brown 9
Harry Moskos...................................10
Robert J. Hively 10
William A. Holcombe............................11
Gardner Pate 12

SCRIPPS-HOWARD BROADCASTING COMPANY
Highlights......................................13
Warren P. Happel...............................14
William J. Brooks...............................14
Robert M. Oxarart 15

SOME SCRIPPS-HOWARD INSTITUTIONS
Highlights......................................16
SHNS Staff Changes 17
Frank Whitehead 18

OTHER PUBLISHING ENTERPRISES
Highlights......................................19
Gerald Lush 20
Patricia Hoddinott 21

ERRATA..22

Published by
THE E. W. SCRIPPS COMPANY
Central Trust Tower, Cincinnati, Ohio 45202

Third revised edition, January, 1981
Supplement to third revised edition, April, 1983

This supplement was set in type and produced by the Memphis Publishing Company. Copy by James H. Wagner and Susan A. Alexander of the Editorial Promotion office of Scripps-Howard Newspapers.

GENERAL MANAGEMENT AND DAILY NEWSPAPERS

1981 HIGHLIGHTS

Scripps-Howard headquarters in Cincinnati expanded to include new executives. **Robert J. O'Connell** came from The Pittsburgh Press Co. to become director of advertising (biography Page 290); **Gilles R. Champagne** came from The Knoxville News-Sentinel Co. to become director of operations/city newspapers; and **Randy Cochran** moved across town from The Cincinnati Post to become graphics director. General business manager **Robert H. Hartmann** added to his duties by becoming a vice president of The E. W. Scripps Co., (biography Page 134), and **J. Robert Routt** was named director of financial analysis. At Baker & Hostetler offices in Cleveland, **John H. Burlingame** was named head of the Scripps-Howard legal team succeeding **Sherman Dye**, who now serves as counsel to The E. W. Scripps Trust (biography Page 163). At the newspaper level, **Harry Moskos** went from executive editor to editor of the El Paso Herald-Post succeeding **Robert W. Lee**, who retired (biography Page 252), while **Banks Leonard** went from Memphis to become president/general manager of the Evansville Printing Corp.; **William A. Holcombe** moved from Cleveland to become vice president/general manager of The Pittsburgh Press Co.; and **Robert J. Hively** left Memphis to become vice president/ general manager of the Daily News Tribune, Fullerton, succeeding Melvin A. Harkavy. (Harkavy's new position is listed on Page 19 of this supplement.)

1982 HIGHLIGHTS

Appointments and retirements marked this year. **David W. Brown** was named editor of the Birmingham Post-Herald and **Angus McEachran**, whom he succeeded, was appointed executive editor of The Pittsburgh Press (biography Page 223). At The Stuart News, **Gardner Pate** moved from The

Pittsburgh Press Co. to become president and general manager. Two longtime executives on the business side retired: **John Feldmann** as business manager of The Cincinnati Post and The Kentucky Post (biography Page 233), and **W. H. Metz** as vice president of the Birmingham Post-Herald (biography Page 226).

1983 HIGHLIGHTS

Banks Leonard moved from president/general manager of the Evansville Printing Corp. to vice president, services/special publications, heading a new division of The E. W. Scripps Co. at its Cincinnati headquarters. **Jimmy E. Manis**, director of circulation for Scripps-Howard Newspapers (biography Page 153), succeeded Leonard at Evansville and **Tony J. Delmonico**, circulation director of the Rocky Mountain News since 1975, replaced Manis in Cincinnati. **Robert A. Eisenbraun**, director of finance at the Newspaper Printing Corp. in El Paso since 1977, was named to the newly-created position of director of operations/metro newspapers of Scripps-Howard Newspapers.

Banks Leonard
Vice President, Services/Special Publications
Scripps-Howard Newspapers

IF YOU WONDER HOW a man could go from the dairy business to publishing, then meet Banks and hear his answer. Both deal with highly perishable commodities.

Born Dec. 1, 1932, Banks was graduated from North Carolina State University where his major was, yes, dairy manufacturing. Post grad study and Army service followed, and then came 10 years in the cost accounting end of firms dealing with dairy products. In 1966 he joined the Memphis Publishing Co. and by 1978 held three titles: controller, assistant to the business manager and assistant secretary-treasurer.

When in March, 1981, the presidency and general managership of the Evansville Printing Corp. opened up and Walter Goeltz retired to become general manager of the Evansville Courier, Banks got the job. He came to his present position in February, 1983, when a new division of The E. W. Scripps Co. was formed.

Banks is a director of The Scripps-Howard Foundation. His wife is Anne. He has two sons, Lee and David, by a previous marriage.

Robert A. Eisenbraun
Director of Operations/Metro Newspapers
Scripps-Howard Newspapers

IT WAS HIS financial background and the operational responsibilities he'd had on newspapers that made Bob the choice to head up the newly-created position of director of operations/metro newspapers, which makes him overseer of the business side of Scripps-Howard's major newspaper properties while reporting to Bob Hartmann.

Eisenbraun, 54, came to Cincinnati from the Newspaper Printing Corp. in El Paso, where since 1977 he'd been director of finance.

A native of Rochester, N.Y., Bob was graduated from the University of Pennsylvania's Wharton School of Finance. For

16 years he held accounting positions in Rochester before joining the corporate staff of Gannett Co., Inc. In 1968, he was named controller of Gannett, a job he performed, in addition to other financial duties, until he went to El Paso.

Bob's family consists of his wife, Joan, and his three adopted children: Mary Jo, Lu Ann and Matthew. He also has four children from a previous marriage: Jeff, Gayle, Eric and Gary.

Gilles R. Champagne
Director of Operations/City Newspapers
Scripps-Howard Newspapers

GIL SKATED through the early part of his life—literally.

Born March 1, 1936, in Hull, Quebec, Gil was raised on ice skating rinks. At 16, he was recruited by the Montreal Canadians and played with its farm teams while attending St. Jean Military College and the University of Ottawa.

In 1961, he moved to Knoxville to introduce hockey to that city. Two years later he joined The Knoxville News-Sentinel Co. Promotions to national advertising manager, advertising manager and assistant business manager followed.

Gil was appointed to his present position in 1981, where he oversees the activities of the concern's smaller newspaper properties. He's also in charge of Scripps-Howard's business relationship with cable TV in its newspaper markets. As such, he is directly responsible for the Tele/Scripps cable operations in Knoxville and Pittsburgh.

Gil and his wife, Magella, have five grown children: Pierre, Gilles Jr., Jo Anne, Jocelyne and Michel.

Randy Cochran
Graphics Director
Scripps-Howard Newspapers

IF IT HADN'T BEEN for the destruction of a bridge spanning the Ohio River in 1970, it is questionable whether Randy would today be in newspapers. His principal means of livelihood that year came from owning an antique store/gift shop, but when money ran short he would moonlight at photography.

He was on the horns of such a dilemma when he persuaded Vance Trimble, then editor of The Kentucky Post, to hire him on a one-day trial basis. His assignment was to photograph 10 news subjects, most important of which was a bridge that workers were blowing up to make way for a new one.

The following day Randy's bridge picture appeared on Page One of The Post, and the day after that he was named photo editor.

In the years since, Randy, now 38, has been assistant managing editor of The Kentucky Post, assistant managing editor/graphics of The Cincinnati Post and, since Sept. 1, 1981, graphics director of all Scripps-Howard newspapers. He describes his responsibilities as "running my mouth and waving my hands a lot."

Randy and his wife Jane have two cats, two dogs and several hives of bees.

Tony Delmonico
Director of Circulation
Scripps-Howard Newspapers

WHEN TONY, 55, came to Cincinnati from Denver to succeed Jimmy Manis as director of circulation, Bob Hartmann said of him:

"In his nearly 26 years at the Rocky Mountain News, Tony has been one of those most instrumental in making the News Colorado's largest daily newspaper and one of America's fastest growing newspapers."

Tony began his newspaper career as a vacation relief

district manager at the News in 1951, after graduating from Colorado University. He later got a master's degree from Denver University.

From 1950-55, he was a high school teacher and coached athletics in Salida, Colo., where he and his wife, Vivian, had the News distributorship to help supplement their income.

Tony joined the News full time in 1957, and climbed the ladder from metro district manager to circulation director.

The Delmonicos have four grown sons: Neal, Doug, Scott and Jeff.

David W. Brown
Editor
Birmingham Post-Herald

IN 1968, DAVID ducked a brick . . . and came up with a career. The place was Ohio University, where he was a junior and a part-time reporter for the school newspaper. One April night, the campus "exploded." A "spring riot" had become the real thing and David covered the story. From then on, he was hooked on newspapering.

His first job after college was general assignment reporter at The Kentucky Post in Covington, near hometown Ludlow. Inside a year he'd won a Meeman Award for a series on pollution and been assigned to Frankfort as capital bureau chief.

He became city editor of The Post in 1972, and four years later was named associate managing editor for news. In 1978, he became managing editor. In 1980, the managing editorship of the Birmingham Post-Herald beckoned and he took it. When editor Angus McEachran moved to Pittsburgh in 1982, David was named editor of the Post-Herald. He was 34.

David and his wife, Donna, have four children: Jennifer, Caroline, Sarah and David Wayne II.

Harry Moskos
Editor
El Paso Herald-Post

WHEN IN THE fifth grade, Harry started his own newspaper because he didn't like the way the school paper was covering the news. Officially, he started his career with The Albuquerque Tribune at age 16 as operator of a UPI telephoto machine.

Harry moves at a break-neck pace and believes in covering the news aggressively and with enterprise. He also believes in community involvement and seldom lets a week go by without giving a speech or attending several community functions.

After graduating from the University of New Mexico in 1958, Harry became editor of the Grants (N.M.) Daily Beacon. He joined The Associated Press in Albuquerque in 1960 and by 1963, was AP's Honolulu bureau chief.

He returned to The Tribune in 1969 as city editor and in 1973 was named managing editor. He went to El Paso as executive editor in 1980, and became editor the following year.

The son of Greek immigrants, Harry was born in Chicago on Oct. 8, 1936. He and his wife, Victoria, have three children: Areti, Xrisanthe and Matthew.

Robert J. Hively
Vice President/General Manager
Fullerton Daily News Tribune

BOB WAS five years old when he landed his first newspaper job on his father's weekly in a small Nebraska town. He picked up ad proofs after kindergarten and carried them to advertisers for corrections. He liked the work because they always had candy for him.

Since then Bob, who was born Oct. 12, 1941, has known few jobs that have not involved newspapers. First came the paper in Great Bend, Kan., where in 1961 he climbed aboard as district manager. Three years later he became circulation manager for the Mercury in Manhattan, Kan. In 1972 he joined the Rockford (Ill.) Newspapers, Inc., and in 1975 Scripps-Howard tapped him as circulation director for The Cincinnati Post. From there he went to the Memphis Publishing Co., where he was circulation director for both newspapers. After five years in Memphis, Bob was offered the position of business manager at the Daily News Tribune, and later was promoted to vice president/general manager.

Bob and his wife, Mary, whom he met at the Memphis papers, both enjoy jogging. Bob has two children by a former marriage: Seth and Angie.

William A. Holcombe
Vice President/General Manager
The Pittsburgh Press

BILL GOT INTO newspapering by writing Boy Scout news for his hometown Trenton Times in exchange for free summer camp. The Army got him after high school and he served three years with the infantry in the Pacific.

After college at the University of Missouri, Bill sold insurance, edited a trade journal, and worked for the American Management Association.

In 1956, he signed on at the Cincinnati Enquirer doing labor relations and management planning work. Next came The New York Times and ultimately the job of assistant to the executive editor. After eight years in the Big Apple, he joined The Cleveland Press. In 1976, he became its business manager. He was named to his present job in 1981.

Bill was born July 8, 1924. He and his wife Jane Ellen have twin daughters: Polly and Susan.

Gardner Pate
President/General Manager
The Stuart News

GARDNER'S GRANDFATHER carried a printing press to Oklahoma in a covered wagon, and his father owned a county weekly, on which Gardner worked at age 12 operating a Linotype machine.

At 22, Gardner owned a weekly himself, but sold it when he concluded it was a good way to starve and work himself to death. Gardner served in the Army Air Forces in WW II, then attended the University of Arkansas and the University of Missouri. He joined the Okmulgee (Okla.) Times and later worked for the Mangum (Okla.) Star, the Madill (Okla.) Record, the Coalgate (Okla.) Record-Register and Mergenthaler Linotype Co.

His Scripps-Howard career began in 1965 as assistant production manager of the Memphis Publishing Co. In 1972, he went to The Cleveland Press as production manager. He transferred to The Pittsburgh Press in 1976 as production manager, and was assistant business manager/operations when the move to Stuart and his present job came in 1982.

Gardner and his wife, Honey, have two sons: Jack, who sells advertising for the Hollywood Sun-Tattler; and Mike, who is general manager of the Myrtle Beach (S. Car.) Sun News.

SCRIPPS-HOWARD BROADCASTING COMPANY

1981 HIGHLIGHTS

The Scripps-Howard Broadcasting Co.'s cable holdings expanded when it acquired **T&W Cable Co.** in DeBary, Fla., and **Lake County (Fla.) Cablevision**. Franchises in Fairfield County, Conn., were won by Cablevision of Connecticut, a partnership of Charles Dolan's Cablevision and Scripps-Howard Cablevision, a wholly-owned subsidiary of Scripps-Howard Broadcasting. (Prior to 1981, SHBCO formed a cable partnership with Daniels & Associates to acquire the franchise in Ann Arbor, Mich.) **Lawrence A. Leser** was elected a SHBCO director (biography Page 125), while **Mortimer C. Watters** retired as a director to become consulting director (biography Page 334), and Robert D. Gordon resigned from the board. Radio stations **KUPL-AM & FM** in Portland, Ore., were purchased and KBMA-TV in Kansas City, Mo., changed its call letters to **KSHB**. **Albert J.** Schottelkotte was elected senior vice president of SHBCO (biography Page 339), and **Warren P. Happel** succeeded James E. Bloyd as the company's director of engineering. **Robert R. Regalbuto** was named general manager of WCPO-TV in Cincinnati (biography Page 357), and succeeding him as general manager of WPTV in West Palm Beach was **William J. Brooks**.

1982 HIGHLIGHTS

Cable was on the move again, with **Tulare Communications Corp.**, Tulare County, Calif., winning a series of cable franchises, and **Longmont Communications Corp.** winning the cable franchise in Longmont, Colo. WNOX-AM in Knoxville was sold. **Edward D. Cervenak** was elected a SHBCO director (biography Page 348) and **Richard J. Janssen** was elected a vice president (biography Page 344).

1983 HIGHLIGHTS

Michael W. Callaghan, assistant to the president of SHBCO, was named president of Scripps-Howard Cable Services Co., a Cleveland-based subsidiary (biography Page 346).

Warren P. Happel
Director of Engineering
Scripps-Howard Broadcasting Co.

WARREN JOINED THE NAVY in 1951 because electronics school was promised as an incentive for enlisting. He was discharged in 1955, and went to work as an engineer at KHQA-TV in Quincy, Ill., his hometown.

Warren attended Valparaiso University and Quincy College before getting a degree in electrical engineering from the University of Michigan. After graduation he became the chief engineer at the East Lansing television station operated by Michigan State University.

In 1964, Warren joined RCA as a broadcast equipment salesman, and while there met his wife Diane. He later worked as a consulting engineer for a telecommunications firm that provided services to the television, radio and growing CATV industry. In 1981, he brought his expertise to Scripps-Howard Broadcasting when he became its director of engineering in Cleveland.

Warren was born Sept. 13, 1931. The Happels have three children: Paul, Eric and Cara.

William J. Brooks
General Manager
WPTV

BILL WAS BORN Dec. 13, 1933, in Boston. Though the men of his family were firefighters and he considered for a time a career as a professional baseball player, he decided on a life of public service, which eventually led to Scripps-Howard's WPTV.

Bill holds three degrees: a bachelor of arts cum laude from Oblate College in Washington, D.C.; a bachelor of divinity from Catholic University; and a master's from Boston College.

His broadcast career began in West Palm Beach in 1972 as host of a weekly radio program. In 1973, Bob Regalbuto discovered Bill and brought him to WPTV, where he became assistant station manager in 1976, station manager in 1977, and general manager in 1981, when Regalbuto moved to Cincinnati to take over WCPO-TV.

Bill and his wife Martha live in Palm Beach.

Robert M. Oxarart
General Manager
KUPL-AM & FM

BOB GOT HIS EARLY JOB training working for his dad, who produced TV shows and sold food merchandising programs for radio stations in the Los Angeles area. From these beginnings, he entered Stanford University, where he met his wife Ann. There was a brief interruption at Stanford for Army service. He returned to finish while doing stints as a radio deejay and selling advertising time.

Bob got his first management chance with a radio station in Fresno, and later worked for a number of L.A. stations. In 1973, he moved to Seattle as general manager of an AM/FM station, and two years later went to Portland to take over KPOK (now KUPL-AM) and KUPL-FM. Today these stations are the number one adult radio combination in the market.

Bob was born June 16, 1936. He and Ann have two daughters: Leslie and Kathy.

SOME SCRIPPS-HOWARD INSTITUTIONS

The Washington Bureau/
  Scripps-Howard News Service
United Media Enterprises
Berkley-Small, Inc.
Scripps-Howard Foundation
SCW, Inc.
Tele/Scripps

1981 HIGHLIGHTS

SCW, Inc., an international newspaper advertising art and copy service based in California, was purchased and added to the roster of E.W. Scripps Co. properties in March. At United Media Enterprises, United Media Marketing Services introduced **TV Extra,** an advertising and promotional service for TV programs via newspapers and cable; **The World Almanac** developed its educational division into a total merchandising program for the educational market; and **Snoopy Place,** the first official PEANUTS retail store, opened in Hackensack, N.J. **Berkley-Small, Inc.** moved into new offices in Mobile, Ala., and added an incentive division. At Scripps-Howard News Service, **James E. Foster** became assistant managing editor (biography Page 179) and **Berl Schwartz** was named coordinator of outside contributions to the Scripps-Howard News Service wire (biography Page 185).

1982 HIGHLIGHTS

1982 was a climactic year for a college and a cat. In an effort to further excellence in journalism through education, **The Scripps-Howard Foundation** donated $1.5 million to Ohio University and its school of journalism, renamed after E.W. Scripps. Garfield, Jim Davis' cynical cat, became a major United Feature Syndicate success story, with the strip now appearing in more than 1300 newspapers, joining only six others that appear in more than 1000 newspapers. Garfield starred in his first prime-time television special in October, and Davis' Garfield books — all seven of them — were listed simultaneously on The New York Times best seller list — a first for any author. Garfield's canine counterpart, Snoopy, received prominence when two more **Snoopy Place** stores opened in Virginia Beach and Fredericksburg, Va. UFS columnist **Miss Manners** (Judith Martin) had a bestselling book published, made hundreds of TV and radio appearances, and her column easily passed the 100 newspapers mark. **Independent News Alliance**, a division of United Media Enterprises, merged with **Scripps-Howard News Service** to expand the SHNS wire and **Dale McFeatters**, while continuing as a columnist, assumed the additional responsibilities of assembling and editing contributions to the wire from non-SHNS bureau sources (biography Page 184). **Frank Morring** was appointed night editor of SHNS. In June, **United Press International** was sold to Media News Corp. **Roderick W. Beaton**, who stayed on as president to help the new owners get started, is now retired (biography Page 193). **Tele/Scripps**, a joint venture in cable by The E.W. Scripps Co. and Tele-Communications, Inc., was formed in Knoxville and Pittsburgh. **Frank Whitehead** was elected president of SCW, Inc., effective Jan. 1, 1983, succeeding **George A. Bolas**, who retired. Berkley-Small, Inc. formed the **Berk-Haul Division** to lease trucks and handle shipments of various products, including newspaper racks.

SHNS STAFF CHANGES
NEW FACES

John Bennett became an investigative reporter after three years as regional correspondent for The Commercial Appeal. Peter Brown, whose beat is politics, formerly covered Congress for UPI. Lance Gay came to Scripps-Howard from the Washington Star and is assigned to the Pentagon. Doug Harbrecht moved to the national desk, where he covers Congress after serving as The Pittsburgh Press regional correspondent.

NEW REGIONAL CORRESPONDENTS

Mary Deibel, The Commercial Appeal; Kathy Kiely, The Pittsburgh Press; Gayle McCracken, Birmingham Post-Herald, Hollywood Sun-Tattler and The Stuart News; and John Reiter, The Evansville Press and The Kentucky Post.

DEPARTURES

Death claimed James P. Herzog (biography Page 181); Ron Royhab moved to the El Paso Herald-Post as managing editor and in early 1983 to The Pittsburgh Press (biography Page 178); Bill Steif retired (biography Page 186); and Gene Basset and J. Stewart Lytle resigned.

Frank Whitehead
President
SCW, Inc.

AFTER MANY YEARS confronting the snow and cold of Chicago, the sunshine and warmth of California are big adjustments for Frank, new president of SCW, Inc.

Frank was born in Chicago on March 31, 1929, and after graduating from the University of Missouri with majors in economics and journalism, returned to the Windy City as an advertising salesman for the Chicago Sun-Times. He later sold ads for the Davenport, Iowa, newspapers, but again returned to his hometown in the mid-1950s to join the former McGiveran Child advertising agency.

In 1960, Frank joined SCW as a sales representative covering Illinois, Iowa, Minnesota and Wisconsin. In addition to selling the company's advertising services to newspapers, Frank led seminars on how best to utilize his product.

His responsibilities changed, however, when he was elected to succeed George Bolas as president of SCW, effective Jan. 1, 1983. He and his wife Bette regretted leaving family and longtime friends in the Midwest, but are enjoying their move to Chatsworth, the home base of the company.

They have five grown children: Howard, Barbara, Robin, Ross and Michael.

OTHER PUBLISHING ENTERPRISES

Cordovan Corporation

Southern California Publishing Company

Scripps-Howard Web Press Company

Kentucky Standard

Jupiter Courier-Journal

1981 HIGHLIGHTS

Southern California Publishing Co. saw the appointment of **Melvin A. Harkavy** as vice president/general manager (biography Page 263) and the start of five new **Orange County weekly newspapers**. Cordovan Corp. acquired the **Pittsburgh Business Journal**.

1982 HIGHLIGHTS

Cordovan Corp. increased its business journals to a total of 12 when it started the **Washington Business Journal** and acquired the **Rocky Mountain Business Journal**. Its president, **Bob Gray**, was named chairman of the board, while **Mike Weingart** succeeded him as president and chief executive officer (biographies Page 307). 1982 also brought the sale of two non-daily newspaper properties — the Campbell County (Ky.) News and Scripps-Howard Press, Inc. in Louisville — and additional publication dates at two others. **Standard Publishing Co.**, Bardstown, Ky., began publishing the Kentucky Standard twice-weekly under the direction of its new general manager **Gerald Lush**. The Jupiter Courier, under the direction of **James L. Overton**, its new general manager (biography Page 301), acquired the Journal to become the **Jupiter**

Courier-Journal and began thrice-weekly publication. **Patricia Hoddinott** was appointed general manager of Scripps-Howard Web Press Co. in Louisville.

1983 HIGHLIGHTS

After 12 years as general manager of the Columbus Citizen-Journal, **Gregory A. Dembski** was appointed general manager of the Courier-Journal, Jupiter, Fla. (biography Page 243). He succeeded James L. Overton, who resigned.

Gerald Lush
General Manager
Standard Publishing Co.

GERALD DECIDED ON A newspaper career while in high school in Calhoun, Ky., where he was born Sept. 12, 1945. After graduating in 1969 from Murray State University, he became sports editor of the Henderson, (Ky.) Gleaner, and later moved up to news editor.

In 1970, Gerald became editor of the Elizabethtown News, a twice-weekly publication in Kentucky, where he was instrumental in converting the paper to five-day publication. In 1982 he joined Scripps-Howard as general manager of Standard Publishing Co. in Bardstown, Ky.

In addition to publishing The Kentucky Standard — which converted from weekly to twice-weekly publication in August, 1982 — the company operates a job printing and commercial web shop as well as a retail office supply store.

Gerald and his wife Bonnie have three daughters: Becky, Stephanie and Gretchen.

Patricia Hoddinott
General Manager
Scripps-Howard Web Press Company

PATTI DENIES that the name she chose for her son, Read, has anything to do with the career she has followed.

"It's a family name," she says. "He was born long before I got into newspapers and printing."

Patti waited until Read and his two older sisters, Cindy and Chris, were settled in school before entering the work force in her native Maryland. Then she joined Landmark Communications north of Baltimore and worked for eight years as its commercial printing sales manager.

In 1979, she pulled up roots and accepted a position with Scripps-Howard Web Press in Louisville. In 1982, she was appointed general manager.

Running the commercial printing operation and managing 33 employees keeps Patti happily busy. The plant specializes in newspaper printing and produces college and religious publications in addition to weekly newspapers.

Still, Patti, who attended the University of Maryland, occasionally feels a twinge of homesickness for her native state. Besides missing her daughters, who live there, she retains a soft spot for the Chesapeake Bay and the taste of its seafood.

ERRATA
Third revised edition, January 1981

On flyleafs, front and back covers, KMBA-TV, Kansas City, should be KBMA-TV. (KBMA has since changed its call letters to KSHB.)

In Section Four of Contents, Page vi, Robert M. Hartmann should be Robert H. Hartmann.

In Section Eight of Contents, Page ix, Robert R. Regalbutto should be Robert R. Regalbuto.

On Page 329, WPTV's location is listed as Palm Beach. It should be West Palm Beach.

On Page 344, Richard J. Janssen is listed as vice president, radio. At the time his title was assistant to the president for radio. His title has since been changed to vice president, Scripps-Howard Broadcasting Co.

On Page 397, Naoma Lowenshon should be Naoma Lowensohn.

On Page 400, Jonathan E. Thackery should be Jonathan E. Thackeray.

Scripps-Howard Handbook

PRICE $9.50

Published by The E. W. Scripps Company,
Central Trust Tower, Cincinnati, Ohio 45202

First issued January 1948.
Second revised edition June 1967.
Third revised edition January 1981.

Library of Congress Catalog Card Number: 80-54072
ISBN 0-9605484-0-8

Copyright© 1948, 1967 and 1981 by The E. W. Scripps Company.
Reproduction in part or in whole forbidden without permission.

THIS BOOK was set in type by The Memphis Publishing Company, Memphis, Tennessee. The text is 10 on 12 point Century Expanded. Headings are Caslon Bold. It was manufactured by Johnson & Hardin Company, Cincinnati, Ohio, printed on Warren's 60-pound Old Style, and bound in Roxite fabric. Cover and end papers were created by Jack Gold.

Scripps-Howard Handbook

Edited and Designed
By Vance H. Trimble

Contents

Preface .... *xi*
Editor's Note .... *xii*

SECTION ONE
Aims, Methods, and Purposes

What Is Scripps-Howard, And How it Operates 3
What Do We Stand For 9
What Is News 24
How To Write News 26
Good Typography 30
Good Promotion 36
Advertising 41

SECTION TWO
Pioneers and Other Personalities

E. W. Scripps 47
Miss Ellen Scripps 65
Robert F. Paine 67
Robert P. Scripps 69
Roy W. Howard 77
W. W. Hawkins 85
John H. Sorrells 86
George B. Parker 87
Walker Stone 89
Jack R. Howard 91
Earl H. Richert 95

SECTION THREE
The Scripps Trustees

Robert Paine Scripps Jr. 99
Charles E. Scripps 103
Edward W. Scripps II 107

SECTION FOUR
General Management and Staff

Edward W. Estlow 113
Gordon Hanna 119
Lawrence A. Leser 125
Daniel J. Castellini 129
E. J. Wolfzorn 131
Robert M. Hartmann 134
B. J. Cutler 138
David Stolberg 140
James H. Wagner 143
Homer E. Taylor Jr. 145
Ralph E. Eary 148
Robert E. Brophy 150
Jimmy E. Manis Jr. 153
William J. Lee 155
William R. Niehaus 159
The General Counsel 162

SECTION FIVE
Some Scripps-Howard Institutions

The Washington Bureau/Scripps-Howard News Service ... 171
United Press International 188
United Media Enterprises 197
Berkley-Small, Inc. 206
Scripps-Howard News 208
Scripps-Howard Foundation 211

CONTENTS   vii

SECTION SIX
Scripps-Howard Daily Newspapers

The Albuquerque Tribune 218
    WILLIAM TANNER, *Editor*

Birmingham Post-Herald 222
    ANGUS McEACHRAN, *Editor*
    W. H. METZ, *Business Manager*

The Cincinnati Post 228
    WILLIAM R. BURLEIGH, *Editor*
    JOHN L. FELDMANN, *Business Manager*

The Kentucky Post 236
    PAUL F. KNUE, *Editor*

The Columbus Citizen-Journal 240
    RICHARD R. CAMPBELL, *Editor*
    GREGORY A. DEMBSKI, *Business Manager*

The Rocky Mountain News 245
    RALPH LOONEY, *Editor*
    WILLIAM W. FLETCHER, *Business Manager*

The El Paso Herald-Post 251
    ROBERT W. LEE, *Editor*

The Evansville Press 255
    WILLIAM W. SORRELS, *Editor*
    JUDITH CLABES, *Editor*, Sunday Courier & Press

Daily News Tribune, Fullerton 260
    ALFRED L. HEWITT, *Editor*
    MELVIN A. HARKAVY, *Business Manager*

Hollywood Sun-Tattler 265
    EDWARD H. WENTWORTH, *Editor*
    ARTHUR SEGALL SR., *Business Manager*

The Knoxville News-Sentinel 270
    RALPH L. MILLETT JR., *Editor*
    ROGER A. DALEY, *Business Manager*

Memphis Press-Scimitar 275
    MILTON R. BRITTEN, *Editor*

The Commercial Appeal 279
    MICHAEL T. GREHL, *Editor*

Memphis Publishing Company 283
    JOSEPH R. WILLIAMS III, *Business Manager*

The Pittsburgh Press 287
    JOHN TROAN, *Editor*
    ROBERT J. O'CONNELL, *Business Manager*

The San Juan Star 293
    ANDREW T. VIGLUCCI, *Editor*
    JOHN A. ZERBE JR., *President and General Manager*

The Stuart News 298
    THOMAS E. WEBER JR., *Editor*
    JAMES L. OVERTON, *Business Manager*

SECTION SEVEN
Other Publishing Enterprises

Cordovan Corporation, Publishers 307
Southern California Publishing Company 311
Grant County News/Campbell County News 312
Scripps-Howard Press, Inc. and
    Scripps-Howard Web Press Company 314
Kentucky Standard 315
The Courier-Highlights 317

SECTION EIGHT
Scripps-Howard Broadcasting Company

History of Scripps-Howard Broadcasting Company 321
Donald L. Perris 331
Mortimer C. Watters 334
James E. Bloyd 337
Albert J. Schottelkotte 339
James E. Smith 342
Richard J. Janssen 344
Michael W. Callaghan 346

CONTENTS ix

WEWS, Cleveland... 348
    EDWARD D. CERVENAK, *Vice President and General Manager*

WCPO-TV, Cincinnati... 351
    ROBERT D. GORDON, *Vice President and General Manager*

WMC-TV, Memphis.. 354
    MORRIS E. GREINER JR., *Vice President and General Manager*

WPTV, West Palm Beach 357
    ROBERT R. REGALBUTTO, *Vice President and General Manager*

KJRH, Tulsa 360
    F. BEN HEVEL, *Vice President and General Manager*

KBMA-TV, Kansas City....................................... 363
    BOB J. WORMINGTON, *General Manager*

WMC and WMC-FM, Memphis................................. 366
    DONALD MEYERS, *General Manager, WMC-FM*
    DEAN L. OSMUNDSON, *General Manager, WMC*

WNOX, Knoxville 370
    CHRISTOPHER T. GALLU, *General Manager*

KMEO AM-FM, Phoenix 372
    STEPHEN C. WRATH, *General Manager*

WBSB-FM, Baltimore... 375
    JAMES P. FOX, *General Manager*

SECTION NINE
Historical Highlights

Spotlighting Interesting, and
  Often Significant, Events in Our Life and Times........ 379

Index 395

Preface

Why We Publish This Book

THE PURPOSE of this handbook is to explain the ideas which shape and guide Scripps-Howard methods and policies.

Those ideas derive from a single standard of values; they represent a harmony of method and purpose. There is a relationship between the way we do things, and the reasons for doing them.

If we are guided by certain standards of decency and good taste in our news columns, those same standards must prevail in our advertising copy.

If we believe in simplicity of literary expression, we are inevitably committed to typographical simplicity.

If we hold to a mature social and political outlook, we cannot reconcile that with a frivolous and irresponsible treatment of the news.

If we choose honest conviction ahead of expediency in our editorials, we cannot strive for circulation through the medium of lurid and lascivious news and features.

FURTHER, we believe there is an intrinsic value in the methods we favor.

Simplicity in writing conveys an idea clearly, earnestly, and with conviction.

A simple and restrained typography is easier to read; it conveys an impression of sincerity. Tricky typography, through an association of ideas, throws a shadow on the verity, or the importance, of a story.

We believe in a mature selection of news because we think mature judgment is required to deal with the problems of our changing times. We do not believe in emphasizing news that is superficially sensational or tainted with moral corruption, because we believe the responsibility for encouraging high standards of public morals is a first duty of the press.

Nevertheless, we are aware of the fact that it is people, and the things they do—noble or ignoble, profound or foolish—that makes news; we understand clearly that passion is the ferment of life, that lust is a bright and familiar thread in our social consciousness. It is no part of our aim to be dull or ponderous or self-righteous or humorless. Our intent is to be interesting and entertaining, alert to all changing phases of public whim and fancy—to mirror without distortion, the humors and passions of our society.

SCRIPPS-HOWARD journalism is not a set of rules, but a thing of the spirit; we believe that spirit thrives best on individual initiative and creative freedom.

This is not a rigid "style book" in the conventional sense. It is a guiding set of principles. The emphasis is on the spirit, rather than the mechanics, of doing things.

As much as anything, this is a statement of our journalistic faith.

Editor's Note About This Revision

IN CONCEPT and basic substance, this revised third edition of the Handbook is remarkably unchanged from the original volume which was published in 1948. That, it seems to me, is a notable reaffirmation of the soundness of E. W.

PREFACE   xiii

Scripps's initial concepts and basic journalistic philosophy. Through the social and economical upheavals of the last one hundred years, the Concern has held steadfast to his ideas, and been quite faithful in following the course he charted.

Some sections of this edition, of course, are vastly different from the revision published fourteen years ago. As in any business, the inexorable march of time dictates some periodic updating. There are scores of new faces in our executive ranks. Editors and business managers are not, alas, immortal; many who were featured in personality sketches in the previous book no longer are active. Many have retired (as in my case), or have died. Consequently passe' write-ups are deleted and new personnel sketches inserted to keep the cast of characters current.

Also the corporate face has a somewhat different look. Several new properties have been acquired or launched, certain subsidiary divisions and operations have been revamped or regrouped or otherwise changed, considerable resources have been committed to new plant and equipment investment, and all of us now work amidst mystical technology, amazingly fast and efficient, that would boggle the minds of most of our Scripps-Howard pioneers.

Yet through the necessary changes, the Concern continues to importantly cling to the old-fashioned but sound credo on which E. W. Scripps got it all started—namely, with a viable business base, to inform and to serve the reader (and now, as well, the TV viewer and radio listener).

The Handbook was conceived during the Scripps-Howard Managing Editors' Conference in 1947. It was to be a composite of technical information. But when the late John H. Sorrells (then the Concern's Executive Editor) started in to produce it a different concept evolved. It became apparent that there was a broad pattern of Scripps-Howard journalism which contained elements of greater significance than a mere assembly of technical data. It was clear that a combination of men and ideas had created a continuity of purpose running through the Concern. A distinctive institutional image began to emerge.

Sorrells had the good sense to let his typewriter give substance and shape to that image—to present a clear and intelligible picture of the structure by bringing together in proper perspective the various elements which give it meaning.

What he wrote more than three decades ago has stood the test of time. His description of Scripps-Howard aims, methods, and purposes—what you call the Concern's philosophy—seem as accurate today as when he wrote them. When Frank Ford was given the task of updating the Handbook in 1967 he undertook to preserve Sorrells's text to the fullest extent possible. Frank also kept as close as he could to John's style in describing changes resulting from promotions, retirements and deaths. I have tried to do likewise.

In the design of the original Handbook, Sorrells took pretty much a plain vanilla approach; and my friend Frank did not greatly alter the format. In contrast, in that respect this third edition has moved uptown a few blocks. The merits of its new appearance should speak for themselves—the book is larger, has somewhat more modern design and typography (yet remains clean and uncluttered), contains for the first time pictures of Concern pioneers and current personalities, includes an index, is case-bound for permanence, and gives belated greater recognition to the broadcast side of the business.

Additionally, this edition is being published in quantities sufficient to provide greater distribution—not only within the Concern, but outside, to public libraries in the communities we serve, to journalism schools, to publishing and broadcast and other professional organizations.

It is an utter impossibility to keep this kind of book current on personnel changes. In a single year there could be a dozen important shifts. Sorrells thoughtfully provided his first edition with screw binding posts so that fresh pages could be printed and inserted when General Management appointed a new editor or business manager, or changed other executives. That proved impractical, for a number of reasons. My proposed solution to that problem, at least within the Concern, is to provide every year or two a small paperback of the same size that can be placed beside this permanent volume on the office bookshelf, thus providing reasonably upto-date info.

Preface xv

Neither Ford nor I found it possible to emulate John Sorrells's rare knack of making the compilation of this book a one-man show. It was a big task, requiring massive assistance from many quarters. People at all levels in Scripps-Howard lent ideas and time to this revision. It simply could not have been done without such teamwork.

The editor of the third edition extends sincere thanks to all who helped, especially Bob Doerr, Randy Cochran, Nancy Tretter, George Alsup, Jim Wagner, Jack Gold, Bob Mathes and Ralph Eary.

—VANCE H. TRIMBLE

December 1980

SECTION ONE

Aims, Methods, And Purposes

How The Scripps-Howard Organization Operates, What It Stands For, And Pertinent Other Info

What Is Scripps-Howard, And How It Operates

Authority Exists Locally, As Well As At The Top

THE NAME "SCRIPPS-HOWARD" both identifies and characterizes the present-day group of journalistic enterprises founded in 1878 by E. W. Scripps.

Clear understanding of the ramifications of the name requires brief historical references plus at least a bare-bones outline of the corporate ownership and administrative setup, as well as a definition of its "spirit." By that is meant what E. W. Scripps and his papers stood for, a creed of straightforward reporting and public service that has faithfully endured the test of a century.

His business initially was limited to publishing newspapers. By the time he had successfully launched half a dozen or so, Scripps saw they needed centralized auxiliary support. So he established his own national telegraphic news wire, and followed that with the nation's first major newspaper feature service. Then he opened a central office through which to buy supplies and equipment. He also set up a national bureau to handle his papers' "foreign" advertising.

He continued to launch additional metropolitan newspapers. Usually he went in deliberately on a shoestring and if successful continued to publish. If not, he was willing to fold his tent in that particular city and concede it was not the place nor the time for a new paper.

SUCH SINK-OR-SWIM "market research" would be financially unthinkable in costly present day big-city newspapering. But that aggressive willingness to gamble start-up capital was—buttressed by his phenomenal foresight and keen public service precepts—the cornerstone of E.W. Scripps's success.

Each newspaper usually was established as a separate corporation. Invariably Scripps retained 51 per cent control, but he would assign as much as 49 per cent of a newspaper's stock to local working partners. These ordinarily were the editor and business manager and one or two others willing to strive mightily to make the venture succeed and pay for their stock out of profits.

Scripps did not think of the group of newspapers and allied enterprises that he controlled as constituting a chain, or a company, but rather as "The Concern." And he wanted mightily for his organization to live on and serve the public after he was gone. His foresight in establishing in 1922 a long-term family trust enabled him to achieve that goal. And even today the business is still called "The Concern."

As he had done on the local level, E. W. Scripps early on sought out an executive to direct nationally the Concern's multitudinous operations. He made a "partnership" contract in 1895 with Colonel Milton A. McRae. The Concern took on the name Scripps-McRae. In 1905 McRae retired and the name fell into disuse.

Later a new fair-haired boy rose through the ranks of United Press—Roy W. Howard. He became the Concern's chairman of the board and business manager and eventually president and chief executive officer. In 1922 Scripps bestowed the name "Scripps-Howard" on the Concern.

To The Edward W. Scripps Trust, the founder assigned ownership control so that what he termed "the children of his brain"—the newspapers he founded—would continue after his death (which occurred in 1926). Under the strict terms of that trust, the Concern remains a privately-held rather than a public business entity.

ALTHOUGH THE NAME Scripps-Howard—and its symbolic lighthouse iogo—has come to represent to the public the source of final ownership and authority in the Concern, the legal and actual power rests in The E.W. Scripps Company. About 89 per cent of this corporation is owned by The Edward W. Scripps Trust, which is administered by three trustees, Charles E. Scripps, Robert P. Scripps Jr. and Edward W. Scripps II, all sons of the late Robert P. Scripps and grandsons of E. W. Scripps.

A majority of the voting stock of each Scripps-Howard newspaper and of each allied enterprise or subsidiary is held by The E.W. Scripps Company, also known—more or less interchangeably—as Scripps-Howard Newspapers.

In recent times, especially in the 1970s, the latter name has become somewhat technically narrower because of the Concern's heavy expansion into allied journalistic fields mainly in the area of broadcasting, community and specialized publications, data processing, news and feature syndicates, and service enterprises.

Essentially the various operations have a great deal of autonomy on the local level, which is a precept established by the founder. Even so, eventually all the lines of administrative control come together in one entity at the top to form "The Concern."

The Scripps-Howard newspapers are separate operations bound together as a group by a single controlling stock ownership and are dedicated to common aims and purposes.

IT IS SCRIPPS-HOWARD practice for the daily newspapers to be administered locally by dual management, consisting of the Editor and Business Manager. Both the editor and the business manager have exclusive responsibility and authority within their respective departments.

The editor has final authority with regard to questions of institutional policy; but in the day-to-day operation such questions are usually settled by joint decision. If the editor and the business manager are in sharp conflict on a major question affecting the welfare of the institution as a whole, the controversy would, in actual practice, be resolved at the general management level.

In several cities Scripps-Howard is involved in an agency arrangement with the owners of other newspapers. Advertising, production, circulation and other business matters are handled jointly in such cases, but the editorial staffs and products remain separate and competitive. In two of these cities, Albuquerque and El Paso, there is no Scripps-Howard business manager on the scene.

THE TOP LAYER of Concern authority—directly below the Trust ownership—consists of the officers and directors of The E.W. Scripps Company. Charles E. Scripps is chairman of the board. Edward W. Estlow is president and chief executive officer. Other officers are Gordon Hanna, vice president and general editorial manager; Lawrence A. Leser, vice president for finance and corporate development; Daniel J. Castellini, vice president and controller and secretary; and E. J. Wolfzorn, treasurer.

The board of directors has nine members. They are: the three trustees, Charles, Bob, and Ted Scripps; Estlow, Hanna, and Leser; Jack R. Howard, chairman of the executive committee, retired president of The E.W. Scripps Company; Earl H. Richert, retired editor-in-chief of the Scripps-Howard newspapers; and Donald L. Perris, president of the Scripps-Howard Broadcasting Company.

The general management level is augmented by operational executives, department heads, and staff, all (except one) operating out of Concern headquarters in Cincinnati. These are: Robert H. Hartmann, general business manager/newspapers; B. J. Cutler, editor-in-chief (in Washington, D.C.); David Stolberg, assistant general editorial manager; James H. Wagner, promotion editor; Homer E. Taylor, president and general manager, Scripps-Howard Supply Company; Ralph E. Eary, production director; William J. Lee, data processing director; Robert E. Brophy, director of human resources; Jimmy E. Manis Jr., circulation director; and William R. Niehaus, director of research.

TO FOCUS ON the Concern's week-to-week administrative problems and to review current operational opportunities, a general management level staff meeting is held usually

Aims, Methods, and Purposes

monthly in Cincinnati. Ed Estlow and Charles Scripps generally are present.

The general editorial manager appoints the editors of the daily and Sunday newspapers, and the general business manager/newspapers selects business managers. Jointly they formulate certain over-all policies—editorial and business—and give counsel and direction to editors and business managers as circumstances require.

The local managers have wide discretion in the formulation of local policy and the direction of local activities. While business practices do not vary greatly between papers and cities, editorial and news policies derive primarily from local and regional conditions and interests. Scripps-Howard editors have broad powers of decision in such matters.

Scripps-Howard editors also have a defined responsibility and authority with respect to certain matters of internal policy on the newspapers. A major concept in Scripps-Howard is the idea that its canons of good taste must apply to all departments equally; hence the final authority, and responsibility, for determining the acceptability of advertising rests on the editor.

SCRIPPS-HOWARD also owns groups of weekly newspapers and shoppers, and some printing plants, in California, Florida and Kentucky. These managers report to the general business manager.

The managers of other Scripps-Howard enterprises report to their own boards of directors and to the president of The E. W. Scripps Company.

In this category are United Press International, the global news agency; United Media Enterprises, which combines two of America's largest feature companies, NEA and United Feature Syndicate; Berkley-Small, a leading producer of newspaper circulation and promotion supplies, and Cordovan Corporation of Houston, which publishes trade magazines and books, and also weekly business newspapers in nine cities coast to coast.

Scripps-Howard Broadcasting Company, which operates six television stations and six radio stations and has interests in cablevision, is 74 per cent owned by The E. W. Scripps

Company. However, Broadcasting is a public company with its own officers and board of directors.

SINCE 1977 THE FORMER general management offices in New York have been combined with the old Central Office in expanded quarters on several floors of the Central Trust Tower in Cincinnati. The headquarters includes the general accounting department.

The General Counsel for all The E.W. Scripps Company enterprises is the firm of Baker and Hostetler, headquartered in Cleveland, Ohio with offices in Denver, Columbus, Ohio, Washington, D.C., and Orlando, Florida.

So much for the statistics.

What Scripps-Howard stands for requires a separate chapter in this handbook. It is next.

What Do We Stand For?

An Attempt to Define the Concern's Spirit and Policies

SCRIPPS-HOWARD is a name identifying a group of journalistic enterprises. It is the symbol of a particular kind of journalism. It is a spirit which expresses and animates a certain journalistic faith.

The original among the group of Scripps-Howard newspapers was *The Cleveland Press,* founded by E. W. Scripps. Said the founder, in his first issue:

> We have no politics, that is, in the sense of the word as commonly used. We are not Republican, not Democrat, not Greenback and not Prohibitionist. We simply intend to support good men and condemn bad ones, support good measures and condemn bad ones, no matter what party they belong to. We shall tell no lies about persons or policies for love, malice or money.
>
> It is no part of a newspaper's business to array itself on the side of this or that party, to fight or lie or wrangle for it. The newspaper should simply present all the facts the editor is capable of obtaining concerning men and measures before the bar of the public and then, after having discharged its duty as a witness, be satisfied to leave the jury in the case—the public—to find the verdict.

Since that was written, we have been referred to by many names. We have been termed reactionary, radical, labor, anti-labor, bolshevik, bourbon, conservative, liberal—the whole range of labels that those who either agree or disagree have chosen to pin on. Yet the one label which seems accurately to express our policy through the years is "independent."

That is a policy which involves calling each shot as we see it, at any time, and under any changing circumstances; for avoiding entangling alliances.

Such a policy, unless grounded in a definite social philosophy, could be used as a refuge for expediency or the aimless exploitation of sheer whim. Although the term "liberal" has been adopted by groups representing almost every shade of ideology, including Communist, we nevertheless cling to fundamental tenets of the traditional liberal faith.

We believe in orderly social progress; we distrust concentrations of power. We believe in the democratic way of life, although we understand that unrestricted democracy would be anarchy, and that society must be governed by rules. We believe in a government by laws, rather than by men. We believe the individual is paramount to the state, and that the purpose of government is to serve society, not society to serve government. We believe it is the duty of the strong to protect the weak—and to champion the cause and support the hopes and aspirations of the underprivileged and inarticulate.

We do not believe in a limited and restricted view of a free press. We conceive it in the spirit—not merely the letter—of the Bill of Rights. We consider it a grant of freedom to the people; and we feel that as journalists, we are the trustees of this freedom.

Democracy is not a body of dogma, but a thing of the spirit; and we believe that a free press in a democracy must accommodate itself to conflicting and contending options. We consider it a public responsibility to give expression in our columns to all shades of legitimate opinion in public matters. By the same token, we feel it is both a right and a duty to express our own views, and gain, if we can, acceptance of ideas which we believe to be in the public interest.

Our newspapers have exercised an independent choice concerning issues and persons ever since E. W. Scripps founded the Concern, but there has been little deviation from our basic philosophy. Specifically:

We supported Woodrow Wilson and his program of social and economic reform.

AIMS, METHODS, AND PURPOSES 11

We supported James M. Cox and the League of Nations in 1920, against Warren G. Harding and his back-to-normalcy philosphy of reactionaryism.

In 1924 we did not believe that either the Democratic or the Republican platforms, or the candidates of those parties, were in accord with our philosophy of social progress and we supported Robert M. LaFollette, the elder.

In 1928 we believed that the issue came down to the individual best qualified by reason of experience and attainments in several areas of social and economic endeavor, and we supported Herbert Hoover.

In 1932 Mr. Hoover's ineptness in the realm of practical politics, and his inability or unwillingness to recognize the fact that prohibition was undermining national respect for the law, caused us to throw our support to Franklin D. Roosevelt. We did not underestimate some of Mr. Roosevelt's shortcomings as a presidential prospect, but we believed he understood the desires of the people, and that this political acumen and boldness seemed more adequate to meet the problems ahead than Mr. Hoover's timid political measures.

The first four years of Mr. Roosevelt's term, and the first year of his second term brought to fruition many things which Scripps-Howard had long contended for—repeal of prohibition, reciprocal trade treaties, soil conservation, governmental development of power resources, social security, minimum wage-and-hour laws, the right of workers to organize and bargain collectively, correction of financial abuses, truth-in-securities legislation, better control of the stock exchange and of the banks.

All of those were measures we had advocated before the New Deal, and we fought on Mr. Roosevelt's side in favor of their enactment. We supported Mr. Roosevelt for his second term. We parted company with him when the loud and aggressive fringe of New Dealers began to depart from our concept of true liberalism. The issue came over the attempt to pack the Supreme Court.

Throughout the years, we had criticized the Supreme Court's hide-bound interpretation of the Constitution, by which much-needed progressive legislation was defeated or deferred; and we had urged a constitutional amendment to limit the power of the court's then ultra-conservative majority. But we could not accept the administration's raw, ruthless and cynical method of accomplishing the desired end. This was one of the greatest constitutional crises of our times.

The attempt to alter the size and the social philosophy of the court by what we considered almost a ukase, was symptomatic of change which came into methods and attitudes of the New Deal—an attitude of contempt for the rights of dissident minorities, an impatience with the restrictions of government by law, a lust for power for its own sake.

We opposed Mr. Roosevelt for his third and fourth terms. We feared an entrenchment of power, always a peril to a free society. Specifically, we were apprehensive of the progressive abuse of power by the President and some of his advisers and administrators.

For similar reasons, believing a housecleaning was overdue, we opposed Harry Truman in favor of Thomas E. Dewey in 1948.

We favored Dwight D. Eisenhower in 1952 and 1956, preferred Richard M. Nixon to John Kennedy in 1960.

Civil Rights was a basic issue in the campaign of 1964. We supported Lyndon B. Johnson's position favoring equal rights for all citizens. Our endorsement also took into consideration his long experience in national affairs, particularly his outstanding record as Senate Majority Leader.

Through the years, when labor unions were weak and employers were strong and arrogant, we fought the battles of labor. We believed then, and still believe, that strong labor unions are necessary for the proper social and economic development of our country. But as labor unions have become powerful, and as many labor leaders have become arrogant and ruthless, we have with equal vigor fought for restrictions of their abuse of power.

In other areas, Scripps-Howard Newspapers in the years following World War II waged successful campaigns for the admission of Alaska and Hawaii as states and for the repeal of state taxes on oleomargarine (which had made margarine non-competitive with butter). During the war years it was a leader in the fight to withhold federal income taxes from paychecks. This was to help provide the funds needed for the war effort.

We supported American involvement in Vietnam until it became clear that the whole affair had become a quagmire with no plan or will on the part of our government to bring it to a successful conclusion. Then we supported withdrawal. We believed that the South Vietnamese people were worthy of our help to keep from being subjugated by the Soviet-backed North Vietnamese.

Our newspapers backed Richard Nixon for re-election in 1972, preferring him to the super-liberal Senator George McGovern. But as the Watergate scandal unfolded, our editorial policy became increasingly critical and when the tapes showed he had been lying to the American people we joined others in calling for him to leave his office. The Concern preferred Gerald Ford to Jimmy Carter in 1976, and Ronald Reagan to Carter in 1980.

The shaping of editorial policy is a day-to-day job; it is a case of facing situations as they arise, measuring them in terms of our own faith, appraising them as to their probable effect on the public welfare. Therein lies the thread running through Scripps-Howard editorial history. We are advocates of the greatest good for the greatest number; our client is the whole public.

Editors of the Scripps-Howard daily newspapers convene periodically and by majority vote adopt or update specific Concern editorial policies on national issues, which all are then obligated to support. A statement setting forth these principles and policies was first approved by the editors at their September 1968 meeting at Stuart, Florida. As of the September 1980 meeting at Williamsburg, Virginia, it reads:

Principles and Policies

Preamble

The one certainty of life is the certainty of change.

Over the years, the Scripps-Howard newspapers have continually sought to adjust to the changing needs of the times.

As chroniclers of change, we do not fear it. Indeed, we welcome it. For although all movement is not improvement, change is the indispensable ingredient of progress.

Thus, a democratic society dedicated to the greatest good for the greatest number must be responsive to the will of the people and pay heed to their demands, their needs, their hopes and their wishes.

In line with this and with our time-tested motto, "Give light and the people will find their own way," we herewith submit this statement of principles and policies.

Government

In a free society, individuals should be allowed maximum freedom.

The needless intrusion of government into the lives of its citizens damages individual liberty. It also runs against the desire of the American people to curb the cost of government at every level.

As a general rule, government should limit itself to doing for its people only that which the people are unable to do for themselves.

Inflation

Inflation may be the most serious threat facing the nation. It robs the thrifty of their savings. It cheats the elderly out of a decent retirement. It drives the cost of houses out of the reach of many working people, puncturing their traditional dreams.

On the political level, it threatens democratic institutions. Few nations hit by severe, long-lasting inflation have been able to avoid authoritarian "solutions" of the left or right.

We cannot expect government to master inflation in every case. Some causes of higher prices, such as actions by the oil cartel or drought and crop failure, are beyond the government's reach. But we can expect authorities not to take steps that directly fuel inflation.

The federal government should balance its budget except during recessions or national emergencies. Certainly it is irresponsible to run large deficits at the height of a business cycle.

The money supply strongly affects price levels. It should not be permitted by the U.S. Treasury and the Federal Reserve System to grow faster than the nation's output of goods and services.

The government must study its own actions to see which are essential and which unjustifiably raise costs. Fertile fields for such examination are regulations, subsidies, rate-fixing, price supports, and protection of special interests.

Statutory spending limits are needed at all levels of government. We prefer this approach to limits on taxation, which can be evaded through debt financing.

Taxes and Fiscal Policies

Fiscal policies and taxes have uses in stabilizing the economy, controlling inflation and protecting the dollar in world markets; nonetheless, the basic goal of taxes should be to raise revenue for essential expenses.

We favor simplification of tax laws and forms. Large incomes, corporate or individual, should never escape reasonable taxation.

The government should refrain from the business of fixing prices, wages and profits.

It is desirable, at times, to give tax incentives to the private sector to advance job training, low-cost housing, pollution control and other goals.

Private foundations and charitable organizations must use their funds in the public interest and for projects which government otherwise might have to undertake. Large fortunes should not be protected from taxation for extended periods through self-perpetuating and self-serving mechanisms.

Energy

America must develop all of its domestic energy resources. The ultimate goal is energy self-sufficiency. Urgent steps should be taken to cut dependence on foreign energy supplies.

We favor the safe generation of nuclear power and the maximum use of domestic coal resources. The country also must rapidly develop alternative energy sources, including synthetic fuels, solar power and the breeder and fusion reactors.

We support decontrol of oil and gas prices to encourage domestic production, reduce consumer demand and promote equitable distribution within the nation.

At the same time, we urge stringent measures to conserve energy supplies. These include enforcing the national 55-mile-per-hour speed limit, fuel-efficient motor vehicles, more mass transportation, and better insulated buildings.

In developing domestic energy sources, we must protect the environment and public safety. But that concern should not serve as an all-purpose excuse for blocking the development of resources vital to the nation.

Conservation

The quality of our life is strongly affected by the quality of the air, the water, the soil we live on — and off. In addition, our life is enhanced by our wildlife and our scenic splendor. So it is essential that we husband them and safeguard them from pollution and destruction.

We are entrusted with a large, but finite, treasure of natural resources as a legacy for all generations to come. The individual who utilizes any of these resources—for pleasure or profit—must discharge his covenant with nature to protect them from plunder and pollution.

State, local and federal governments should enact and enforce legislation to ensure proper use of resources.

Transportation

It is necessary to improve and promote mass transit to conserve energy and relieve our polluted, automobile-clogged cities.

We support the use of highway trust funds for this purpose, as well as for continued construction of necessary highways. We urge proper maintenance of roads and bridges.

We strongly oppose government regulations leading to inefficiency and waste in transportation.

We continue to oppose bigger and heavier trucks on our highways because they damage public roads, cause traffic problems and imperil life and limb.

Firm enforcement of traffic regulations is needed to lessen the terrible slaughter on our roads.

We support highway-beautification efforts, particularly those aimed at reducing junkyard and billboard blight.

Cities

Many of our cities are plagued by serious problems, including bad housing, high unemployment among the young and poor, and crime and drug abuse. A coordinated effort by individuals, local institutions and government at all levels is required to attack these problems.

Because they have the resources, state and federal governments must continue to provide money for solving local

Aims, Methods, and Purposes

problems. How these funds are used normally should be decided at the local level.

There are continuing local responsibilities as well. Community services should be consolidated to give taxpayers the most effective government. Police and fire protection, sewage disposal, building-code enforcement, mass transit, pollution control and other services vital to the proper functioning of cities should be coordinated on an areawide basis.

We favor rational, long-range zoning that considers the quality of life as an important criterion for land use, and we look forward to the revitalization of our central cities.

Crime and Courts

People look to law-enforcement officers to protect them from crime and to courts to administer swift and certain justice. They have a right to expect even-handed justice at both police and court levels.

We urge further improvement and professionalization of local police forces.

The FBI and drug-enforcement agencies should be kept at a high professional level to prevent and solve federal crimes and to suppress illicit drug traffic and organized crime.

Such effective police work must be supported by effective courts. Public confidence in the courts is shaken by abuse of legal technicalities, by delay of trials and by interminable appeals.

We support open courts and condemn moves to close court proceedings.

While protecting individual rights, courts must show equal concern for public safety. To that end we favor stern punishment of repeat offenders. Capital punishment, within the limits defined by the U.S. Supreme Court, sometimes is necessary.

Gun Control

All levels of government should try to retard the traffic in deadly weapons to reduce crime and violence.

We support laws that impose heavy penalties on those who use guns in committing crimes, and we urge stringent enforcement of these penalties to deter armed violence.

Education

American society has an obligation to assure every child equal opportunity to develop his talents. Support of local public schools and of higher education is of utmost importance.

All school districts must recognize that academic achievement of the student is their main goal. To this end we urge greater emphasis on basic educational subjects and more effective discipline.

Since its founding this nation has been an English-speaking society. We believe that English should remain the primary language of classroom instruction. Attempts to promote bilingualism can harm the nation's long-term interests.

We deplore that court-ordered busing has shaken public confidence in some school systems and frequently has proved counter-productive to its goal of desegregated classrooms. Thus it should be used only as a last resort.

In higher education, private or independent universities should be encouraged and supported as alternatives and complements to state and community colleges.

Continuing education should be available to adults so they may master new subjects, pursue new careers and make better use of their leisure.

Science and Technology

In an increasingly complex world, our progress often is paced by developments in science and technology. It is important that the United States remain in the forefront of these fields.

Our quest for pure knowledge should be accompanied by a search for practical knowledge, and the objectives should be to learn more about the universe and to enrich our lives and those of our fellow men.

When practical, we should cooperate with other nations in joint research efforts, such as those involving vast expenses in outer space and under the seas. In this way we can advance world peace and brotherhood as well as universal knowledge.

Health and Safety

Though more people are receiving better health care than earlier, the costs of delivering medical services are distressingly high. For many families major illness brings financial catastrophe, and too many Americans still lack adequate medical care.

All suppliers of health care—physicians, dentists, nurses, drug firms, hospitals, nursing homes, health insurers—should do everything in their power to hold down costs. Needless duplication of expensive health facilities and equipment must be avoided.

Most important, there should be increased emphasis on keeping people well, and out of hospitals and doctors' offices, through health-maintenance organizations, ambulatory clinics, etc.

Also, we favor a national health-insurance program to protect all Americans against financially catastrophic illnesses.

We endorse continued federal support for the training of necessary health manpower, and for medical research.

The Aged

The aging of our population is an inevitable result of the increase in our life expectancy and the decrease in our national birth rate.

As more people live longer, we must try to make these added years more meaningful than mere existence.

Our older citizens are particularly vulnerable to chronic illness and chronic inflation. It is imperative to protect them from such ravages as much as possible.

Those who served their nation for most of their lives in factory and field, office and home, deserve financial security, physical comfort and peace of mind in their later years.

Welfare

American society has an obligation to help those citizens who cannot help themselves. But it should not help anyone who won't help himself. We should care for the unable but not the unwilling.

In addition to distributing welfare funds to the poor, there must be a greater, more imaginative effort to help people lift themselves out of poverty by using their energies and talents.

The inordinate cost of the present system of welfare for the poor and its obvious failure to free many from the bonds of poverty make reform imperative.

Illegal Aliens

Our wealth and other nations' poverty have led to an intolerable increase in illegal aliens in the United States, damaging the interests of our citizens.

To combat this invasion, we urge necessary manpower increases for the Immigration and Naturalization Service. We favor strict penalties for employers who knowingly hire illegal aliens and for smugglers of aliens.

Since alien labor may be beneficial in specific cases, we recommend that the temporary-work-permit program be simplified and expanded.

The United States should support efforts by developing countries to increase job opportunities at home.

Equal Rights

We believe in equal application of all laws to all persons in all phases of life, and stand for equal opportunity and equal pay in employment, education and housing. In line with this, we favor ratification of the Equal Rights Amendment to the U.S. Constitution.

All local and state governments must protect such rights and uphold them. But whenever such rights are denied, it is the ultimate responsibility of the federal government to see that they are secured.

Business and Labor

We believe both business and labor have a responsibility to the public to produce goods and services at reasonable costs. Moreover, both business and labor share the responsibility of upholding America's position in world trade.

Just as workers in private industry have the right to organize to bargain collectively, so do public employes— but protecting the public's health, safety and welfare, and the education of our children, must always remain paramount.

All businesses and all labor unions should eliminate unfair hiring and advancement practices.

Both labor and business should be required to abide by their contractual obligations. For the protection of the public, the antitrust laws should apply to big labor as well as big business.

Agriculture

Our test of any farm proposal shall continue to be: Does it tend to get the Government out of the price-fixing business and agriculture back to the free market?

Electoral Process

In a democracy, every citizen should be encouraged to vote. To this end, we favor making it easy for citizens to register and vote, while avoiding electoral fraud. To strengthen the political-party system, which aids stable government, we oppose cross-over voting in primaries.

We favor states conducting presidential primaries on a regional basis and revising the Electoral College system to outlaw the so-called "faithless elector." We want shorter presidential campaigns.

We support use of public funds in presidential campaigns and would extend the practice to congressional elections. Also, we back reasonable ceilings on campaign spending and on campaign contributions by individuals and organizations in local, state and federal elections. There should be complete and timely disclosure of campaign contributions and expenditures.

Puerto Rico

We continue to support Commonwealth status for Puerto Rico until statehood becomes feasible and the people ask for it.

Probate Laws

All states should have probate laws that permit estates to be passed on to heirs without undue expense and delay.

Estates of persons who die without leaving a will should be divided along lines suggested by the uniform probate code of the American Bar Association.

International Relations

The United States has responsibility to provide its share of leadership in international relations.

But we are not obliged to be the world's keeper nor the

world's policeman. We have not the economic, military or spiritual strength for such exalted and lonely roles—nor the wisdom.

Our efforts to aid friendly nations and peoples should, to the extent possible, be channeled through appropriate multinational agencies.

Our treaties and other foreign commitments should be kept under review so that, in any confrontation, American troops shall not be expected to enter the front lines first.

We should not shrink committing our armed forces when our own national interest is imperiled, and we should be ready to help countries struggling for causes that coincide with our goals with moral and economic support and military supplies.

The commitment of U.S. armed forces to combat should be based on the collective judgment of the President and Congress, who should share responsibility for it. The President has the right to take emergency action as Commander-in-Chief, but Congress should terminate undeclared wars when it deems this in the national interest.

A strong Central Intelligence Agency is needed. So long as other nations engage in covert activities harmful to the United States, our interests may require the CIA to engage in such activities. At the same time adequate congressional supervision of the CIA and its activities is called for to guarantee that they stay within the law.

Defense

We believe that national survival, as well as avoiding global war, depend on our military strength, particularly on our nuclear deterrent. We and our allies must maintain our military power until there is effective arms control by all nations.

We approve of military forces manned by volunteers, who should be adequately paid to make such service attractive. The authority and basic machinery of the draft should be kept on a standby basis for use if necessary.

Middle East

The objectives of America's Middle East policy should be to bring about complete Arab-Israeli reconciliation and to make the Middle East a peaceful area free from domination by any outside power.

The United States should furnish friendly nations in the area military and economic aid needed to help them maintain their independence.

The settlement the United States should press for ought to assure national sovereignties, secure borders, a just resolution of the Palestinian problem and unrestricted international commerce. We condemn all terrorist activities, which only increase the obstacles to a settlement and victimize innocents.

China

We support the policy of improved relations with Mainland China. Much benefit can result from encouraging China to play a wider, peaceful role in world society.

At the same time, we should maintain close ties with Nationalist China, an old and valued friend of the United States, and we look forward to the day when Taiwan will be readmitted to the United Nations.

We believe that Taiwan's future should be resolved by peaceful means and in keeping with the wishes of its people.

Population Control

Overpopulation of the earth is a serious threat to humanity's future. The United States should encourage family planning at home and abroad.

Newspaper Shield Law

We urge Congress and state legislatures to strengthen free-flow-of-information laws and other measures to protect newsmen and the confidentiality of their sources.

The Right To Know

The Constitutional guarantee of freedom of the press is not a special boon to the press alone; it is a guarantee of freedom of information to all citizens.

As editors, we believe this fact must be stressed to the public, and we accept the obligation to fight attempts to erode the people's right to know.

What Is News?

Its Values Lie in a
Newspaper's Standards

NEWS IS EASIER to recognize than to define. News is an overt act; it is an animated picture of people doing something, not a still-life of the condition of society. As a matter of Scripps-Howard principle, the other fellow's side of the story is also news.

News is a record and a measurement of current human affairs. It is an event or a situation which is of importance or significance in the life of a community. It is a happening or a development—national, international, regional or local—which affects the public welfare, or claims the public interest.

News is a daily recording of the efforts of human beings to adjust themselves to their environment, and to each other. It is a chronicle of human frailties and human failures—of their perfections and triumphs; it is a record of their greed and lust, of their love and generosity, their wisdom and their stupidity. It is a report of their strivings and aspirations, their hopes and their fears and their courage.

News is created out of shifting elements: it is relative, not absolute. It is an ingredient in the human awareness of related circumstances—not an isolated fact or incident suspended in time. Something might be news today, and not tomorrow—or an event might be news next week and not today.

Certain events, such as a legislative debate, a fire, a robbery, a murder, a riot or a catastrophe, a crisis at city hall, have elements of immediacy and become news on the instant. They require no relationship to other events in order to establish their significance.

But facts or events which do not contain the element of immediacy must fall within the public awareness of other happenings in order to become news. They must be relevant to known motives or associations; they must coincide with a certain trend in human affairs, a certain turn of events. Timing is the essence of such news.

The highest form of reporting is the ability to understand and fit together certain isolated and apparently unrelated trends before they become news. The public knows what news is after it becomes news. Only the accomplished and skilled reporter or editor knows what it is *before* it becomes news—and the most experienced reporter or editor will look to the timing of his reports so as to gain a maximum of public interest through public awareness of the coincidence of facts and events.

News is a recording of the substance, as well as the spirit of things by which men live: a report of their buyings and sellings, of the things they create and build; it is a chronicle of their cultural and social yearnings. It is a report of their heartaches and tragedies, a record of their spiritual quest—and their goings to hell.

News is something unusual or fantastic or bizarre—or so uniquely commonplace as to be extraordinary.

News is a fist fight or a dog fight or a political fight; news is a contest between men, or between men and nature.

News is adventure, it is mystery; it is high drama and low comedy, it is wealth and poverty; it is splendor, and frequently squalor.

News is a description of what men pay for, and women wear; a report of what people eat and drink, and how they live. News is the death of a person—and the birth of one. News is what your editor says it is.

How To Write News

No 'Rules' Here But You
Might Find Some Pointers

THIS IS LIKE trying to tell how to write a novel. There are lots of ways to do it. In a news story, the idea is to arrange a set of facts in such manner as to attract attention, and cause someone to read what you have written. There are no fixed rules for doing that, but the best way to start is to have all the available facts at hand.

It is an axiom—a bromide, almost—that a news story should answer the question who, what, where, when and sometimes how. The rush of some reporters and rewrite men to hurry these elements into a story—to crowd everything into the opening sentence—often results in some extremely dull writing. Few readers are going to spend their time poking around in a literary junk pile on the chance of finding some deeply buried item of interest.

A WELL—CONSTRUCTED news story will have dramatic interest, the narrative will be arranged in proper sequence, and it will be written in simple language. The term "dramatic interest" should be defined—it might be contended that there is no dramatic interest in a routine real estate transfer, or a listing of people attending a luncheon of a welfare organization. What is meant here by "dramatic interest" is simply the main thing that happened.

It is not always necessary, or desirable, to state the main dramatic fact in the opening sentence, but if that is not done, then everything which goes ahead of it should be skillfully fashioned to sharpen interest in the main dramatic fact when it does appear. Further, if the statement of the main point of interest is delayed, the reader should understand that he is being deliberately drawn along with the promise of something worth while to come. A story should not seem aimless.

The technique of the leisurely beginning is chiefly used as a device to create a mood, or set a stage. It should also achieve a note of expectancy.

AFTER THE MAIN FACT of dramatic interest has been stated, the rest of the story consists of expository and explanatory detail. The details are the most important elements in a well-written news story.

Details should be exact. The exact time and place, the exact distance, the exact thing that was said, the exact height, or color of hair or eyes or cut of garment are facts which sharpen interest and give movement and imagery to a story.

These details should be not only explicit, but arranged in such sequence as to give clarity and meaning to everything that goes before, and to everything that follows. Each paragraph should relate to the paragraph ahead, and to the whole of the story; and the value of these details should be graduated from the bottom of the story up. Don't let the make-up man kill a vital detail, or a reader miss it behind a jump line.

In the hands of a skilled craftsman, the leisurely beginning and the delayed cracker are sometimes effective; but that sort of technique is a mere mannerism, which confuses and annoys a reader. A flowing, rhythmic style is preferable in any kind of writing, unless the subject matter, or the circumstances of the story indicate a special sort of treatment.

GOOD NEWS WRITING does, however, presume the establishment of a mood to conform to the subject matter. A story involving tragedy or sorrow would be written in a sombre tone, not flippantly or lightheartedly. The report of a Senate debate on the atomic bomb would not be handled in the same mood as the story of a boy and a lost dog. There are subjects which indicate a whimsical treatment, others which call for words at a gallop, and others which require acid—but rarely does one story call for a combination of such moods and tone.

Although it cannot classify exactly as NEWS-writing, there is the "interpretative" story which also requires distinctive treatment, and tone. An interpretative story is not a recital of the writer's personal opinions—it is an objective and impersonal analysis of the facts, designed to cause the reader to reach his own conclusions, or form his own opinion of the merits of a controversy.

Interpretative stories are usually written by men with strong personal opinions, but these personal opinions of the writer do not necessarily conform to the conclusions derived from his arrangement and appraisal of the facts. Ray Clapper's articles often led to conclusions which he did not sentimentally or philosophically embrace.

But whatever "style" or mood or tone one uses in newspaper writing, it is achieved through the impact, or the imagery of written language. Words are the raw materials of language. A newspaperman, as the illiterate said of the Squire, ought to have enough words to write his name, with a few left over. The simpler a man strives to write, the more words he should know. It does not require a very wide, or exquisite knowledge of words to write in a fat, windy style. It is the little words that develop a lean, hard prose.

BUT SIMPLE WRITING, in order to be good writing, requires more than the stringing of little words on a short thread. It requires the use of the exact word.

Some words are hard as rocks, others soft as clay. There are words as direct in meaning as a pointed pistol. Some words are iridescent, giving color and tone to other words. Unless he is miraculously endowed with intuitive knowledge, a newspaperman who wants to write well must devote much labor to the study of words.

But words alone cannot make a story, despite the fact that clever and facile writers can make it appear so. It is

Aims, Methods, and Purposes

facts that make a news story—the energizing element of something happening, or about to happen. The purpose of words is to give the happening movement and meaning.

COMMENT: This chapter seemed, on casual first reading, a trifle outdated. For instance, perhaps only Concern graybeards might recall Ray Clapper—though the noted Scripps-Howard national reporter left an indelible mark of excellence on journalism in the Twenties and Thirties. Did the passing years and advent of electronic journalism do serious harm to this treatise, written for publication in the 1948 first edition of this Handbook?

That question was put to four senior Scripps-Howard editors, all of whom are excellent writers and keen students of our craft. Not one felt it should be updated or revised. As one observed: "The more I read this chapter the more I am persuaded it remains as valid today as when it was first written, presumably by the late John Sorrells. It's a good piece of writing itself and to tinker with it or squirt bits of our own wisdom into it would bitch it all up." —The Editor.

Good Typography

A Matter of Taste, But We Have Our Own Standards

THE SIXTIES and the Seventies, marking the demise of hot metal and the advent of electronic composition, brought monumental upheaval in newspaper typography, design and graphics.

But nothing that has happened, or possibly will happen, has altered the time-honored Scripps-Howard principle that type is a medium for the expression of ideas—not a substitute for ideas. Great newspapers are not created in the composing room.

Since the era of John Sorrells—in the late Forties—the Scripps-Howard estimate of what is good typography has been more a matter of taste than of rule. However, there are some generally accepted practices—and their fundamentals have survived the free-thinking vagaries of so-called modernism.

It was Sorrells's assessment in the 1948 edition of this handbook that nearly everybody agrees that a carefully constructed page, with simplicity of design, and a balanced contrast, is a sounder principle to go by than a page in which there is no design, no point of focus, and no contrast; and that a restrained arrangement of type is more effective, and easier to read, than a tricky arrangement.

The more-or-less universal pressure to resort to just-gotta-be-different gimmicks in typography and design has been felt in Scripps-Howard the same as in other shops, and adjustments have been made to accommodate the shift from an eight-column page to six columns, and to acknowlege the attendant new dimensions and possibilities in offset printing, computer composition, greater availability of color, etc.

The ideas of John Sorrells—totally sound for his day and the then state of the art—were later updated by Jack Howard and Jack Lockhart. But that, too, occurred some years back, and much more has changed. It was time in 1976 to update again—and that fell to Gordon Hanna.

He found many of Sorrells's suggestions still sound. It remains perhaps even more imperative to pay serious attention to typography, both to invite attention and to make reading easier. There seems to be merit in some uniformity among the Scripps-Howard Newspapers. Not that any one should be a carbon copy of another. Each must have its own identity and personality. But the Concern has a personality, too, and there should be an underlying theme that identifies each newspaper as a member of the Scripps-Howard family. This can best be accomplished by following certain basic standards throughout.

Recent years have brought considerable change in the way we live. Our readers are different. So are their interests and habits. With that has come change in the way we produce our newspapers and in the product itself.

The content, as always, is the most important ingredient of a good newspaper. But today appearance plays an important role in attracting the reader in the first place, in making him feel comfortable with it, and encouraging him to return tomorrow.

Ours should be a clean and open appearance, neither too black nor too gray. It should be one that invites the reader in, and encourages him to stay. By avoiding clutter we can accomplish this.

Hanna and Dave Stolberg reworked the former appearance concepts into a set of broad guidelines, deliberately avoiding making them too detailed so as to leave some room for innovation and experimentation.

There have to be exceptions, Hanna pointed out, to the general rules. They are guidelines, not gospel. For instance, in Memphis *The Commercial Appeal* has to be different, and tabloid editors have their own special problems.

Most of the following guidelines, however, can and should apply to all:

Format

Use six columns to the page for editorial matter—throughout the paper when on a 9-column ad base, and on all open pages and wherever else possible when the ad base is 8-column. Except for agate, avoid narrow one-column set when on the 6-9 format. Cooperation from the advertising department in laying out the pages can help eliminate the need for this.

Makeup

The trend is away from strictly vertical display, and that is good. But avoid going overboard on the horizontal. The best design may lie somewhere in between. Open pages and pages with few ads require several points of focus. Try to square off stories. When you can't, don't allow wraps to stray beyond two levels. Carefully dummy every page. A good overall appearance depends upon close attention to detail. Advertising should not be carried above news matter.

Boxes/Rules

Use boxes sparingly; no more than two to any page. Avoid using boxes next to art and/or ads. Eliminate cutoff rules, as we have dropped column rules.

Booking

The number of sections will depend on the size of the newspaper, of course. Try to keep section fronts open. There should be some news on Page 2 and 3 of the first section. The basic booking categories—main news, opinion, finance, family, amusements, and sports—should keep their relative position every day, when possible. Try to group items of like geography or subject on inside pages of each department. The lead page of each department should have the most open space allocated to that type of news. Comics, television schedules and other standing features should be anchored if possible.

Headline Type

Stick to one family of type throughout the paper. Our headline survey shows a trend toward the use of Spartan, medium and bold (the black is too black). This corresponds to

Harris Intertype's Futura medium and demibold. No matter what the brand name, the important element is a sans serif legibility which avoids the opposing pitfalls of laciness and blackness. We are not encouraging anyone to rush out and buy all new headline type, but if yours is substantially different, we urge you to consider Spartan when making a change. With a variety of sizes, and italic for relief (especially over features), there seems little need to use several different faces.

Headlines

We approve the trend toward all lower case heads (except, of course, for the first word and proper names). All caps and outsized heads may be appropriate for street sale editions, but we see no reason to shout at our home-delivered readers. Headlines should be flush left. Exceptions are one-liners or boxed heads, which may be centered. Headlines should never bulge into the margins. Tombstoning and bumping heads should be avoided. All heads should have an adequate and consistent amount of white space above, below and between lines. Head counts should not exceed 40 units per line.

Kickers

Kickers (or overlines) should be flush left, at least half the point size of the main head (which then must be indented one quad), and italicized if the main head is Roman (and vice versa). Limit letter count to that of the main head. Decks and hammerheads, when appropriate, should conform in appearance to the clean and simple look sought by these guidelines. Kickers should not be used when the head has a deck.

Standing Heads

We recommend uniform style for all logos and standing heads. They should identify the regular feature simply, directly and cleanly. Avoid arty graphics. Features with standing heads need news headlines, too. Section logos always should run above the fold, the higher the better.

Subheads

Subheads or bold-faced lead-ins may be useful to break up gray type, but avoid stars and asterisks in this role.

Air
Used judiciously, white space can make the newspaper page more appealing to the eye. Overdone, it dilutes graphic impact and wastes newsprint.

Nameline/Masthead
One cutoff rule between the nameline and news on Page One is enough, and we see no need to box ears. Limit information in namelines and mastheads to what is essential, avoiding clutter. Other desirable data can be printed in the postal notice box.

Indexes/Summaries
Indexes can be too skimpy. They should be detailed at least to the degree that the reader can find all regular departments and features. When references are carried as part of the index, they should give the reader an idea of what the story is about. Summaries of news events should be just that and not a catch-all for miscellaneous shorts. They demand careful writing and editing.

Jumps
Keep to a minimum, and group them inside. Never jump out of the section.

Art
Pictures should be judiciously cropped, carried in adequate size, and have something to say. Faces are interesting, but not if six of them are crowded into two columns. A liberal use of maps and other graphics makes the news clearer to the reader and helps relieve the grayness of type. Reader surveys show there is less confusion when stories are placed under accompanying photographs.

Cutlines
Cutline style should be consistent throughout the newspaper. When a picture accompanies a story, say what's in the picture and avoid repeating what's in the headline or the lead.

Spot Color

We encourage use of spot color when it is available from the pressroom. Generally, it is not suitable for big headline type. And tint blocks can inhibit readability. Used tastefully, color can add impact to the page.

Opinion

Don't let the importance and seriousness of editorial commentary trap you into dullness. Graphics and attractive makeup have a place on editorial pages, too.

Classified

When more than three columns of classified ads are to be carried on the slop page, try to square them off. This will avoid wasted space caused by varying column widths, and at the same time give display room at the top of the page.

Business Review

Business review pages are still with us in some places. They must be properly and clearly labeled as advertising, or at the least carry a disclaimer line across the top making it clear that the advertisers pay for the space. Headline type must be different from that used on news pages. Positioning opposite editorial or other premium pages should be avoided. This same philosophy applies to advertising sections. They should be clearly labeled for what they are. And, unless the content is legitimate news, a different headline type should be used. We should get away from the "puff" stories and produce the content of these sections for the reader, not just the advertiser. Better readership will benefit him more than a free plug.

Good Promotion

Not Floats and Floozies,
But Service to The Public

IT USED TO BE A GIRL—any pretty, well-figured girl doing anything at all, or nothing at all, so long as she did it with her legs crossed and her skirt above her knees. Standard equipment for a promotion editor was a well-filled address book.

That was in the "gee whiz" era, when it wasn't people but city editors who made news, and a front page looked naked without Railroad Gothic type. If a Chinese got carved up in a cutting scrape it was called a Tong War, and a picture wasn't worth a thousand words unless it showed a lifeless body with an X marking the spot. Police went around with "dragnets" and it became a "manhunt" when the call went out to bring in some two-bit sneak thief. If he dusted out of town in a T-model Ford, he invariably escaped in a "high-powered" automobile. Comic strips consisted of "wham" and "biff" and if a man could spell the three words *smash, blast* and *drive*, he was qualified for at least a trial at writing heads. News was served up juicy rare, well peppered and sizzling hot.

It was a time when no new feature or enterprise could be properly introduced to the public without a floozie, a float and a basket of roses. The purpose of *promotion* was to drum up a crowd and it had some of the characteristics and flavor of a medicine show, with barker, shills and somebody in tights.

That period—Pegler's "Era of Wonderful Nonsense" —disappeared in the maw of the Depression. Editors emerged from that social cataclysm with a soberer and a sounder standard of news values, and from the same conditioning, no doubt, acquired a different concept of the possibilities and techniques of promotion.

PROMOTION ISN'T cheesecake any more. It is an instrument of policy. It is the machinery for setting in motion a newspaper's ideals of public service. It is the medium through which a newspaper solidifies its relations with its readers. Promotion paves an avenue of approach to public good-will.

There is, of course, a place in the over-all concept of promotion for the drum-beating type of stunt promotion, but it should not be considered a substitute for the day-by-day, long-range program of public service, by which a newspaper sinks its roots into the life of the community.

PUBLIC SERVICE PROMOTION is infectious. It becomes an institutional attitude; an attitude that transcends a promotion editor or a promotion department. It becomes a journalistic concept and creed, and when that creed becomes a part of the newspaper's character, every staff member will consciously or subsconsciously seek ways in which to participate.

The person in Scripps-Howard who is responsible for the Concern's institutional promotion, and whose Cincinnati office serves as a conduit for promotion ideas for the newspapers, is the editorial promotion director, James H. Wagner. He, in turn, has an opposite number at most Scripps-Howard newspapers with whom he maintains a liaison, sharing ideas with them, and when occasion demands, working with them at their newspapers.

Institutionally, Scripps-Howard for more than five decades has bought the outside back cover of Editor & Publisher magazine for a full-page promotion ad. These ads appear weekly and usually feature an achievement by one of our newspapers, United Press International or Scripps-Howard News Service.

The ads also are used to promote the awards program of The Scripps-Howard Foundation. The editorial promotion director turns them out, often with the help of promotion departments at the newspapers and at UPI.

MOST RECOGNIZABLE of Scripps-Howard promotions institutionally is its symbol, the lighthouse. The lighthouse has been guiding readers of our newspapers since 1927. Its origin is credited to the late Carl C. Magee, crusading editor and publisher of the *New Mexico State Tribune,* now *The Albuquerque Tribune.*

Magee wrote a column on Page One of *The Tribune* under the headline, "Turning on the Light." The column gradually took on a lighthouse, which was featured at the top, together with the line, "Give Light and the People Will Find Their Own Way—Dante."

Scripps-Howard, which bought *The Tribune* in 1923, adopted the lighthouse and slogan as its trademark in 1927. "Dante" was dropped from the quotation the next year when Scripps-Howard could not verify the origin. Researchers have since traced the quotation to a similar passage in Dante's "Divine Comedy," but some persons still say Magee invented the line.

THE NATION'S BIGGEST and most prestigious newspaper public service promotion in the Eighties is owned by Scripps-Howard. It is also one in which, besides most of our own newspapers, numerous other dailies outside Scripps-Howard participate. It is the National Spelling Bee where, at the grassroots, it is estimated eight million school children compete.

The Louisville Courier-Journal founded the National Spelling Bee in 1925 with nine sponsoring newspapers. Twenty-nine newspapers were participating when Scripps-Howard took over the program in 1940.

By 1960 the number of sponsoring newspapers had reached 73, but there the figure leveled off. For the next decade the Spelling Bee would gain a few sponsors one year and lose a few the next. At best it stayed even. It was a period in American education when schools put subjects like spelling on the back burner.

By 1970, however, spelling began enjoying a resurgence as an important subject in elementary and junior high schools, and with this resurgence came renewed interest in the National Spelling Bee. More and more newspapers added the promotion to their community service programs, and in 1976 the real explosion came. Sponsorship leaped from 79 to 87. The next year it climbed to 94, and the next year to 106. In 1980 there were 112 sponsorships.

THE FINALS OF the National Spelling Bee are conducted, usually late May or early June, in Washington, D.C. Contestants spend one and a half days spelling, and the rest of the week sightseeing, attending mixers and an awards banquet. Most spellers are accompanied by their families, so the size of the group is close to 500. A White House visit is always scheduled and they are frequently greeted by a member of the First Family.

One phenomenon of the National Spelling Bee is the practice spelling booklet, *Words of the Champions*, which is made available to sponsoring newspapers at modest cost for promotional and study purposes. The booklet is updated each year and its cover given a new look. It has become a "little best seller" with sales of nearly one-half million copies.

The Spelling Bee is directed nationally by Wagner, and his assistant, Laurel Maag-Sakai.

WHILE THE SPELLING BEE is the big promotion at most Scripps-Howard newspapers, by no means is it the only promotion.

The late Seventies saw the emergence of Book & Author Luncheons and Health Seminars as major promotional vehicles, and at newspapers like *The Columbus Citizen-Journal* and Fullerton *Daily News Tribune* marathons drew thousands of participants as jogging became a national pastime. Crime Solvers became another propular promotion in cooperation with police departments.

The Pittsburgh Press and *The Kentucky Post* proved that a promotion didn't have to be space-consuming and costly to prosper. These newspapers were front-runners in refining what became known as the "mini promotion." Valentine's Day, Mother's Day and Christmas were especially suited to these promotions.

Long-time promotions like the Maid of Cotton at The *Memphis Press-Scimitar* and recognition of Straight A Students continued popular.

THE TERM "IN-HOUSE AWARDS" became part of the Scripps-Howard vocabulary in 1979 when, on a monthly basis, it was decided to recognize outstanding spot news writing, headline writing and news photography on the Concern's daily newspapers.

The next year the number of prize categories was increased to include reporting, and writing, when time is not a factor.

Monthly winners receive a $100 prize and a certificate, and qualify for grand prizes of $1000 and a plaque and second prizes of $500.

PROMOTION OF The Scripps-Howard Foundation's contest awards, which have grown annually in the number of entries, continues under the editorial promotion director's office, and in 1980, *Scripps-Howard News,* the Concern's monthly employee magazine edited by Sue Porter, became a part of the office.

It is frequently said that no promotion is really new, but with polishing, almost any good idea can be given a new twist and upgraded. To make Scripps-Howard newspapers aware of what others are doing promotionally and in their news columns—both inside Scripps-Howard and outside—Wagner's monthly "Clip Tips" package is a mine of good suggestions.

Advertising

How It Serves The Public
And The 'Free' Press

THE USE OF NEWSPAPER advertising in America got its start in three paid notices in the May 8, 1704 issue of the weekly *Boston News-Letter*. One posted a reward for capture of a thief. The second offered a reward for return of stolen goods. The third:

> At Oysterbay, on Long Island in the Province of N. York. There is a very good Fulling Mill to be Let or Sold, as also a plantation, having on it a large new Brick house, and another good house by it for a Kitchen & workhouse, with a Barn, Stable &c. a young Orchard with 20 acres clean land. The Mill is to be Let with or without the Plantation; Enquire of Mr William Bradford Printer in N. York, and know further.

These little ads doubtless put mere pennies into the *News-Letter's* till. But from this quaint beginning, advertising has become of paramount importance to anyone who makes a living from newspaper work, because it helps meet the payroll and keep newspapers solvent.

There's no reason to be apologetic about that. Financial independence is the first requisite of a free press. An insolvent newspaper can't stay in business; a subsidized newspaper is neither free nor independent. The only kind of a newspaper that is authentically free and independent is one which derives sufficient revenue from the sale of its product—and its by-product—to operate profitably. Modern newspapers require heavy capital investments, and it is a basic necessity to make adequate profits.

Advertising has a profound significance in our society. It is inextricably woven into the whole economic and social pattern of our way of life. It is the channel through which the producer and the seller can reach a free and open market for their wares. It is the thing which gives life and vitality and endurance to our system of free enterprise.

American businesses are thoroughly convinced of the effectiveness of newspaper advertising. Testimony to that truth is how much is spent annually in the United States for advertising in newspapers—more than fifteen billion dollars.

ADVERTISING is an intrinsic instrument of democracy. What we call a "free" society comes down to a system of habits and customs involving the performances of many small acts. These acts bear directly on the way people live their daily lives—how and what they eat, what they wear, how they get about and what they do for entertainment.

In our form of social organization, no one is required to trade at a specified store, or accept a specified brand of food. Ours is a system which promotes the theory of free choice in the purchase of goods and services, and merchants compete among themselves for patronage. Advertising is the passport to this free market.

It not only provides the opportunity for free choice, but it protects the buyer against discrimination in price and quality; it is a social force, a democratizing element in our way of life.

A NEWSPAPER has only two things to sell. One is the product—the newspaper itself. The other is advertising—a by-product. The product is sold to the reader, the by-product to the merchant, or to the man whose message is not "news" and who is willing to pay for addressing the newspaper's audience.

The advertiser's purchase of this by-product is limited and restricted: he buys a specified amount of space, and that alone. He does not buy a newspaper's influence, or its good will, or its news and editorial columns; a newspaper will guarantee to him that a given number of people subscribe to the paper, and charge him a rate based on that number of people, but it will not guarantee that a single one of them will read or be impressed by his message.

The hoary and flimsy charge that newspaper policy is influenced or controlled by the advertiser has no support either in fact or in logic. An advertiser's primary interest is in creating a market for his wares. To do that, he wants to attract the attention of a maximum number of people, with a maximum amount of buying power. He is greatly interested in the amount of a newspaper's circulation, and in the loyalty of its readers.

HIS BUSINESS INTEREST in a newspaper's policy derives solely from the question of whether that policy will attract or alienate readers, whether it will cement or destroy public confidence in the newspaper. The latter is important to him, because it affects the quality as well as the quantity of a newspaper's circulation. He knows such confidence would be destroyed if the public suspected that the newspaper's policies were controlled or influenced by purely commercial interests.

The political and social views of a liberal newspaper might be personally distasteful to a conservative merchant, and a merchant with advanced social views might be personally contemptuous of the policies of a conservative newspaper.

But, liberal or conservative, if the newspaper has a large enough audience to give wide distribution to the advertiser's message, and if it enjoys the confidence and respect of that audience, the merchant's needs and wants are served. If a newspaper's policies are such that the paper cannot serve those wants and needs, the merchant is not concerned with changing the paper's policies—he merely changes his advertising.

Scripps-Howard solicits advertising and seeks to make profits in order to preserve financial independence. By the same token we have always sought to give adequate service in return.

But our papers and our space is offered to reader and advertiser on our own terms. Those terms are that there will be no compromise with what we conceive to be journalistic integrity, or public responsibility.

Our Code of Ethics

FOLLOWING IS THE POLICY of the Scripps-Howard Newspapers for all editorial personnel concerning outside work, junkets, political activities:

1. Prohibited:

Paid work of any sort for any branch of the government, any political organizations, any candidate, any politician.

Preparing or handling publicity for pay for anyone the employee might have occasion to deal with as a reporter or an editor.

Doing correspondence for any direct competitor of his own newspaper or of any other Scripps-Howard newspaper.

Participation of an employee in a prominent or leading role in party politics, in a way which could raise questions as to the newspaper's objectivity.

2. Permitted, but ONLY on prior approval of the editor:

Teaching, lecturing or speaking for pay.

Regular or guest appearances on radio or Television.

Outside writing for magazines, trade publication, house organs.

Sale by photographers of prints, or by artists of their work, done for the newspaper.

All outside work not included here must have prior approval.

Any junket or trip on which the staff member's expenses are paid wholly or in part by someone other than the newspaper.

3. Gifts:

When the gifts exceed the limits of propriety, they should be returned. We do not expect, and in fact discourage gifts or free admission in return for fair treatment or coverage in our columns.

September 24, 1976

SECTION TWO

Pioneers And Other Personalities

Lusty EWS, Gentle Miss Ellen,
Brash RWH, And An Array
Of Luminaries Who
Molded Concern
Tradition

E. W. Scripps at Miramar about 1922

E. W. Scripps

Tough-minded, Realistic . . .
a Product of His Times.

Some OF HIS biographers have created an image of E. W. Scripps as a farm boy sitting on a rail fence, contemplating the whole range of his ultimate purpose. This is a doubtful idealization of a genuinely precocious intellect. Like most men with the capacity for mental and spiritual growth, it is more probable that his philosophy of journalism and his sense of social justice flowered as he grew in stature.

Neither would it be an exact picture of E. W. Scripps to imagine him a bowed, sorrowful figure, brooding over the miseries of mankind. As a young man he was serious in purpose, but was of a lively disposition. He liked horses and drove a fine span. He smoked cigars and drank whisky until almost the day of his death. He enjoyed wholesome pleasures of the flesh. He liked a rowdy game of poker. In his later years, he was gruff of manner; he wore boots and dribbled cigar ashes on his vest. His language was not always elegant. He was, in fact, a tough customer.

He was a humanitarian, but not a sentimentalist. He was tough-minded, tough-fibered and realistic. His idealism was intellectual, not emotionalism. He didn't strive to make people better—he sought to make them better off. He wasn't so interested in improving people as he was in improving the conditions under which they lived.

E. W. Scripps was no soft-hearted paternalist. He strove to provide jobs, not charity. He believed the laborer was worthy of his hire, but he would hire him at the market rate and expect a full day's work for a day's pay. He wanted a man to feel free to quit his employ any time he wished, for whatever purpose he desired; and he figured that when a man had worked a week, and been paid for a week's work, there was no continuing obligation on the part of either party. He believed self-reliance created self-respect.

Men looking for soft and easy journalistic careers rarely sought service with E. W. Scripps. It was hard, tough work. The hours were long; and good men more often than not worked for less pay than they could have drawn for commensurate work on the opposition paper.

But for men of a particular breed, there was a quid pro quo—men who considered journalism an exciting adventure, or who had instincts for social reform, or who liked to deflate pomposity and pretense. Scripps papers stood in awe of no person or institution; they were often rowdy, and always aggressive. There were no sacred cows.

Scripps men worked in an atmosphere of journalistic and creative freedom. A man could try out his ideas. And since the Scripps policy was to sell stock to editors and managers, there was a chance for substantial financial rewards to those minded that way.

It won't do to jerk E. W. Scripps bodily out of the context of his times. He was the product of a peculiar era in American history. The principles on which he founded his first newspaper, and his concept of journalism he intended to practice, were shaped by the conditions of his environment.

He was born in Rushville, Illinois, June 18, 1854. Franklin Pierce was in the White House. It would be only seven years until the American people were to decide, in the convulsion of Civil War, the question of whether men could govern themselves in a democracy. A decade or so before, the technique of national politics had changed, making way for the politician and the development of the party machine.

Within the twenty years prior to his birth, the nation had fought a war with Mexico, from which the United States bagged a vast territory—Texas, New Mexico, California, Arizona and a part of Colorado. It was a rough, tough, brawling young nation, a nation of restless people on the march. The Oregon Trail was opened, traders drove long caravans on the road to Santa Fe. Gold was discovered in California. Two

Pioneers and Other Personalities 49

working parties met at Ogden, Utah, and hammered a spike which united the nation in a single railway line.

THE TWO DECADES following the birth of E. W. Scripps was an era of unbridled economic lusts, of incredibly brazen corruption, both in business and in politics. Congressmen auctioned off their votes, an American ambassador to England sold stocks in fake mines to Britishers. Railroads fleeced the taxpayers and then gulled the public with watered stock. It was the era of the *credit mobeliere*, the age of Jim Fisk and Jay Gould and Commodore Vanderbilt; there was plunder and greed on every hand, with a trail of scandal leading to the White House. It was a period of political venality, symbolized by the "Tweed Ring" in New York, an organization which practiced thievery with an abandon that would shame a Dick Turpin.

IT WAS AN economic jungle, in which the common man —the little merchant and the wage-earner—were helpless to cope with the problems of their environment. It was this era that saw the rise of vast corporations which devoured the smaller ones, or consolidated with the larger ones. Trusts were formed in sugar, in meat packing, in oil. Railroads made special rates to favored corporations, thus riveting their absolutism.

It was a period marked by an arrogant, ruthless abuse of economic power. Wages were low; prices were high. Two great industrial protests—a railway strike in Baltimore and the Pullman strike in Chicago—were broken by Federal troops. Labor organizations were intimidated, demoralized, destroyed. Discontent and rebellion were in the air.

It was also in this era that a new type of immigration made its impact on American society. The older types of immigrants—German and Irish for the most part—were eager and quick to assimilate. The new elements came from Poland, Hungary, Russia, Italy. They were inclined to cling to the industrial centers and to form tight little islands of racial and nationalistic culture.

It was in 1878, under the influence of these times and conditions, that E. W. Scripps started his first newspaper. It was The Penny Press in Cleveland, Ohio. His first editor was Robert F. Paine, a rugged, courageous, rough-hewn newspaper man, who continued for many years confidant and adviser to E. W. Scripps.

E. W. SCRIPPS'S father—James Mogg Scripps—emigrated to America from England in 1844. He was a widower with six children, ranging from three to thirteen. He bought a farm in Illinois and soon thereafter married his second wife, Julia A. Osborne.

E. W. Scripps was born of James and Julia. When he was eighteen, he went to Detroit with $80 in his pocket and a determination to make his way in the world. He clerked in a drugstore briefly, then, with his brother, James E. Scripps, started a newspaper. It was called the *Detroit News*, and still is. Associated with Ed and James in this venture were another brother, George, and a sister, Ellen Browning Scripps.

E. W. Scripps was put to work in the circulation department, but soon gravitated to the editorial department. The *News* was a two-cent paper. It was successful at that price and E. W. Scripps probably reached some profound conclusions as to the possibilities of mass sales through low rates.

By the time he was ready to launch his paper in Cleveland, he must have formed some clear and fixed concepts as to the kind of paper it would be. Out of the vast intellectual ocean which represented the mind and personality of E. W. Scripps, certain huge land masses of essential truth and wisdom from time to time emerged. His concept of *The Penny Press*—later to become *The Cleveland Press*—was the first of these.

It would be a paper designed to reach the greatest possible number of people. It would be cheap in price and popular in appeal. It would be simply and clearly written. It would be a medium of popular education. He sought from the start to bring to the level of common understanding the whole range of human knowledge. He would translate social progress into simple and understandable terms, and give a certain animation and meaning to public affairs.

He understood the inability of the common man to deal with the ruthless and predatory forces of his times. His paper would fight the alarming concentrations of corporate power.

One way to fight this gargantuan system of trusts was through organization among the people whose economic lives were affected. He encouraged workmen to organize into unions and championed their cause. He believed there was a relationship between political and economic injustice, and he conceived that his paper would fight to cleanse the courts and the political machines of corruption.

He understood the history of Europe, with its conflicts of language and race and culture. He believed America's welfare required a prompt assimilation of these foreign groups.

He visioned a daily newspaper as a practical medium for the establishment of a common community denominator. It would have to be candid and direct in its approach; it would have to be genuinely democratic in spirit. And it would have to be independent.

IT IS NOT CLEAR whether at the time he launched *The Penny Press*, E. W. Scripps had any idea of projecting his activities beyond a single city. His son, Robert P. Scripps, once told an associate that after *The Press* began to return a comfortable surplus, his father began to cast around for a place to invest his savings, and considered putting some capital into a coal business. He consulted a trusted adviser about this, and was asked if he knew anything about the coal business. Upon replying in the negative, he was advised to put his spare capital in the newspaper business—something he had demonstrated an ability to manage successfully. Shortly afterward, according to Robert P. Scripps, his father acquired the controlling interest in Cincinnati's *Penny Paper*, which later became *The Cincinnati Post*.

Whether that move was a decision casually arrived at, or actually was the result of long and thoughtful deliberation, the fact remains that the result was profound. It was a turning point. It not only determined the scope of Scripps journalism, but it influenced the quality and character of it, because the theory of putting his spare capital into newspaper projects became a basic principle of E. W. Scripps's concept of independent journalism.

So long as his money was invested in newspaper enterprises under his control—instead of in utilities, for example or in real estate, or bank stocks—he knew that his journalistic judgments would be influenced and affected only by factors which derived from newspaper publishing. He understood that "where your treasure is, there your heart is also."

E. W. SCRIPPS realized also that the first requisite of journalistic independence was financial independence. He had to make his papers pay. He also understood that journalistic independence is dissipated in a dilution of financial control. He could not be free to execute his ideas, many of which were considered radical in his time, if he surrendered the power of ownership, or if he admitted into his financial framework, business or other elements which had private interests in conflict with his broad concept of public duty.

He confined ownership in his properties to people within his organization—chiefly to his editors and business managers, who understood and shared with him the risks, and sometimes heart-breaking, and often back-breaking, struggle for public acceptance. He never surrendered his financial control and fixed it so that Scripps control would endure through two succeeding generations.

As he began to expand his group of papers, he launched and operated some which were cheap by standards other than price. He made-do with old equipment; he insisted on a strict system of expense control; he denied his papers many mechanical and journalistic luxuries which would have made them more attractive to the eye and more complete and entertaining to the reader. But he was driven by stern necessity, and he made a virtue of it. His papers, and his chain grew.

E. W. Scripps grew personally wealthy as his papers prospered, but he did not hobnob with rich men, or seek the company of bigwigs. Consistent with his theory of journalistic independence, he wanted to be free of personal entanglements which might be alien to his aims and purposes. He wanted no commitments in friendship which might influence his judgment, or stay his hand. He believed news should be appraised without fear, but also without favor.

Nevertheless, he indulged himself in some of the comforts and tastes of a rich man. He spent a great deal of his time on his ranch in California. He owned a yacht. He entertained great numbers of people who interested him. He lived well, and traveled in style. He was not a hypocrite, and while he fought for a richer and fuller life for underprivileged people, he did not consider it necessary to endure a dull man, or choose him for a companion, because he was improvident.

But, as a rich man, E. W. Scripps was neither a profligate nor a voluptuary. There was a hard core of purpose in him, never softened by the comforts of personal wealth. He never departed from his concept of his newspapers as mediums of education, as instruments of public welfare, as advocates of the man who was unable by his own honest means, to combat the excesses of his greedier or less honest fellow. He kept this sword sharp to the end.

THE ABILITY of E. W. Scripps to start or acquire papers depended in part on the availability of adequate telegraphic news reports. He held several early-day Associated Press franchises, and was one of a group of publishers called to discuss and effect a reorganization of the policies of the Associated Press. A basic policy under consideration revolved around the question of exclusivity.

From the outset, E. W. Scripps discerned where that road would lead—what it would mean in terms of independent journalism. He wanted to be free to start papers wherever he wished; and he wanted other men to be free to start newspapers, because he believed in newspapers as such. He saw that a single, powerful press association could become such a monopoly in the gathering and distributing of news as to hold the power of life and death over a publisher whose social and economic views might be at odds with the publishers who were in control of the news monopoly. A man could not start a newspaper, or operate one, except by sufferance of an association of publishers who, inevitably, would judge circumstances in the light of their own special interests.

He determined to fight this development. He organized a little news service of his own, acquired another. He brought several puny little services into a single press service. He

When *EWS* prospered in Detroit he "bought a silk hat and moved into a hotel." This photo is from that period.

PIONEERS AND OTHER PERSONALITIES

E. W. Scripps at Miramar with his sons, left to right, John, Jim, and Bob. Circa 1898.

Mrs. E. W. Scripps with Dolla, left, and Nackey.

Catching up on the news at sea

The Scripps yacht Ohio

PIONEERS AND OTHER PERSONALITIES

Portrait by John Young-Hunter, 1922

*Bust by
Jo Davidson,
1922*

EWS with a group of his execu

Robert is visible over EW's right shoulder. Roy Howard is fourth from right.

forfeited his Associated Press franchises in the process. His central idea was that telegraph news should be furnished to any publisher who desired it, and could pay for it, without regard to competitive interests. He felt that there should be a free flow of information.

It was a costly fight in many ways. Sometimes he would see a competitor subscribe to his service, and use it to the disadvantage of his own newspaper. But he never faltered, and his idea endured and prevailed. That was one of his last fights for journalistic independence, and by any measurement, one of his greatest. It required great courage and vision.

E. W. SCRIPPS conducted a voluminous correspondence; he wrote essays, tracts, observations, disquisitions; he put many of his reflections and cogitations on paper; he "thought out loud" in writing. Many of the ideas he advanced did not represent fixed or final conclusions. He used ideas as tools to carve, to create, to build—not as pronouncements of final and immutable judgment.

He often tried out some of his ideas on his associates, with a force which caused some of them to accept literally what he himself recognized at the time to be nebulous, fallacious, or unsound. He appeared to be a man of contradictions. That might have been because he was prolific in ideas, and one idea might overtake and conflict with another one previously expressed. In viewing his career, it does not seem that it was what he said that counted most—it was what he did. It was what he actually stood for—as against what he reflected upon, or toyed with in his moments of intellectual contemplation.

THERE ARE SOME cynics, some ill-wishers, and some more-in-sorrow-than-in-anger friends of Scripps-Howard who from time to time express their disapproval by invoking the spirit of E. W. Scripps, and conjuring an image of his consternation or disapproval of some line of Concern policy. Nobody knows, of course, what attitude E. W. Scripps would take with respect to specific questions today, but one thing seems clear from his character and personality as he revealed it in his own time and in his own works: he would be realistic and practical in his approach. He would develop his attitudes and concepts from conditions as he found them. He was a man of his times, and he would be a man of his times today.

It seems clear from the principles on which he started, and operated his newspapers during his own lifetime, that he would oppose waste of taxpayers' money; that he would fight political and economic corruption; that he would strive to destroy concentrations of power, irrespective of what persons or organizations wielded that power. He would fight the tyranny of union bossism over the individual and over the public as he once fought concentrations and abuses of corporate power. He would fight for the right of a man to work and get ahead by his own efforts. He would fight for a conservation of national resources for the welfare of many, as against the self-seeking of the few. He would fight subversion of national security, regardless of what name it went under.

It is safe to believe he would do all those things today, because those were principles on which he founded his newspaper enterprises, and the basis on which he operated them.

Scripps lived to be seventy-one. To the very end he left no doubt who was in charge. On March 12, 1926 his yacht *Ohio* was anchored in Monrovia Bay, Liberia. His health was poor; he had a hunch this might be his last voyage. "If I die," he had told his secretary, "bury me at sea." After dinner Scripps complained of feeling ill, and in twenty minutes was dead of apoplexy.

As he wished, the crew slid his body into the Atlantic Ocean. They wouldn't have dared not to.

E. W. Scripps, indeed, was truly one of a kind.

THREE WEEKS AFTER getting his first paper started, E. W. Scripps wrote this letter to his sister, Julia Anne, who was seven years his senior and a confidant.

Office of The Penny Press
12 & 14 Frankfort St. Cleveland, O., Nov. 23, 1878

DEAR ANNIE:

Your letter was handed me last evening just as I was about leaving the office.

You want to know how I think of me as I am situated. For several hours each morning I think you would be unable to think of me as you would be asleep. I wake at 5 o'clock, go to the office and work till 8 or 9 a.m., laying out the work of the day, reading the papers and writing. Then I go to breakfast 15 minutes and return with a cigar, the first of the day.

I do little other work till the first edition goes to press except reading and revising copy, giving a few instructions, looking after the composing room, keeping the printers supplied with copy and pushing the foremen up to his work so as to be down to the press in time with the forms. At 2 o'clock, 15 minutes for dinner, then my second cigar and back to the office. Work is now light. Only a couple of columns of copy to be handed out, unimportant local and telegraph. Men come in to see me, and bore me.

At 3 o'clock our second edition goes to press. From that time until 4 o'clock, the time of going to press with the third and last edition, I am too weary to do much of anything and the third edition is made up of scraps and ends, a little telegraph, a few local items, etc. I give out "time" copy for next day, story selections, etc. mostly reprint.

At half past 4 o'clock, completely fatigued, I do nothing but take a little walk, talk with the men and visitors, or go over to my room and take a little nap. Supper at 6 o'clock with John (Sweeney, his cousin and business manager). Then lie down on sofa for a rest—my third and last cigar of the day. Then back to the office, letter writing, revising copy and preparing for next day. Go to bed at 10 p.m.

Such is my life on weekdays.

An Editor's Day

On Sunday I lay abed late, spend a few hours at the office writing letters, talking with John and smoking. Sunday evening go to church. I seldom or never attend places of amusement, never any social gatherings. Business is enjoyment enough for me just now. How long this feeling will last I know not.

I pay $8 for board and do not get my money's worth. Have tolerable comfortable office quarters. My position in Cleveland has hardly yet been settled. People are beginning to have confidence in us and business prospects are improving, though they are by no means assured.

Have been noticed by every paper in town. The Herald has been complimentary. The Leader has tried to ignore me but Saturday tried to set down on me editorially, but was not successful. The Sunday Voice puffed us. The Times lied about us. The Advance gave us half a dozen screeds, but then no one ever reads The Advance. The Universe has denounced us, but that has not hurt. The Plain Dealer has squibbed us and thereby shown how we are hurting it.

We are selling more papers than any other concern in the city. Some persons in high authority have commended us. Some have condemned us. But still, on the whole, I have been received better, met with better success and done better myself than I had expected. I never thought myself brilliant or capable of doing any brilliant work. I have simply thought I could make a tolerable fair paper and be tolerable successful.

James says he is satisfied. Ellen is delighted and some of the (Detroit) News men who never thought much of my ability are a little surprised. Even Mr. Little who came with me owns now that he never had much faith in my being able to make things swing as well as I have.

Hoping that I have interested you for a half hour, I remain.

Your affectionate brother,
Ed. W. Scripps

Ellen Browning Scripps at her desk, 1919

Miss Ellen Scripps

Her Sage Counsel, Love and 'Miscellany' Helped EWS

ONE OF THE earliest and most lasting influences in the life of E. W. Scripps was that of his half-sister, Ellen Browning Scripps.

Born in England October 18, 1836, Miss Ellen was eighteen years his senior. She "adopted" the boy Edward. She read to him from the library their father, a failed London bookbinder, had brought across the ocean to his new home at Rushville, Illinois. Under her tutoring, E. W. learned to read when he was four or five.

Miss Ellen became his lifelong confidant and adviser. She was, in the words of a respected biographer, "a short, ill-proportioned and homely woman, whose sweetness, common sense and serene assurance made her a family mainstay." Through seventy years, his love for her never wavered.

Their relationship was all the more close because the boy carried on something of a running feud with his mother, who had to contend with a huge family—two daughters and three sons of her own (of whom E. W. was the last), and four step-sons and two step-daughters, one of whom was Miss Ellen.

Miss Ellen taught school and was graduated from Knox College at nearby Galesburg, Illinois, at age twenty-three in 1859, one of America's first women college graduates. After her father's death in 1873, she joined her brothers in Detroit in founding *The Evening News*. She began as a proofreader, but soon was producing a page one column of tid-bits. She combed other newspapers and periodicals at night for these human-interest shorts. They were known in the office as "Miss Ellen's Miscellany."

She sent a copy daily to E. W. Scripps who had gone on to Cleveland to found *The Penny Press*. His idea was that a readable newspaper ought to contain about four hundred to four hundred fifty items daily; his sister's report helped achieve that aim.

On the basis of her "miscellany" E. W. Scripps in 1902 founded what was perhaps the nation's first important newspaper syndicate, The Newspaper Enterprise Association. For a time it supplied features and *must* editorials to the growing chain of Scripps papers, and in 1921 went commercial, eventually serving one thousand client publishers. The durable NEA, vastly expanded, is a key component of today's United Media Enterprises.

Through the years Miss Ellen maintained close contact with her brother Edward. They exchanged thousands of letters; many of hers contained wise counsel which he heeded. They traveled together over much of the world. She took a year's leave in 1881 to tour Europe, Asia and Africa with E. W. On the trip she became a "foreign correspondent" for his *Penny Press*.

She mailed regular descriptive letters to the Cleveland paper. One depicted a bullfight in Madrid. It was a long story, perhaps five thousand words. The editor ran it in full and said his readers applauded it as "the dangdest finest description" ever written of a bullfight.

So great was E. W.'s respect for her that when returning from a long cruise he would steam his yacht past her oceanside home in California and fire a salute with his deck gun.

She joined him in other newspaper ventures and invested her savings in them. In time she realized she was becoming a wealthy woman. It was then that she began to put funds aside as a "trust for the benefit of humanity."

She lived a simple life, and gave away millions of dollars. Her benefactions include schools, colleges, hospitals, research institutions, children's playgrounds, churches of all denominations, natural history societies, and the like. She underwrote books on California wildflowers and birds.

Miss Ellen never married. Her own comments on the subject were, "As a child I hated to be forced to do anything . . . I hated the word *must*. If my elders could only have understood me better, things might have been different."

She died in her home at La Jolla, California on August 3, 1932 at the age of ninety-five.

Robert F. Paine

EW's First Editor, Lifelong Mainstay

WHEN E. W. Scripps started The Cleveland *Penny Press* in 1878, Bob Paine tackled him for a job. E. W. was his own first editor. Soon he turned the job over to Bob, a hometowner born March 8, 1856. The association thus formed lasted through life.

As Scripps expanded his newspaper holdings, "Uncle Bob" Paine became editor-in-chief of the Ohio papers. He directed Concern telegraphic news service as first general manager of the Scripps-McRae Press Association. When this was consolidated into United Press in 1907, one of his "boys," John Vandercook, became first president of UP. Paine also was first president and general manager of Newspaper Enterprise Association (NEA).

Uncle Bob was in Sacramento at the time of the San Francisco Earthquake in 1906. He walked most of the way to Oakland, across the bay from the fire-ridden city, set up headquarters in a livery stable to resume publication of *The San Francisco News*. He put up a sign "Ohio Registration Headquarters" and helped Ohioans to get word to relatives through the Scripps papers in Ohio.

In his mature years he established his home in San Francisco and his office in a corner of *The San Francisco News* editorial room. From that headquarters he conducted a wide correspondence on journalistic philosophy with the editors and general management, wrote an occasional editorial. He died in San Francisco, August 29, 1940. Uncle Bob ranks with E. W. Scripps and Miss Ellen Scripps, as one of the founders of the Scripps-Howard tradition in journalism.

Robert Paine Scripps, circa 1936

Robert P. Scripps

He Dreamed of Being a Poet,
But Took Command in His Twenties

WHEN BOB was about twelve, E. W. Scripps thoughtfully sized up the gangling, somewhat stoop-shouldered lad who stood better than six feet and concluded this was the son who would turn out to be most like him. E. W. was correct.

E. W. told an editor visiting Miramar he wasn't sure the frail youngster, his fourth and last son, would ever fill out and be strong. Scripps, making a "biological" analysis, confided that he expected "a hell of a lot of trouble with Bob until he develops, finds himself, and gets his stride."

This was 1908. E. W. had just begun "retirement" at fifty-four, handing over business control of his newspapers to eldest son Jim, barely twenty-two. E. W. was correct in predicting some difficult times with Bob—Robert Paine, named after E. W.'s great Cleveland editor. The trouble came from the boy showing a headstrong streak and a short burst of wanderlust, neither a surprising trait in the light of his paternal heritage.

It was a brief period of annoyance, far less hurtful to the old man than the real tragedies that overtook his other sons. John, No. 2, two years younger than Jim and groomed to become editor-in-chief, died at twenty-six. No. 3, Edward Willis McLean, didn't live to his eighth birthday. And Jim later stunned his father by blowing up over a World War I policy dispute, walking out and taking with him five of their West Coast newspapers and *The Dallas Dispatch*. They never got to heal their rift; Jim also died early, at thirty-five.

Bob was the only son to out-live E. W.—but by a mere dozen years for he too died in his prime.

The boys attended nearby Pomona college, but didn't stay to graduate. E. W. considered his personal "university" superior. At Miramar he supervised their education, laying out serious books for them to read three hours a day. He trained them in business. His style was down to earth. His goal was to prepare them to serve humanity by carrying on his publishing empire. He discovered the ideal classroom in which to teach them to direct men and manage property and earn money—Miramar.

It was a 2000-acre ranch. As soon as each son became fifteen, E. W. turned the place over to him to run. Jim, of course, got the job first. He actually hired and fired, directed a big crew of ranch hands, ordered supplies, paid the bills, and tried to turn a profit.

John took his turn and when Bob (born October 27, 1895 in San Diego) turned fifteen the job was wished off on him. There was natural sibling rivalry—which E. W. encouraged —and Jim booby-trapped Bob on his first day as the new ranch honcho; he incited the ranch hands to strike for a pay raise.

From age twelve Bob wanted to become a poet. E. W. abhorred the idea, fearful it would finish his son as a useful newspaperman. He hoped Bob would outgrow the adolescent urge. Bob tried to be dutiful and please his father. In 1912, before he was seventeen, he went to work on a new Scripps paper in Philadelphia, the ill-starred *News-Post*.

Bob started—as had his father—as a circulation canvasser. Later he became a reporter. In 1913 he visited Europe to study Continental municipal government. In January 1914 he was assigned an editing job in the Scripps San Diego office.

The boy grew restless. The poetry bug was still biting. It also troubled him, having no desire for ostentation, that he had been born rich. Finally, he struck out on his own.

Bob went to the oilfields at Bakersfield, California and tried to get a job as a reporter. The only work he could land was as a circulation hustler. Rival papers were giving premiums in the battle for customers. One gave a washboard for a month's subscription; the other an iron. Bob got on the washboard paper, and toted one of the contraptions around while signing up customers.

The work wasn't all that thrilling. Bob turned in his washboard and took an oilfield job. Finally he became a contractor, building foundations for gas engines, and hauling iron pipe. Disaster overtook his new career. One of his workmen broke a leg on the job; the hospital bills wiped out Bob's assets.

Moving north, he landed a $1-a-day reporter's job in Eureka, Humbolt county. His beat included the waterfront, but once he hurried with the sheriff to a town forty miles away where a circus got in trouble with lumberjacks, who killed three roustabouts. The editor splashed Bob's story across page one—and promptly chewed him out for not getting his regular shipping news.

In February 1916, he went to Hawaii (where he met Jack London, who became a lifelong friend) and on to Australia where he worked on a newspaper and studied political, social and business conditions. He regularly wrote his father, telling what he was thinking and learning. Bob came home that fall. E. W. asked Bob to write a novel based on his travels— within six weeks. Bob wrote it.

E. W., still anxious about the boy's strength, hired a physical instructor to come to the ranch, teach Bob boxing, take him on long hikes, and generally build up his muscle. Bob went along until he thought he knew enough about boxing, says a biographer, "and then knocked the stuffing out of his trainer; the trainer threw up his job."

Once again Bob was under E. W.'s tutelage. In March 1917 Bob married Margaret Culbertson, a lumberman's daughter. One month later America got into the World War.

That brought E. W. out of his nine-year "retirement." Scripps hurried to Washington in May and resumed active command of his Concern. He threw the strength of his newspapers back of President Wilson's government in all its war activities. Bob was with him night and day.

Differences were developing between E. W. and Jim, who had been in nominal command since 1908 as chairman of the board. The father abruptly appointed Bob editor-in-chief, responsible only to him. It was sink or swim—and Bob swam. Jim walked out. Bob, over E. W.'s protest, went to Camp Sherman, Ohio to join the army. He was exempted from the draft, and returned to Washington as full-fledged editorial director.

RPS with son Charles in Washington, circa 1922

Bob collected a small group of seasoned journalists, established in a back room at the old Washington Daily News. He called this the Editorial Board. It was the beginning of the present day Washington bureau and Scripps-Howard News Service. The aim was, and is, to create a composite of Concern expression.

Three years later E. W. Scripps gave Bob full charge of the Concern as his agent and attorney in fact. Roy Howard was persuaded to resign as president of United Press and team up with Bob as chairman of the board and general business manager.

Bob was a big, quiet man with strong conviction that the power of the press was a public trust which should be used for the benefit of society. He was almost fanatic in his insistence on the independence of his editors from any outside influence, including that of the business department. Thus he crystalized a Scripps-Howard tradition which had been initiated by his father.

With his administrative chores becoming increasingly complex, Bob, in 1924, placed Roy Howard in full charge of the Concern as head of both business and editorial operations. When EWS died, in 1926, Bob was left as sole trustee.

Bob found time to write some verse. Under different conditions he might have been a scientist. When a subject interested him he would follow it to the end, through countless reference books and consultation with authorities in the field. Attracted to law, he read his way through Blackstone.

Mr. and Mrs. Robert P. Scripps on a cruise

RWH and RPS around Labor Day, 1935

Pioneers and Other Personalities

He was casual in manner, easy to know, liked to visit the papers (usually by auto) and chat with staff members. He especially liked printers and was on a first-name basis with many.

Roy Howard described him as "kindly, considerate of others, always generous in his business dealings, possessed of a great sense of humor, a genius for friendship and a zest for life." A man's man, he had no yen to be a newspaperdom dictator.

One passion was his yacht *Novia del Mar*. On a leisurely cruise *Novia del Mar* was visiting Cabo San Lucas on the southern tip of Baja California March 2, 1938 when Bob began bleeding from the throat about 1 a.m. His companions and crew were instantly alarmed; just the summer before in Honolulu Bob had suffered a similar attack, diagnosed as a varicose condition of the esophagus.

A physician was summoned to the yacht from a nearby island. He found Bob's blood loss critical. He did what he could. Three more hemorrhages occurred, and at 1:30 p.m. Bob Scripps died—only forty-two.

He was buried on a hill at Miramar after a brief service in which one of his poems, "An Epitaph," was read.

Bob was the father of the three present Scripps trustees, Bob, Charles and Ted.

RPS aboard "Novia Del Mar", late Thirties

Roy W. Howard in a relaxed mood, circa 1955

Roy W. Howard

Brash Hoosier Ran The Show,
Treasured Journalistic Integrity.

Roy WILSON HOWARD was born in Ohio in 1883. His forebears on his father's side were Scotch-Irish. On his mother's side they were Scotch and English.

He attended Manual Training High School in Indianapolis; he delivered papers, worked in the high school cafeteria, did string work on *The Indianapolis News* and engaged in other remunerative activities. His father died when Roy was a boy, leaving him the only support of his mother. He did not have the time or the money for a college education. He had to hustle.

That's a familiar story in American life, a perfect setting for the Horatio Alger theme. But a lot of mediocre men have gone through that mill and it doesn't explain Roy Howard. His boyhood experiences helped shape some of his thoughts, habits and outlooks, but whatever he was originated from some deep, elemental spring of intuition and energy; it flowed from an inner reservoir of natural endowments.

He was a complex personality, full of contradictions. He was considerate by nature, but would call important conferences for the end of the day when his associates were fagged; he formed quick and positive opinions, but often put off making a decision. Roy was realistic yet had an infinite capacity for rationalization; he was persuasive in argument but a soft touch for a salesman. He was skeptical and wary, but could be taken in by sheer charm; he formed instant likes and prejudices, but had little capacity for nursing a grudge.

THE KEYNOTE in Roy's temperament was action. In the vernacular of sports, his instinct was to get rid of the ball. Yet in Roy action was harnessed to imagination; he could plan the course of his action and vision the end result.

Like a great many newspapermen, Roy wanted to be a writer—but he always wound up managing something. However, he was no frustrated victim of fate in that respect; he liked to manage and his administrative interests covered a wide range. He once took an associate to task for permitting his wife to endure the birth of a ten-pound baby; Roy thought his associate should have managed things to have a child of lesser weight.

Roy would arrange your itinerary, get you rooms, diagonose your ailment, show you how to bone a fish or pronounce the name of French cuisine, just as readily and as competently as he would analyze the fit of your jacket, edit your story or tell you what was wrong with your front page.

THIS READINESS to shoulder a wide variety of responsibility manifested itself in other ways. Roy had a quick sympathy for anyone in trouble and he was not content merely to stand by. He dropped everything and devoted himself aggressively and unstintingly to remedying the trouble or trying to. He was as quick with his purse as he was with advice; and while he might privately question the brightness of a man who got himself into avoidable difficulties, he was no moralist, and had no urge to censure. He was a doughty defender of people and things he believed in.

Candor was something Roy didn't cultivate; it sprang unbidden to his tongue. Unless you could take the strong medicine of frankness it was unwise to ask him what he thought about your shirt, your haircut, your ideas or your work. Frequently you didn't have to ask.

WHEN ROY finished high school he went to work for *The Indianapolis News* as an $8-a-week cub. He was raised to that dignity after a week during which his returns as a string correspondent netted him $35—approximately what the city editor received. Roy was a skinny kid, lacking the thews for football and baseball. It must have been some sort of wish fulfillment, because he went into the sports department on *The News* and was devoted to sports, especially boxing, all his adult life.

He later became sports editor of *The Indianapolis Star* but, after a couple of years desiring to broaden his experience and feeling his wings would stand a takeoff, he went to St. Louis and got a job on the telegraph desk of *The Post Dispatch*. Prior to going to St. Louis he had made a trip to New York in an unsuccessful attempt to land on *The New York World*. Failing to get into *The World* by the front door, he decided to try to get in by the back door—via *The Post Dispatch*, from which men were frequently transferred to New York, both papers being of Pulitzer ownership.

Roy had a friend, Ray Long, who was managing editor of *The Cincinnati Post*—then as now of the Scripps group. When Roy was in St. Louis he got a bid from Long and went to Cincinnati as assistant managing editor of *The Post*.

Despite his better job, he still had the incandescent stars of Broadway in his eyes. He started in to sell the editor on the desirability of *The Post* and its Ohio associates having a special correspondent stationed in New York. After about six months effort he made the sale and was sent to New York in March 1906 as the special New York correspondent of the Ohio Scripps-McRae papers—Cincinnati, Cleveland, Columbus and Toledo.

ROY HAD a few simple hobbies. They were fishing, hunting, photography and collecting. But whereas some people collect old washstands and the chinaware that goes underneath, Roy collected celebrities. He corresponded with important people in all parts of the world, people whose acquaintance he had made in nearly two million miles of globe trotting—about half of it by plane.

But it would be inaccurate to say that he was merely a collector of big shots. Many of his correspondents never made *Who's Who*. It was enough if they knew what was what. He liked important people partly because he was stimulated in the presense of a first-rate mind, partly because he considered it his job as a journalist to know and to get from the leading figures of his day whatever they had that would contribute to the journalistic development of the Scripps-Howard newspapers. He got a lot of good tips by knowing people.

IN THE EARLY summer of 1906, E. W. Scripps bought the Publishers Press, a news-gathering agency which, in 1907, merged with the Scripps-McRae Press Association to form the United Press. Roy was made general news manager of Publishers Press on its purchase by Scripps. A year later when the United Press evolved he became the first general news manager. He became president of the UP in 1912.

Roy had a sense of humor that always was cocked. He enjoyed a joke on himself almost as much as he did on someone else. But his manner should not have deluded anyone into believing that he lacked earnestness: There was nothing superficial or frivolous in his attitude toward his journalistic or his public responsibilities. He was a student of the labor movement and other social developments. His interest in such matters was quick and genuine.

HIS HIGH evaluation of the importance and significance of foreign affairs was reflected in a consistent effort to enlarge the area of interest among Scripps-Howard editors and readers in such material.

An important contribution to American journalism was made by Roy, who was the first American press association man to sense the danger to American journalism of the long-accepted system of international cartels and tieups of press associations with the subsidized and government-controlled news agencies of Europe. That was when he was president of United Press.

At the time when he was appointed to that position the United Press still was experiencing lean years. Roy was an adapter to necessities. He understood that it was impossible for the United Press to cover everything completely, so he developed a technique of covering certain types of news superlatively well. He pioneered in developing the human interest press association story; he gave bylines; he sought to inject a vivid, warm and relaxed quality into United Press

PIONEERS AND OTHER PERSONALITIES

RWH and New York Mayor LaGuardia at the fights, 1937

RWH tries out his Leica on Tom Sidlo

Interviewed at La Guardia on return from Pan-Am's inaugural round-the-world flight

stories; he encouraged a lean, compact style of news writing, featuring interviews and human interest stories which up to that time had been regarded as out of bounds for press associations.

ROY NEVER was casual about matters he considered important; he would not seek an interview or a meeting with a person of consequence unless he had something at hand he felt would justify taking up the man's time. He also liked for people to come to him with matters of more moment than a discussion of the weather. Roy liked for things to have meaning and purpose. He took calculated risks; he was audacious but not foolhardy.

Sportsmanship was instinctive with him—almost an obsession. He thought a newspaper should be prompt and generous in correcting errors of fact, and that necessary retraction should be direct and forthright. Some of his closest friends were men he fought politically in times past.

In 1921 E. W. Scripps emerged from eight years of retirement to reorganize his newspaper commonwealth. He persuaded Roy to resign from the United Press and become chairman of the board and business director of the then Scripps-McRae newspapers in association with E. W. Scripps's youngest son, the late Robert P. Scripps, who became editorial director.

Pioneers and Other Personalities

On November 3, 1922 the name of the concern was changed from Scripps-McRae to Scripps-Howard. E. W. Scripps retired and through a power-of-attorney vested his stock control in Robert P. Scripps, who, in 1925, extended Roy's authority to include jurisdiction over both editorial and business departments. Roy relinquished the title as board chairman to W. W. Hawkins some years later but continued as head of the Concern, as President, until December 31, 1952, when he also gave up that title — to his son, Jack R. Howard.

These various retirements in theory should not prompt the conclusion they were retirements in fact. Until his final illness he was at the office daily, often seven days a week. Title or no title, where he sat was the head of the table.

Roy sometimes was criticized by his close associates for paying too close attention to detail, for being overly impulsive. He usually pleaded guilty to both indictments and by so doing saved a lot of argument. He did and said impulsive things frequently; but his impulsiveness was disciplined and sometimes was the studied effect of a calculated plan.

ROY HAD an assertive and waspish manner that frequently was a trial to his associates, especially when he felt that his judgment was based upon personal experience or upon the record; yet few men studied themselves with more meticulous candor, or devoted more care to correcting or improving their technique of human relations.

Roy was positive in his opinions but generally accepted the majority view of his associates even when it conflicted

Frank Ford watches RWH try to get his birthday wish

with his own best judgment. But he always took full responsibility for the result of any course of action, irrespective of whether he deferred or prevailed in council. He had no fondness for "I told you so."

ONE characteristic was that he never believed what it said on the outside of the package. He had to open it and see. Whether he was trying to chivvy a statement out of a general or a profound reflection out of a taxi driver, or to get to the bottom of a problem in a board meeting, his methods were the same. He didn't try to arrive at the core of truth through ivory-tower cerebration, or by clairvoyance or calculus—he simply leaped upon it and started tearing it to shreds. If thwarted at one spot, he circled and circled, pouncing again at another point, tearing off layer after layer of extraneous or collateral matter, until he clawed his way to the bottom of the business.

Roy had a touchy pride concerning matters he considered fundamental, such as the good name and the good intentions of himself and the Scripps-Howard papers. He considered the most priceless thing a newspaper or a newspaperman can have is a deserved reputation for integrity and good faith. He burned under criticism touching on those things. He never allowed himself to brood over mistakes, his own or those of his associates. He readily admitted that some of his own had been colossal. He rarely made the same mistake twice. He contended that quick and decisive action frequently is essential to journalistic success. This necessarily involved some measure of error. He had no respect for a safety player who stalls or sidesteps the difficult decisions. He measured a man not by his errors but by his percentage of attempts successfully completed.

Roy died of a massive heart lesion in Doctors Hospital in New York City early in the evening of November 20, 1964. He was eighty-one. He was first stricken in the lobby of the Pan American Building at 200 Park Avenue and was given first aid in his upstairs office headquarters.

As he lay dying he sternly questioned the methods of attendants arranging an oxygen mask. Roy Wilson Howard never took anything for granted. He wanted to make sure they knew what they were doing.

W. W. Hawkins

He Always Made
A Team With RWH

IN THE same year—1901—that Roy Howard got his first steady job on a newspaper, in Indianapolis, William Waller Hawkins went to work as a reporter in Springfield, Missouri, his home town. Roy made a somewhat sharper deal than Bill. His weekly wage was $8. Bill started for $2.

Both took dead aim on New York City. Both arrived there in the same year, 1906, Bill by way of a job on Henry Watterson's *Louisville Courier Journal* where he worked up to city editor.

The two men met at the start of United Press, forming a comradeship, business and personal, that lasted for forty-six years. Bill succeeded Roy as president of United Press, later succeeded him as chairman of the board of the E. W. Scripps Company. He resigned from that job the same day—December 31, 1952—that Roy resigned as president.

Bill was a big man, quiet of manner and slow to wrath. In the words of the late John Sorrells, he had the solid, implacable manner of an army tank. He wrote little, was considered one of the best copyreaders in the business when he was operating United Press. In a sense he was the editor of this two-man team, Roy the reporter. Roy was the innovator, Bill the one to determine whether Roy's ideas added up.

Bill could multiply fractions without a slide rule, quote yards of verse from memory, liked people, never missed a Kentucky Derby. He had a great deal to do with the development of Scripps-Howard as it stands today.

Bill and Bob Scripps's widow, Margaret, were married October 21, 1943 and lived at Miramar. He died at the ranch February 19, 1953 at seventy. When the ranch was sold in 1968, Margaret Scripps Hawkins moved to La Jolla where she died April 15, 1977 at eighty-five.

John H. Sorrells

Park Avenue Link With The Papers

JOHN likened his job to playing shortstop. It was his assignment, he said, to go after everything that came his way and make the double play at second with the business office. The language of baseball came naturally to him. He did some barnstorming as a semi-pro right out of Washington and Lee. On the university football team he played fullback.

John's title was executive editor. His position in the Concern was what he carved out for himself after being called to New York in 1930. Immediately before that he had been editor of *The Fort Worth Press*, before that managing editor of *The Cleveland Press*.

He became the intimate contact of Park Avenue with the papers. He handled budgets, advised on labor contracts, personnel and staff handling, promotion, etc., including typography at which he was a recognized expert. He was a constant traveler, visiting the papers periodically and getting acquainted with their staffs. He knew literally hundreds of Scripps-Howard employes by their first names, watched their progress and helped get them better jobs when these opened up in the Concern.

John was born in Pine Bluff, Arkansas, in 1896 and started newspaper work there on a paper founded by his grandfather. His pay was $3 a week. He worked on half a dozen papers in the Southwest before joining Scripps-Howard, in Cleveland, in 1925.

In 1941, during World War II, he was called to Washington where he organized the Press Division of the Office of Censorship. He compiled the original censorship code for newspapers. John was an omnivorous reader, a talented writer though he found little time for that. He traveled by train, being quite frankly suspicious of airplanes. He was patient, tolerant, friendly, played a little poker though not with any great degree of skill. He could do practically anything around a newspaper better than anyone else. In the apt words of Deac Parker he was a "superlative craftsman." He died in his New York apartment February 25, 1948. He was fifty-one.

George B. Parker

His Pencil 'Sang'
And Won A Pulitzer

D<small>EAC</small> PARKER goes into Concern annals as the philosopher whose scholarly researches gave a definite trend to modern Scripps-Howard policy.

He acquired his nickname early in life because his father was a deacon in the First Baptist Church of Ithaca, Michigan and he was "little Deac." He was born in Ithaca, spent his first eighteen years there.

An older sister married a professor at Oklahoma University, which was why Deac went to Oklahoma, started newspaper work on *The Oklahoma News*. Eventually he became editor of that paper, next editor of *The Cleveland Press*, then editor-in-chief of the Southwest group which included Memphis, Oklahoma City, Houston, Fort Worth, El Paso and Albuquerque. Next he went back to Cleveland as executive editor of all the papers. He was appointed editor-in-chief in 1927.

Deac was tall, angular and slightly stooped, his usually solemn expression concealing a broad, earthy sense of humor. His temperament was judicial. He read voraciously, had a retentive memory for historical precedent and apt quotation. His writing had a musical swing and a special style which was readily identifiable. He won a Pulitzer prize in 1935 for "distinguished editorial writing."

In his later years in Washington Deac did not concern himself greatly with the daily operation, delegating that job to Walker Stone whom he had picked as his successor. He continued his reading and wrote but seldom, concerning himself particularly with the relation of Scripps-Howard policy to nation-wide trends in politics and economics.

His editorials tended to go to the heart of the question, building a framework within which day-to-day policy could be expressed. One of his great writing campaigns helped frustrate the efforts of Franklin D. Roosevelt to "pack" the Supreme Court.

Deac liked to play poker and liked even better to lecture on the science of the game, particularly after an opponent had beat him out of a pot by what he considered unsound play. He never got used to a typewriter, doing his editorials on yellow tablet paper with a soft lead pencil. He died, aged sixty-four, from an internal hemorrhage, in Washington, D.C., October 10, 1949.

Walker Stone

He Liked to 'Whip Easy And Ride Slow'

IN FORT WORTH several years ago, a guest debouched from an elevator, walked unhurriedly to the desk and in a quiet voice told the clerk he was dissatisfied with his room and was checking out at once. That was in the days when it mattered to hotels. The clerk, eager to appease, asked solicitously what was wrong. "The room's on fire," the guest replied.

That anecdote is not an exact description of Walker Stone's unruffled manner of dealing with a crisis, but it is illustrative. He never was one to ring bells or blow whistles, or act like a man with ants in his undershirt when unexpected trouble descended. He just took care of the situation. His soft voice, non-committal grunts and dead-pan manner deceived some. His colleagues knew that behind that seeming detachment was an alert steel-trap mind. Walker was incisive and could be, if necessary, tough.

He preferred, as he said, to "whip easy, and ride slow." Born in Okemah, Oklahoma March 8, 1904, Walker grew up around horses but yearned to be a lawyer. He was graduated by Oklahoma A. and M. (now Oklahoma State) in 1926. He was editor of the college paper.

He drifted into the newspaper business. He went to Washington, D.C. to study law at George Washington University from 1927 to 1929. In order to eat regularly, he found it necessary to get a job. He landed on *The Washington Daily News* as a copyreader. He was a greenhorn. "I just looked over the other guy's shoulder, and saw what he did, and caught on," Walker related.

He caught on pretty good. He became city editor and later transferred to SHNA as a regional correspondent. When Deac Parker, editor-in-chief, moved his headquarters to Washington in 1935, Walker was writing editorials. Deac took Walker under his wing. He gave Walker the title of SHNA associate editor in 1936 and made him editor in 1943. All the while training Walker as his successor.

After Deac's death Walker was named editor-in-chief December 31, 1952. Walker knew Washington, and the people in high places, better than most newspapermen of his time. He also knew the little people, too—and never lost the common touch. He was a man's man, with the chivalry instincts of a knight.

Once a prolific writer, Walker tapered off doing daily editorials. But he often presided at the staff meetings, adroitly appraising ideas, counterpunching and forcing the discussion to reach below the crust to the essence of the matter. He traveled widely, and wrote about how he found the world. He interviewed scores of world leaders. Once he even set Premier Khrushchev straight—about the Baruch atomic bomb treaty.

He was a great recruiter of talent—in one week he brought into SHNA Bill Newton, Jim Lucas and Robert Ruark.

Walker was married to his college sweetheart, Donna Smith of Stillwater, Oklahoma. They had two daughters.

He was one of the architects of Scripps-Howard's mandatory retirement policy. He believed in making room at the top for rising younger executives. He retired in May 1969, when he became sixty-five, and spent virtually all his time at his 520-acre farm called "Hawthorn" in the Blue Ridge mountains eighty miles west of Washington.

He kept his interest in the Concern alive by serving as president of the Scripps-Howard Foundation. He dabbled in growing apples, quail, fish, grapes, trees for timber, and tried his hand at horse-breeding and birddogs and the like. He loved the clean air and the solitude of the mountains.

At Hawthorn on March 18, 1973 he suffered a massive heart attack and died almost instantly. He was sixty-nine.

RETIRED PRESIDENT
Jack R. Howard

**Broadcasting Chairman,
And a Scripps Director**

THE OVERPOWERING personality of Roy W. Howard was, in some obvious ways, an advantage to his son, Jack. In other ways it was a severe handicap which Jack worked stubbornly to overcome.

Jack is a native New Yorker, born August 31, 1910. He attended Phillips Exeter Academy, graduating in 1928, then attended Yale University where he was graduated in 1932. He served a pretty rigorous apprenticeship before achieving executive position in the Concern.

Roy Howard had a sense of dynasty and wanted his son to carry on with his chosen career. Besides shop talk around the house, Jack read some of his father's correspondence and met many of his father's acquaintances who either were figures in journalism or in the news. His training was deliberately pointed for a newspaper career. This was Jack's initial advantage.

On the other hand Jack developed, rather early in life, a pretty strong preference for doing things his own way. As Roy once remarked somewhat wryly, "His one obsession is not to be a Roy Howard Jr."

In school Jack had to depend on a family allowance but carefully stayed inside it. Once he was out of school he paid his own way, even though the salary of a beginning reporter did not afford the same comforts he had at home.

HIS FIRST newspaper job was working the summer of 1928 for United Press in London, at the Olympic Games in Amsterdam and in Paris. To get to London, Jack got a job as a steward in steerage on the SS *Leviathan*. His job was waiting table.

The summer of 1930 he worked for UP in New York. The next summer he worked for United Press in Paris, with a side trip to Moscow.

From 1932 on he was variously a reporter, copy reader, telegraph editor and news editor. He first was on the *Japan Advertiser*, an American-owned newspaper in Tokyo, later was reporter for the *Shanghai Evening Post and Mercury*. Before leaving the Orient he was sent by United Press to Harbin, Manchukuo, for a spell of friction between Japan and Russia over the operation of the Chinese Eastern Railway.

Having thus learned his trade, he returned to the United States and got his first steady job with the Scripps-Howard Newspapers on the copy desk of *The Indianapolis Times*. Later he became courthouse reporter, by chance, the same beat his father had covered thirty years before. He also worked as police reporter and on rewrite. Next he moved to *The Washington Daily News* as telegraph editor.

It was in 1936, after returning from a Congressional trip to the Philippines for the inauguration of the Commonwealth and while he still was technically on the staff in Washington, that he became interested in radio. Possibly it appealed to him as offering a chance to test himself in a line of endeavor that was independent of the newspapers, hence a little out of the family tradition. The stubborn streak also may have been involved. Roy Howard initially was cool, or even hostile, to the prospects of this new-fangled contraption. Perhaps Jack welcomed a chance to prove to his father he now was a grown man.

Karl A. Bickel, former head of United Press, had come out of retirement to launch Scripps-Howard in the radio field as Continental Radio Company. Bickel gave Jack a job with WNOX in Knoxville, where he familiarized himself with everything from programing to sales. From Knoxville Jack went to Washington, where he studied the general broadcasting picture and its relationship with the FCC. By now it was March 1937; Bickel resumed his retirement and Jack Howard

Jack and RWH meet aboard the "Oakland" at Leyte in June 1945

was elected president of Continental Radio. He moved back to New York.

With the exception of the war years, Jack headed up the rapidly growing broadcast endeavor which became Scripps-Howard Radio, Inc. in 1937 and the present Scripps-Howard Broadcasting Company in 1961.

In 1939 he returned to newspapering also, as assistant to John H. Sorrells, executive editor of the Scripps-Howard Newspapers.

IN WORLD WAR II Jack chose the Navy. He was commissioned Lieutenant (jg) in February 1943.

On the U.S.S. *Fletcher* for eight months he saw action in the South Pacific—Morotai; the initial landings at Leyte; a sweep of the Camotes and Coral Seas; bombardment of enemy positions on Ormoc Bay; Mindoro; San Antonio; the initial landings in Lingayen Gulf; Nasugbu; Subic Bay; Zamboanga, Palawan, Cebu and Tarakan, Borneo.

Later he was transferred to the U.S.S. *Oakland* and took part in the final operations against the Japanese home islands and occupation of Yokosuka Naval Base. For his part in this he received a commendation from Admiral Halsey.

Returning to civilian life early in 1946, Jack resumed as president of the radio company and as assistant to John Sorrells. He also was elected executive vice president of The E. W. Scripps Company. In 1948, following the death of John Sorrells, he was appointed to the newly-created position of general editorial manager of the Scripps-Howard Newspapers.

When Roy W. Howard stepped down as president of Scripps-Howard, Jack was elected to succeed him, effective January 1, 1953. He continued to serve also as general editorial manager and as president of Scripps-Howard Broadcasting Company.

Jack reached retirement age in 1975. He gave up, effective January 1, 1976, his positions as president of The E. W. Scripps Company and general editorial manager. He remained, however, a director and chairman of the executive committee of The E. W. Scripps Company, and continued as chairman of the board of Scripps-Howard Broadcasting Company.

Back in his reporter days—April 5, 1934—Jack was married to Miss Barbara Balfe, of New York City, who died June 19, 1962. They had two children, Pamela, who was a reporter on *The Washington Daily News*, and Michael, who worked for United Press, *The Commercial Appeal*, and *The Rocky Mountain News*, including five years as editor in Denver. In January 1964 Jack married Miss Eleanor Sallee Harris, a well-known magazine writer and TV personality.

The personal relationship between the Howards, Roy and Jack, always was very close — but often quite spirited. It was Roy's nature to stir things up, prodding vigorously to discover whether his opponent in discussion knew what he was talking about and would stick to his guns. Jack is more of a harmonizer, trying hard to put himself in the other fellow's shoes. He is tolerant and generous in his estimate of people, suffered when forced to the conclusion he had put a square peg in a round hole and must make a change. He is reluctant to offend, rarely speaks unkindly of anyone. His temperament, in short, greatly resembles that of his mother, the late Margaret Rohe Howard, a nationally-distinguished newspaperwoman in her younger days.

Jack likes people; he is intensely loyal to his friends. He likes parties that generate fun of a slightly rowdy sort. He is of medium height, compactly built, with dark brown eyes. He goes fishing and hunting, used to play some tennis, smokes a pipe, enjoys driving a car, an art at which he is expert, despite one bad spill.

DIRECTOR
Earl H. Richert

THOUGH BORN in Oregon (September 20, 1914), Earl grew up on a wheat farm in Blaine County, Oklahoma. As a boy he milked cows, weeded the garden, knocking potato bugs into a can of coal oil at a dime a can. He rode a horse four miles to get the bus to school. Earl decided he wanted to get off the farm—and stay off.

At Oklahoma A. and M. College (now Oklahoma State) Earl prepared himself to teach and write history. He became interested in the college daily and was elected editor twice by the students. After graduation in June 1936 he went to work for the Scripps-Howard *Oklahoma News* at $15 a week as a copy boy. The paper hired the college editors from both O.U. and A. and M., telling them one would be eliminated by September 1. Earl made the pastepots fly, won the contest.

Two and a half years later, while Earl was covering the statehouse, *The News* was suspended. He got a job on rewrite at *The Tulsa Tribune* and five weeks later was back in Scripps-Howard on general assignment at *The Indianapolis Times*. He covered most of the Indianapolis beats and on the side was capital correspondent for *The Evansville Press*.

He caught Louie Seltzer's eye and went to Washington as Ohio regional correspondent in 1944. Two years later he was on the SHNA national staff. He covered Truman through the 1948 campaign.

In November 1951 Earl went back to Indiana as editor of *The Evansville Press*. Eight years later Walker Stone summoned him back to Washington as editor of SHNA. Earl was elected a director of the E. W. Scripps Company in 1962. On

Stone's retirement in May 1969, Earl was named editor-in-chief. He retired December 31, 1979 but remained a director.

Earl is studious, serious-minded with a strong back for responsibility. He has always been a hard news man with complete dedication to exact facts. In Washington he suffered from a constant anxiety lest he hurt the tender feelings of some careless staff members. "Not to nit pick," Earl would say, "but shouldn't that budget deficit be $5 billion instead of $5 million."

Earl is five-ten and tips the scales at 185. He likes attending and giving parties. He has one of Scripps-Howard's champion hostesses in wife Margaret (nee Vincent) whom he married in the Oklahoma days. Earl is a bridge and poker player, wields a mean tennis racquet, and a close student of the stock market and financial pages.

It was no surprise that the Richerts pulled up stakes in Washington after retirement and bought a big, roomy house in Evansville. They have two married daughters, one in Greenwich, Connecticut, and the other just around the corner in Evansville.

They need a big house because the latchstring is always out for the visiting friends they've accumulated en route from Oklahoma to Indiana to Washington—and back to Indiana.

Oklahoma hasn't forgotten Earl. In 1978 he was elected to the Oklahoma Journalism Hall of Fame.

SECTION THREE

The Scripps Trustees

Bob, Charles and Ted Carry Out Their Grandfather's Wish to Keep Alive The Children of His Brain

Bob Scripps

Charles Scripps

Ted Scripps

Bob, Charles and Ted Scripps

As EW's Trustees They Hold the Power in the Concern

THREE GRANDSONS of E.W. Scripps share final responsibility and authority for major matters affecting the Scripps-Howard organization. They are Robert Paine Scripps Jr., Charles E. Scripps, and Edward W. Scripps II. They have spent virtually their adult years as trustees of The Edward W. Scripps Trust which holds voting control of the parent operating company, The E. W. Scripps Company.

Two were mere children of eight and six—and the third was not yet born—when E. W. Scripps died in 1926 leaving their father, Robert P. Scripps, as his sole trustee. Barely a dozen years later their father died at age forty-two. His untimely death catapulted his sons onto a succession path to assume the heavy ownership/executive roles. The three young men literally grew up in the company.

With time out for military service in World War II, Bob and Charles became active full-time trustees around the start of 1946. That translates into having been in command through more than three decades. Ted, the youngest who was born three years after his grandfather's death, has been a trustee only nine years less than Bob and Charles.

For brothers they have rather diverse characteristics and interests; but on one significant point they are firmly united. That is their unwavering dedication to the spirit of their grandfather's creed and to the success and well-being of the Concern he deliberately left for his heirs.

BOB NEVER WANTED to be a newspaperman as such and has been firm about it. From boyhood he had his heart set on farming. However, he has a clear understanding of the responsibility invested in him as trustee, which he conscientiously conceives in terms of a personal trust. He keeps himself informed of all major matters pertaining to the Concern, and takes justifiable pride in his record of attendance at meetings of the trustees and the board of The E.W. Scripps Company, on which the three brothers sit.

In about thirty years Bob has missed only one board meeting—although his getting there usually meant flying from his home in West Texas to New York about once a month, and in recent years to Cincinnati or, occasionally, to some other city where Scripps-Howard operates. He is mainly a listener, but in board meetings his infrequent but pertinent comment reveals a clear grasp of the fundamentals of the question involved.

Bob has a quick sense of justice; his integrity is an integrated quality in his character—in his thinking, his actions, even in personal habits and manners, he is true to his beliefs and his institutions.

He has made his principal career as a farmer—and certainly not as a "gentleman farmer." Those who have visited Bob out in Texas know you don't find him supervising a crew of field hands from the air-conditioned seat of a Lincoln Continental. The tall husky fellow striding across dusty furrows in baggy, sweat-stained khakis and a straw cowboy hat, or working on his farm machinery—that will be Bob.

FARMING IS LITERALLY in Bob's blood. E. W. grew up on a farm, and his brothers, too, were farmers. Bob is mindful that his grandfather tackled some of the roughest land on the California coast and turned it into a garden spot, Miramar Ranch. Growing up on Miramar, Bob had land aplenty on which to practice farming, and he started while still in high school. One of his first crops was squash; and he must have had a heavy hand with the seed. Brother Ted recalls: "My gosh—we had squash for breakfast, lunch, and dinner!"

Bob was born March 1, 1918 in Washington, D.C. during the first World War. He was old enough to toot his tin whistle when the Armistice in the "war to end all wars" was signed. Twenty-three years later—a few days after Pearl Harbor—he sailed from San Francisco as a private in the 161st Infantry. He served in the Pacific throughout the war and returned to San Francisco on V-J Day, in time to celebrate the end of another war to end all wars.

While living at Miramar, Bob attended Webb School in Claremont, California during the years 1932-37 and took a course in the University of California College of Agriculture at Davis.

Though intent on a farming career, Bob suddenly found himself being literally dragooned into the newspaper business in late 1939. The nation was in the Great Depression. Lawyers were looking after the interests of The Scripps Trust. The legal minds decided it was about time for Robert P. Scripps's sons to get involved—to at least be knowledgable about the business.

"Things seemed pretty bad at the Concern," says Bob, "and they wanted me to come to Cincinnati and work in the Central Office to learn about the business." Bob went reluctantly, out of a sense of duty, after only a year and a half of ag school.

HE GOT THE SAME $20 a week paid other beginners in the Central Office. "Someone" did provide him a hard-to-find room at the Cincinnati Club. Bob says he found "running the calculators" a lot of fun but his supervisors were so unimpressed with his handwriting they sent him to night school to learn typing.

"I didn't mind working in Cincinnati," says Bob. "It was a change."

But the new job lost its allure in about eight months. Bob's dream of being a farmer kept nagging him. He left and went back to Miramar. He was about to start farming when he was drafted.

Bob saw action in the Guadacanal and New Georgia campaigns. In the Solomon Islands Bob volunteered to act as a scout in combat. "I'd had an education, knew how to read maps, had studied surveying and more or less considered myself an engineer," says Bob. "I figured I was a lot safer out front knowing what was going on than I was in back."

He won his chevrons as a corporal in 1944, was promoted

to sergeant during the Philippines show in 1945, and placed in charge of a regimental reconnaissance platoon.

Bob went back to his farming immediately after discharge from the Army and his first crop turned a nice profit. His uncle, Ed Culbertson, an oil man in West Texas, discovered artesian water while drilling for oil and prevailed upon Bob to come join him in a project to irrigate the arid plains and raise cotton.

Unfortunately the wells produced sulphur water and the artesian venture failed—though the discovery eventually became one of the Duval sulphur mines.

THERE WAS SOMETHING, though, about the desert and the rocky hills around Pecos, Texas that appealed to and challenged Bob. He was determined to make the land produce something besides cactus and rattlesnakes.

He developed an irrigation system and went into extensive cotton growing and later became a commercial bee-keeper. He also set up a small machine shop and iron foundry where he has built a steam engine to drive a boat, and manufactures engines and parts for other steam buffs.

In Bob's shop at the ranch is a powerful, expensive Cincinnati Milacron lathe and other machine tools. They are well-used, and Bob can make them do everything but talk. He is a member of the American Foundryman's Association.

Bob married the former Mariana Rocha in 1948 and they live in the small town of Balmorhea, Texas where they have raised eleven children, including twins, Adam and Eve, born in 1959. The others are Rebecca born 1949, Robert Jr. (1952), Bill (1953), Corina (1954), Margaret (1956), Jim (1957), Mariana (1962), Henry (1963), and Virginia (1965).

He is not what you would call gabby, but if you ask him a question about something in which he is interested, look out! His interests run from how to melt and pour iron to building steam engines to the love life of bees. He plays a deadly game of poker, and never seems to tire in an all-night session.

CHARLES SCRIPPS was born January 27, 1920 in San Diego, California and grew up at nearby Miramar Ranch. His father didn't try to pressure his children into going into journalism; but Charles has since youth been deeply interested in the newspaper business.

He also was graduated by Webb school in 1937 and on advice of Editor-in-Chief Deac Parker to try a change of scene picked out a college in the East—William and Mary in Virginia. The death of his father and a general homesickness for the West Coast prompted him to transfer in 1940 to Pomona College in California.

At the end of his junior year in June 1941 he married his college sweetheart, but they were divorced in a few years. With an obligation to become a trustee on the horizon, Charles went to Cleveland as a cub reporter on *The Press* to begin his matriculation in actual journalism. He covered police and handled some courthouse assignments. "I got some feel of reporting," says Charles.

When the Japs hit Pearl Harbor, Charles turned in his press card and headed West to join the Coast Guard. He and Bob had learned as boys to sail in San Diego bay with a twenty-nine foot sloop their father gave them. Charles enlisted in January 1942 as Yeoman Third Class. The Coast Guard was not as much interested in his skill as a seaman as it was that he could type twenty-five words a minute.

"They put me right behind a typewriter and that kept me out of boot camp," Charles recalls. He was in the cutter *Alert* and later assigned to the training school for Coast Guard reserve cadets in New London, Connecticut. He was commissioned Ensign in February 1944 and served in the USS *Mintaka*, a Liberty ship converted for troop as well as cargo carrying in the Pacific.

HIS SHIP WAS ENGAGED for the most part in gathering up troops that the war had left behind in the Solomons area. He finally caught up with the war at Buckner Bay, Okinawa. In September 1945 he was advanced to Lieutenant (jg). He got word from home that Bob's outfit was training on New Caledonia for the Philippines campaign. When the *Mintaka* put in at New Caledonia, Charles got shore leave, hitched a ride in a jeep out to Bob's camp and the brothers had an hour's visit.

When he left the Coast Guard in February 1946, Charles intended returning to *The Cleveland Press* to pick up where he left off. Instead he visited Denver to observe how the Scripps-Howard paper there operated. He dropped by Oklahoma City. He spent the summer at *The Fort Worth Press.*

Eventually he returned to Cleveland but soon gave up his reporter's job; the lawyers were anxious for him to devote his full attention to corporate business, which was piling up. "Being a trustee meant doing a lot of nitty-gritty chores, but they were important and necessary," says Charles.

In 1946 he was elected a vice-president of The E.W. Scripps Company, in 1948 elected chairman of the trustees and assigned to the corporate staff at the Central Office. His move to Cincinnati slightly preceded his marriage October 14, 1949 to Lois Anne McKay, daughter of two practicing physicians in California, and universally known by her childhood nickname, "Beano."

Since then Charles has lived in Cincinnati and had an office in the Central Trust Tower, where the former New York headquarters is also now located. On January 1, 1953, Charles, not quite thirty-three, became chairman of The E.W. Scripps Company board. He is on the boards of directors of most of the individual papers.

CHARLES APPLIES HIMSELF to the job seriously and earnestly. He tried to learn the business from the bottom up but, by turn of circumstances, found himself at the top, working his way to the bottom of all the intricate affairs which a group of newspapers and allied properties involves.

This he did in his own way, listening diplomatically but not relishing too much kibitzing by earnest well-wishers in the higher Scripps-Howard echelon, most of whom were many years his senior. It's probably unneccessary to say that everybody was willing to knock off any time and give him an earful of advice, suggestion and criticism.

Besides attending meetings of General Management and the directors of The E.W. Scripps Company, Charles receives and studies reports of Concern business and sometimes visits the properties to learn from direct observation how things are done in different operations. Research designed to improve editing and publishing methods long has been one of his special interests. He used to make talks about it, but in recent years has ducked most speech-making. He has an easy,

At Miramar Ranch March 28, 1947, left to right, Bob Winkler, Deac Parker, Bob Scripps, Roy Howard, Charles Scripps, Hugh Baillie, and W. W. Hawkins.

Charles and Bob aboard "Novia del Mar".

friendly, even modest manner. People around the papers, clear down to the copy boys, find him easy to get acquainted with on a first name basis. He wants to spend more time "on the trail" but finds it difficult to escape the daily corporate grind.

Like Bob, Charles cares little for show, but he likes good clothes and wears them well. He is partial to a shower, good shaving lights and three good meals a day. He is a hair under six feet, an excellent swimmer, plays some golf. After the war he learned to fly, got a commercial license and an instrument rating and, for several years, piloted his own plane. He also liked to sit up front as co-pilot when Scripps-Howard had a company plane. In 1955 Charles gave up flying. "It became too much like work," he says, "not fun any more."

Charles will take a drink and stay up most of the night and talk. He is fond of good music—which he identifies as classical. "I don't like rock at all. When you are young noise is exciting. I think it was a French philosopher who said, 'I hate all noise except that which I am making.' " He would prefer to take a phonograph apart than listen to it, though solid state stereo would probably buffalo him. He has an urge to see what makes things run. He used to doodle with a T-square, and has drawn some intricate mechanical dingbats. He candidly admits, "I like gadgets."

CHARLES AND "BEANO" have four children: Charles E. Jr. born in 1950, Marilyn (1952), Eaton (1954) and Julia (1956).

There is much in the mannerism and character of Charles to remind people who knew him of his father. Like RPS he has brown eyes and used to have brown hair. It is gray now, and so is his beard, a strong reminder of his illustrious grandfather.

Charles is still a sailor. He and Beano had a thirty-nine foot ketch berthed in Florida and became frustrated because they couldn't go down and sail often. They bought a trimaran about 1965 but that proved not too useful. They now own the sixty-foot *Rainbow*, a beautiful Rhodes-designed, Cheoy Lee-built sailboat. But they are still frustrated because there isn't enough time available for sailing her.

EDWARD WILLIS SCRIPPS II—Ted for short—is the youngest of the three trustees. In fact he is the youngest of a family of six children, four boys and two girls. Ted is deeply interested in newspaper work, particularly the editorial side. He has served his apprenticeship faithfully in a variety of jobs, as reporter and copyreader. His credentials as a full journeyman journalist are all in order.

He was born in New York City November 26, 1929. When he was three the family moved to Miramar Ranch, near San Diego, California. He grew up there and at Lake Tahoe, Nevada, where he formed his love for the water. He's seldom been without some kind of boat ever since.

Following the grades he prepped at Chadwick School, entered Stanford University, earned his degree from the University of Nevada in 1952. After graduation he joined the United Press bureau in Reno where he helped cover such stories as the Redfield burglary, famous at that time, and one of the big snow storms of the century, which stranded a trainload of passengers in the Sierras and isolated many Nevada towns for weeks.

The UP job lasted but six months. The Korean war was on and he was called into active duty in the Navy, spending the major part of two years on a destroyer in the Pacific as a member of the flag staff of Destroyer Squadron One where he had such assignments as regular radar watches and publication of the ship's newspaper.

UPON DISCHARGE from the Navy Ted moved to Cincinnati for a six-month stint in the Central Office. Next he joined the staff of *The San Francisco News* as a general assignment reporter, then moved to Denver where he worked on the *Rocky Mountain News* on the statehouse beat and as an editorial writer. A year on the desk of United Press in Washington rounded out his training.

Ted is a gregarious, friendly type, likes to give parties and meet people. When he set up offices in Washington's National Press Building he was right across the hall from this kind of opportunity. His willingness to work at any job handed him brought his appointment as National Press Club luncheon chairman. Notables from all over the world appeared at the famous luncheons. Ted met and welcomed them.

In the 1964 election he was voted in as secretary which

meant that, in the usual course of events, he would be president a year or so later. He had, however, to forego a chance at that honor. Early in 1965 he transferred his base of operations to New York City. With his wife Jean, whom he met at the University of Nevada and married in the fall of 1954, and their three children, he made his home during the New York period in Greenwich, Connecticut. The children are Cynthia born in 1956, Edward W. Jr. (1958), and William H. (1960).

During his undergraduate days, Ted took a working interest in Sigma Delta Chi, serving as chapter president. He was elected to national office in 1955, serving successively as secretary, vice president in charge of expansion and finally, in 1961, as national president. In this capacity he spent a year visiting Society chapters across the country, greatly enlarging his acquaintance with newspapers and newspapermen, in and out of Scripps-Howard.

TED IS TALL—six feet one inch—slender, weighing 195 pounds, intense in his fascination with public affairs, domestic and international. Intellectually Ted is an experimenter, not too respectful of the way the world is being run and not reluctant to suggest plans for improvement. He is tolerant of dissent, unabashed when associates argue forcefully that some of his notions are visionary. His skin is thick and he learns fast. He is also persistent. He won his battle to establish a Scripps-Howard research and development department. "You know I love gadgets—all Scrippses do."

Ted spent nine years in New York headquarters as vice president and assistant secretary of The E.W. Scripps Company. He didn't feel the job was enough of a challenge, or that he was achieving his corporate goals.

"I finally stepped back from the frustration of wearing two hats," explains Ted, "and said I'm going to sit back and be an owner and director and not part of the day-to-day management. It was a very real decision for me."

And, Ted feels, a wise one. Most of the proposals he argued for futilely as a veep, he says, have gradually been adopted since by the board of directors.

TED'S LOVE FOR the water "is still as deep as ever" —and he has owned a variety of sailboats and cruisers. But

Ted Scripps at a 1978 conference

Charles Scripps as Coast Guard officer

Ted as a tyke with his Miramar pal

the sky is his new interest. He was already forty, living in Connecticut, when he decided to learn to fly, mainly because of the challenge. "I didn't think I could do it because I'm a *Nervous Nelly*. A flier friend of mine assured me that if you aren't a Nervous Nelly, you're a lousy pilot."

When Ted took his first lesson, the instructor thought he was a FAA inspector checking up on him. Ted was that much of a natural-born flier.

Ted moved back to Nevada and opened up an air charter business in Carson City. He has a twin-engine Cessna 340 and a Cessna 182, both of which are leased out for forest fire patrol, ambulance runs, and general passenger service.

"I'm not a guy to sit idle," says Ted, "so I've got very involved in other projects, especially in the area of R and D. My mind never relaxes."

One project was production of a TV movie, *Trap Beneath The Sea*, in 1976. He is proud of taking over a company that was losing $250,000 a year in the oceanic newsletter business and bringing it out of the red. With the help of "very able editors," he has added a successful weather newsletter. "There's no competition left. We ran 'em all out of the market. I'm damn proud of that."

Ted feels just like his father did—that you don't push your children to follow in your profession. But their daughter Cynthia turned out to be something of a chip off the old block. She went into the communications field, first as an assistant producer for a television station. Now she works for United Press International.

SECTION FOUR

General Management And Staff

The Corporate Officers and Executives Who Keep The E. W. Scripps Company Going Ahead Steady And On Course

PRESIDENT
CHIEF EXECUTIVE
OFFICER

Edward W. Estlow

TWENTY-SIX YEARS before he became president of Scripps-Howard, Ed Estlow was publishing a weekly in Lovington, New Mexico, selling and writing ads, shagging news, laying out a "circus" makeup, engraving news photos, coaxing production out of boomtown printers, a balky linotype and a cranky press, drawing his own page one cartoons, rawhiding the governor, making loyal friends—and not working over ninety to one hundred hours a week.

Ed was gung-ho. He had a ball, but it was a grind. "When people on dailies complain about working their tails off," says Ed, "I just laugh. There's no work like running a weekly."

It was Ed's debut in newspapering. His father-in-law had bought the paper. He needed someone to run it. He gave Ed, at thirty and untrained in journalism, a quarter-interest and turned him loose. It was 1950. Ed had one reporter, a society editor-bookkeeper, two and a half printers. He leaped in.

Ed turned the paper into a nice little gold mine. First he took all the grocery ads—two pages from Piggly-Wiggly and one from Shorty's Superette—away from the opposition paper by offering a frequency discount. Lovington was in the midst of an oil boom. Each start of a new water well required the state engineer to publish three notices. Ed was the first publisher to go ask for these legals, so he got 'em. Ditto for city, county and school board legals. Ed regularly ran 16 pages.

Ed knew how to get along in a small town. He joined

Rotary, and the Lions, too. He decided his readers didn't want dull makeup. He jazzed up page one. Once he shot a picture of a sunset with eerie flat clouds and ran it with a headline MYSTERIOUS OBJECT SIGHTED OVER LOVINGTON. *Look* magazine sent a reporter to check up on that hint of flying saucers.

Ed took his scissors and made a montage out of Fairchild plastic engravings. He sent a story about that to *Editor and Publisher*, claiming a first. Someone read *E & P* in Havana, Cuba and wrote for info. Ed promptly printed a page one blurb, LOVINGTON PRESS GETS INTERNATIONAL RECOGNITION.

THE TOWN WAS WARM and friendly; people liked the way Ed had shaken up the paper. So did other publishers. His father-in-law had bought the paper for $24,000; within a year they had offers of $120,000. Ed sensed, after a couple of years, the oil boom might play out. The paper was about at its peak. They decided to sell. Ed got his cut, and started looking around.

He heard about a job as retail ad salesman at *The Rocky Mountain News* and landed it, at a hundred a week. It was 1952, and that was his start with Scripps-Howard. (Lovington hated losing Ed. A few months later local businessmen offered to buy the paper and give it to Ed if he'd come back and run it. He thanked them, but he'd found his niche—daily newspapers, no more back-breaking weeklies.)

Ed was born March 20, 1920 in the little tumbleweed and sagebrush town of Snyder, Colorado. His mother was a rancher's daughter and his father a Methodist preacher who had come west in 1900 from New Jersey. They had a series of homes in the mountains beyond the Continental Divide —where his father was pastor in such towns as Crawford, Fruita, Glenwood Springs and Monte Vista.

"We moved about every two years," Ed recalls. "Before we could even unpack, I was usually challenged to a fight— —being new kid on the block."

Ed took his first step, his mother told him, on Grand Mesa, the world's largest flat-top mountain, where the family had gone to fish. Ed's father was a great fly fisherman, and a college track star. ("I saw him do hand-springs after fifty.") So Ed grew up loving the outdoors and sports.

General Management and Staff 115

HIS BOYHOOD reads like pages from both Frank Merriwell and Horatio Alger. When he was a high school sophomore, Ed's family went back to New Jersey—Collingswood, near Philadelphia—because his grandfather was ill. Ed played halfback on his high school football team, and ran the 110-yard high hurdles, eight-tenths of a second off the world record.

At the end of his junior year Ed's family moved. That put Ed on the spot. He figured the only way he could get a needed college scholarship was through a good showing in football or track. He stayed behind to finish at Collingswood High. His parents paid his rent, and Ed worked for his food—as paper carrier, church janitor, mower of lawns.

"I never made more than four or five dollars a week," says Ed. "That bought one meal a day and dry cereal for breakfast. My mother sent cookies."

He got scholarship offers—in track from University of Pennsylvania, and in football from Swarthmore, Rutgers, Maryland, University of Colorado, University of Denver, and from Pop Warner at Temple.

"I picked the one that really offered the most and seemed more interested in me," says Ed. It was the University of Denver. That summer Ed went to Colorado and worked as a cowboy "for a dollar a day and all I could eat." By time college started, Ed had saved fifty bucks. He bought a sports coat, new slacks, shoes and socks, and reached Denver with only $6—and had no overcoat that first winter.

BECAUSE OF his speed, Ed played halfback and wound up with an outstanding record. He set the Denver U. mark for most yards rushing in a single game. As a senior he was selected "most valuable player" in football and was captain of the track team.

He pieced out his scholarship with part-time work. His summer jobs included building a cattle fence, running a jack hammer on a streetcar track repair gang, and hard-rock mining.

As he received his A.B. degree World War II was raging. Ed joined the Army Air Corps and soon was a staff sergeant. He was sent to officer candidate school, emerging in March 1943 a second lieutenant. Ed promptly married the vivacious brunette he'd met at Denver University, Charlotte Schroeder. She had been a freshman beauty queen when he was a senior football hero. "I met her at the Student Union—where else," says Ed.

Ed helped set up air cadet preflight courses at colleges around the country. Later he instructed pilots in parachute jumping. The closest he came to personally hitting the silk were the practice jumps off a twelve-foot tower.

Out of the service as a captain at the end of 1944, Ed started studying law at Denver U. He supported his family by working mornings as a sales rep for a manufacturer of western jeans and shirts. He was a senior and just three courses short of graduation when the Lovington challenge caused him to leave law school.

WHEN ED STARTED at *The Rocky Mountain News* his New Mexico training in writing and selling ads quickly paid off. In less than a year he was top lineage producer. Ed volunteered to help out the business manager on labor negotiations because of his law schooling and Lovington experience, and in 1955 found himself installed as *The News* personnel manager.

That was at no increase in pay. "Things were tough, and I was raising three kids," Ed says. "I needed a new car. I walked into Safeway one day and saw they were having a contest for an Oldsmobile. 'Why I like Skylark Bread . . . in twenty-five words.' That night I went home and wrote three pieces of copy, with every other word having a double meaning. I knew I could write."

He got some bread wrappers and mailed his copy in—and won.

To shine up the new Olds, he went to buy a can of polish and saw Johnson Wax had a contest giving away one hundred gallons of gas. He ripped off twenty-five words—and won the gas.

As personnel manager, Ed was soon drawn into the paper's business affairs, and decision-making. In April 1964 on retirement of Wally Lewis he was made business manager. He faced instant problems: stabilizing revenue, gaining employe loyalty, and averting a press capacity crisis. He sold

General Management and Staff

General Management on installing new presses, and increasing press capacity.

Four or five times a week Ed walked through the plant, talking with people. He got to know many on a first name basis. He had already earned their respect as a "fair and square" labor negotiator. Ed worked fifty or sixty hours a week, but considered that duck soup after his grind on the weekly.

"The reason *The News* is successful is because they've got a great bunch of people," Ed says. "That's the only reason. It isn't any one individual."

On growth properties as soon as one problem is solved a new one usually springs up. But *The News* eased its pains, Ed feels, by careful foresight, getting ready in advance for coming new technologies. Ed got to know his paper, he thinks, better than any one else did.

GENERAL MANAGEMENT noticed. Ed was asked to go to New York as assistant general business manager. He had mixed emotions. He loved *The News* and living in Denver. He and Charlotte fortunately faced no family complications in a move. Their four daughters—Susan born in 1944, Nancy (1946), Sally (1949) and Mary (1953)—were either married or in college.

Ed could visualize the challenge New York offered. "I'd had eighteen years' experience on a daily newspaper, but with eighteen newspapers that would be like having eighteen years' experience every year. And that sounded really exciting to me."

Ed went to New York in April 1970 as assistant general business manager. He was named general business manager in November 1971. And on the retirement of Frank Powers in June 1972 he was also elected vice president and director of the E. W. Scripps Company. On January 1, 1976 on retirement of Jack R. Howard, Ed became president and chief executive officer.

As the complexion of Scripps-Howard operations changes, Ed spends 40 to 60 per cent of his time on newspaper matters, perhaps 20 to 30 per cent on service organizations such as United Press International, United Media Enterprises, Berkley-Small, Scripps-Howard Supply Company, 5 per cent on broadcasting, and about 10 per cent on industry matters, such as being chairman of the board of the Newspaper Advertising Bureau.

Ed and Charlotte have lived in Cincinnati since January 1977 when Concern headquarters were combined there. They have a getaway place in Colorado. Ed still has the knack of fly fishing learned from his father—and he's taught Charlotte. They're both proud of some fine trout catches.

FOR YEARS Ed has been a Sunday painter. He works on a large drawing board in his den at home. He always has a canvas underway. He's self-taught. "I have a daughter with a fine arts degree and she says 'Dad, I don't understand how you know to do this technique. Where did you learn?' Well, I just figured it out. I read books, and talk to other painters and get good tips."

Ed works in watercolor, tempera, acrylic and oil. His best result is in something called *tempra resist*—which involves a layer of paint that works against an added material. He paints some at night and finds artificial light no handicap.

From his travels Ed has brought home twenty chiming clocks. He sets them to go off simultaneously. Charlotte is patient about the bonging. The clocks compete for space in the Estlow home with the paintings. It should be no surprise that much of the art brought to life by Ed's brush are landscapes right out of the old West.

VICE PRESIDENT
GENERAL EDITORIAL
MANAGER

Gordon Hanna

ALTHOUGH CORPORATE records don't reflect this historical tidbit, Gordon Hanna did his first work for Scripps-Howard—albeit rather indirect—as a ten-year-old sitting obviously tall in the saddle in a little Texas ranch town.

Astride his pony he saw to it that fifty citizens of the countyseat of Jacksboro got their daily copy of Scripps-Howard's *Fort Worth Press* come rain or shine. He delivered the route about a year. That was long enough to get used to reading *The Press*, and to develop some sense of its vitality and integrity. The experience didn't inspire him to rush into journalism. That came later; an aunt steered him.

Gordon did decide early about one career—negatively. He had no hankering to become a cowboy or, as was his father, a rancher.

"I had a horse from the time I was seven or eight until I was sixteen," says Gordon. "I lived much of my early life on a ranch and horses were work animals. I've ridden as long as twelve hours a day, moving cattle, and it's not a sport. Being in a rodeo didn't appeal to me. I guess that's the same reason you don't find many retired Navy people going out in sailboats like I do."

Gordon was born February 22, 1920 on a ranch in Jack County, seventy-five miles northwest of Fort Worth. He went to high school in Jacksboro. His aunt lived across the street from the publisher of the weekly *Gazette* (circ. 1,306). She told Gordon that looked like a good line of work.

Acting on her idea, he went down to the *Gazette*. She thought he might start as a printer. The friendly publisher talked to him, showed him around the shop, but had no job to offer.

"I was intrigued by it," says Gordon, "and started hanging around the paper a lot." This was late in his high school days. Gordon figured he'd better go on to college if he wanted to get into newspapering. Times were too lean for his parents to send him.

Another aunt loaned him $200—and Gordon was off to Texas Tech at Lubbock. About the first thing he learned was how to type. He studied journalism and got quickly involved with the student newspaper, a semi-weekly.

His finances were dreadful in his three years at Texas Tech. He worked summers in the wheat harvest. His aunt loaned him another $150 (and eventually got paid back). He got $10 a month "government assistance" for sweeping out the student newspaper office and typing its mailing list. His mother managed to send him $2 a week for personal expenses. He worked his way up to associate editor of the college paper.

WHEN GORDON went home at the end of his junior year his parents lived in Fort Worth. He tried to get on as a reporter at *The Fort Worth Press*. Editor Don Weaver chatted for an hour. He explained the Depression was still on, he was feeling a budget pinch. No opening. Gordon tried to get other jobs. At length he found one—selling Jewel Tea products door to door. "I didn't sell much, but it was a liberal education."

Just then—late July 1939—his luck changed. Two college friends summoned him to Lubbock to join in starting an off-campus sports-amusements paper they'd dreamed of. Gordon hitch-hiked out there and wrote the amusement articles. The paper was catching on. Two more Tech friends joined the staff.

"We were beginning to do well," says Gordon, "but the paper couldn't support all of us. I got a call from a friend in

Beaumont offering a job on a weekly that had just gone daily. It paid $17.50 a week. I took it."

Gordon paid a travel bureau $7 for the 350-mile ride to his new job. In six weeks the new daily folded. Gordon tried for a job on the nearby *Port Arthur* (Texas) *News* and the New Orleans papers. No luck. To eat, he hocked his watch for $3. He got coffee and a short stack of pancakes for 15 cents in a Beaumont cafe and hitch-hiked 300 miles home to Jacksboro. "Rides were easy to get. Nobody had much, but people were very obliging."

Two days later *The News* sent a wire offering a police reporter job at $20 a week. Gordon promptly thumbed his way to Port Arthur. He was nineteen.

Gordon not only succeeded as Port Arthur's crime reporter but also in the romance department. He discovered a local brunette beauty, Annie Lou Guidry, and they were married April 22, 1941.

GORDON STARTED stringing for Scripps-Howard's *Houston Press*, ninety miles away. That brought in only $20 to $30 a month. But it offered good contacts. From boyhood days of reading *The Fort Worth Press* he felt comfortable with what he discerned to be the Scripps-Howard philosophy.

As he saw it: "They were aggressive but I thought they were fair. I was impressed by the fact they didn't have local financial interests that influenced their handling of the news. That sort of thing. I thought I could see that in some other publications where the publisher might be a big wheel in the community and have a lot of property other than the newspaper. It seemed to me it was a freer, more honest type of journalism."

After he'd spent three years in Port Arthur, *The Houston Press* hired him October 1, 1942 as a reporter at $45 a week and promptly put him on city desk rewrite. World War II was slow to catch up with him because he was a father with a second child on the way. Finally he went into the Air Force in April 1944. In pre-cadet training, he qualified to go on and become a pilot, navigator or bombardier. But the war ended in Europe and all training was frozen. Though stationed at San Marcos, Texas, he managed to get home many weekends by "stretching" his 50-mile pass to 175.

Gordon spent his last six months in service at Ellington Field, near Houston. He edited the base newspaper. He returned to *The Press* in the fall of 1945. He got a variety of assignments from covering the Legislature to being oil editor.

HOUSTON WAS JUST beginning its phenomenal growth. The booming town came alive with one news sensation after another. Gordon was made city editor in July 1949 and plunged into five of the fastest-paced years of his career.

The Press thrived on investigative reporting and crusades. Gordon had a hand in plenty of action: the story of a Hispanic dictatorship in Duval County—a crusade against organized crime in Houston, with page one photos of actual racket payoffs—the revelation that Houston schools were being sold horse meat for children's lunches.

Gordon had the double privilege of rolling out of bed at 4 a.m. to get an early start on the city desk, plus sitting in a neighborhood cafe and drinking coffee until 6 p.m. with Editor George Carmack, a tireless dynamo, plotting strategy to get the jump next day on the rival *Post* and *Chronicle*.

Gordon's success caught the eye of Frank Ahlgren, editor of the Memphis *Commercial Appeal*, who was looking for a managing editor. In July 1954 Gordon moved to *The Commercial Appeal*. "Frank was very smart in the way he brought me up there," says Gordon. "I started as a copy reader, then was night makeup man, and finally spent a month on the night managing editor's desk, the fellow who stays till the paper is out.

"So when I became managing editor on October 1, I was reasonably familiar with the town and the newspaper. I had been m.e. about a week when Ed Crump (famous political boss) died. It was the biggest story of the decade in Memphis. We put out an extra—and I guess it was the real test of my performance and my authority. We did a good job, and after that everything went smoothly."

Five years later—October 1, 1959—Gordon went to Evansville as editor of *The Press*, succeeding Earl Richert who moved to Washington as editor of Scripps-Howard Newspaper Alliance and to later become editor-in-chief.

WITHIN A FEW WEEKS Gordon was flying to Hershey, Pennsylvania for his first editors' meeting. The late Ludwell Denny, then the scholarly dean of our Washington foreign staff and a former editor, took the trouble to check Gordon's flight and get the seat next to him out of Washington. En route Lud patiently and earnestly counseled the freshman editor, who listened attentively.

"He talked all the way, even in the car," says Gordon. "I remember him telling me I wasn't a managing editor any more, I was an editor—and they were not paying me to put out the paper. They were paying me to think. Which I thought was pretty good advice."

After nine years in Evansville, Gordon was sent back to Memphis to become editor of *The Commercial Appeal* when Frank Ahlgren retired at the end of 1968.

"I believe," says Gordon, "that I was a better editor of that paper, having been there and having gone away and come back, than I would have been had I just stayed. This is one of the reasons I believe in this cross-fertilization—as we sometimes refer to it—in moving people from one paper to another.

"You know if a man already on the paper moves up he isn't going to do things a lot differently from what he and his predecessor had been doing; basically the pattern is there. If you come in from the outside after exposure to other places you have ideas that you might not otherwise have thought of."

When Jack Howard announced his decision to retire as president and general editorial manager in late 1975 the board elected Gordon vice president and general editorial manager effective January 1, 1976. Ed Estlow became president and general business manager.

GORDON AND ANNE lived in New York until the headquarters shift to Cincinnati in January 1977. Ohio proved a good location, familywise. Both their daughters, Judy born in 1942 and Harriet born in 1944, and their families are within driving distance. The Hannas have five grandchildren.

Asked to define his policy as general editorial manager, Gordon says: "Basically what we are all trying to do is improve our products and win greater reader acceptance. We want to be thought of as we think of ourselves—what is stated in the front of this Handbook.

"We want people to know that we have integrity and that we are trying to serve our communities. And at the same time we want to be thought of as interesting and sprightly publications. I think this takes constant work. We can't arrive at any special place and say we've got it whipped and this is the kind of paper we want to put out for the rest of our lives. Circumstances keep changing.

"So it's a fight every day to put out a better paper than we did yesterday.

"I think of my role as one of being here to encourage, to back up editors. But the last thing I want to do is try to edit any of our newspapers from Cincinnati. I think that's the editor's job, and I'm here to help when they need help."

AN EARLIER BIOGRAPHER, commenting on Gordon's six-four and two hundred-twenty-five frame, calculated he could have easily bulldogged a Longhorn steer. It's for sure, Gordon hasn't grown any smaller. Despite his size, or maybe because of it, Gordon is soft-spoken, mild-mannered, slow to wrath; though once he's made up his mind he's hard to budge. He plays golf, tennis, poker and bridge. He reads a lot—at the office, reports, mail, news wires, newspapers, and at home chiefly wine and sailing magazines and books.

He also relaxes as a do-it-yourselfer, having learned carpentry, plumbing and wiring, mainly to build a wine "cellar" in his basement. He's a self-taught wine connoisseur stemming from exposure to a Memphis gourmet club. He also built wine rooms in his Memphis and Manhattan digs. He keeps his racks pretty full, and has some rare bottles.

Sailing is his greatest avocation. He bought his first sloop and learned to sail on a lake near Memphis. He had the boat hauled to New York when he moved, joined the Larchmont Yacht Club, and cruised on Long Island Sound. Anne is not so enthusiastic about the water, but he taught her to man the tiller and how to tack.

He keeps a twenty-two-foot Catalina at Panama City, Florida where they have a getaway condominium. On holidays and vacations he sails Gulf waters. Gordon chartered a forty-one-foot ketch at Saint Thomas in 1978 and skippered Anne and two other couples on an eight-day cruise of the Virgin Islands.

Gordon doesn't itch to set out single-handedly across the Atlantic. But his eyes glitter when he sees sleek, bigger sailboats. And somewhere in his stack of navigational charts at home is one of the South Pacific with check marks on Tonga and some of the other romantic islands.

FINANCIAL VICE PRESIDENT

DIRECTOR OF CORPORATE DEVELOPMENT

Lawrence A. Leser

P ERHAPS THE BEST WAY to identify Larry Leser is to dub him Scripps-Howard's "bottom line man"—who knows not only where the money now comes from and to where it disappears, but, more importantly, also where it will come from in the distant future.

He has a head for figures, and faces—and he dreams dreams. That is all part of his job.

Larry is responsible for organizing and nudging along the Concern's "wish list"—areas targeted for development down the road. He sees on the roster some "quite promising" opportunities.

In the business world about all he's ever known are books and ledgers; but his experience has given him some superb perceptions about financial management and forecasting.

Larry's father was an accountant in the automotive field. That was not an early career influence on Larry who was born in Cincinnati May 15, 1935. But by the time he got out of Saint Xavier high school in 1953 he realized he had a knack with math and concentrated on it when he went to Cincinnati's Xavier University.

HIS PARENTS HELPED him go to college but Larry worked, too. For three years he was a parttime sales clerk at Sears, putting in twenty hours a week at minimum wage.

Sears didn't know they were shuffling a budding financial whiz kid from department to department. But his professors at Xavier recognized his talent. When he was graduated in 1957, Larry was first in his accounting class of forty seniors.

That meant being lured by several top national accounting firms. Right out of Xavier he went with Haskins & Sells as a junior accountant at $4500 a year.

In college he had joined ROTC and he was barely settled in his new job when he was yanked away to Fort Bliss, Texas for six months' reserve training as an artillery officer. It was an uneventful experience, as Larry tells it, but he did emerge as a captain who knew something about making Nike missiles zero in on the enemy.

One of his first assignments at Haskins & Sells (now Deloitte Haskins & Sells) was to do some auditing for one of the firm's major long-time clients—Scripps-Howard.

"It was routine," says Larry. "I can't remember now just what it was."

LARRY WAS BRIGHT ENOUGH to move up rapidly. After four years at Haskins & Sells he was a senior accountant, which is one step below management level. In 1961 he qualified as a CPA, and in 1965 became a manager, one level below partner.

All the while he had been involved in Scripps-Howard auditing and got to know several Concern executives on a personal basis. He was friendly with Barney Townsend, financial vice president, and Sherman Dye, chief general counsel.

In the late summer of 1967 Townsend asked Larry if he'd bring his expertise over to Scripps-Howard on a permanent basis. "I had no inkling they were going to make an offer," says Larry. "I was surprised and flattered."

He talked it over with Sherm.

"I could see the opportunities," says Larry. "What swayed the most were the people in Scripps-Howard. I had dealt with a lot of them. They were all first-class. There is a feeling of integrity that permeates the whole Concern. I've certainly had no regrets."

On retirement of L. C. Wessel, Larry became secretary-treasurer of The E. W. Scripps Company January 1, 1968. He was elected financial vice president January 1, 1975 and made a board member in May 1977. In June 1980 he was given the additional responsibility of Director of Corporate Development.

THIS IS WHERE Larry gets a chance to dream. He's not a guy to prop his feet on the desk, smoke a pipe and stare out his 11th floor office window at the busy Ohio river. He takes the more practical approach.

His first shot at corporate development was to assemble top executives who run the various Concern enterprises and conduct a brainstorming session that looked into the future.

"It was the first time we'd ever done that," says Larry. "Out of that came a whole market-basket of ideas. There are several excellent prospects that appeal strongly to all of us."

These have become what Larry calls the Concern's "wish list." Another result of the meeting—a decision to hold similar sessions on a regular basis.

Meantime, Larry puts on his own thinking cap, usually devoting specific periods to study in mornings at the office and also as the day winds down.

Because of his overseer role on finances of the far-flung Scripps-Howard operations, Larry spends 30 to 40 per cent of his time traveling. Usually he works a nine to ten hour day.

FOR HIM TO HOP an airplane and skitter to a distant town can at times become traumatic. He suffers from claustrophobia. Three times in recent years he had to hurriedly get off planes that were too small.

"If I have an aisle seat and can stand up without my head touching the ceiling, I'm okay," he says.

It takes a bit more than average space to accommodate Larry because he's six-two and weighs about 200. He's fine on most commercial planes; it's usually the infrequent hurry-up charter flights that plague him.

He plays golf but has never been deeply into other sports or the outdoors life. He reads a lot. For relaxation—and mainly on plane flights—he dives into whodunits; Robert Ludlum is his favorite author. At the office he pores over "every periodical that comes my way."

ED ESTLOW SAYS that one of Larry's greatest attributes is his memory. "I can always remember faces and names, especially," says Larry. He hasn't taken any memory-training courses. "It's just a knack. I must have been born with it."

Larry was married in June 1974 to Anne Johnson and they live in Cincinnati with his four children and her one: Kathleen born in 1958, Lawrence M. (1959), Sharon (1961), Nancy (1966), and Charles Johnson (1968).

VICE PRESIDENT, SECRETARY, CONTROLLER
Daniel J. Castellini

ALTHOUGH HIS FATHER was a lawyer, Dan Castellini didn't know he had the hidden talent of a Perry Mason until the U.S. Army brought it out.

Fresh out of Notre Dame with his accounting degree, and an ROTC obligation, Dan in 1962 began two years of active duty as platoon leader and executive officer of a 900-man special troops company at Fort Eustis, Virginia.

His duties kept Dan hopping. He was assigned to defend a soldier accused of robbery. "Funny thing about that court martial," says Dan, "the defendant was a lawyer himself. I didn't get him off, but I did get him a light sentence. He was happy."

After defending another soldier, Dan was switched over to "prosecutor." His task was handling court martials for fifty or so deserters and AWOLs from the "goon platoon."

Next he was delegated to set up the Transportation Corps first temporary processing center. He did such a good job his scheme became a Second Army model.

DAN RATED SO HIGH on military proficiency when he ended his tour of duty, the FBI offered him a job. "I was tempted," says Dan. But he was destined to be in the newspaper business.

In his fourth grade days, Dan hawked *The Cincinnati Post* (at 5 cents with his profit 1.45¢) in the 5 o'clock traffic rush at a surburban intersection.

"I didn't have to. But there were five kids in the family

and my folks believed we ought to do something to earn a little money."

For Dan that meant driving a truck summers for the large produce business his grandfather built in Cincinnati, and also peddling Christmas trees.

Dan was born in Cincinnati January 15, 1940. At St. Xavier High he was a first string football tackle and forward on the varsity basketball team. (He's six-two and a half, weighs 190.) After graduating in 1958 he went on to the University of Notre Dame to study accounting.

In the top 15 per cent of his graduating class, Dan was recruited by Haskins & Sells (now Deloitte Haskins & Sells). The summer of 1962 was a busy time. Dan married Joyce Rendler, a registered X-ray technician, and they were off to Fort Eustis. The first of their six children, William, was born in the Army hospital there the next May. So was their second, Mary Elizabeth in 1964.

RETURNING TO CINCINNATI and his desk at Haskins & Sells, Dan found himself doing a lot of newspaper auditing. In addition to working on the Scripps-Howard account, he was sent to Huntington, West Virginia to make audits on *The Herald-Dispatch & Advertiser.*

In the evenings Dan hung around the plant and learned production, computers, and circulation techniques inside out. The publisher called him in to calculate potential revenue and expense ratios on proposed circulation price increases. Dan developed a pretty accurate pencil.

Dan enjoyed his newspaper work so when Larry Leser offered him the post of assistant treasurer in 1971, Dan said yes. He had been a CPA since 1966, and went to night school to get his MBA in finance from Xavier University in 1973.

He went from assistant treasurer to secretary-treasurer and in June 1979 to vice president, secretary and controller.

Dan not only has coached a kids' soccer team, but built the only existing covered bridge in Anderson Township, where they live on a couple of acres in the Cincinnati suburbs. The bridge traverses a creek running across the back of their property which flows only when it rains hard.

A HAMMER OR A SAW fits Dan's hand neatly. He has added on, remodeled, and generally improved their home. He built a stone wall. It all took about seven years.

Dan likes sports, especially biking, and most of the Castellini activities are family-oriented. Their other children are: Michael born in 1966, Dan (1967), Peter (1970), and Todd (1971). Dan also reads a lot, mostly light fiction.

As controller he is responsible for all corporate accounting, financial reports, tax returns, internal audits, the central data processing center, Central Office payroll (for 2000 employes), and does some work on acquisitions and investments.

He records the minutes of the board meetings, handles stock transfers, and has responsibility for operation of the Central Office.

That must not be a back-breaking load after all, because you seldom see Dan when he isn't wearing a big smile.

TREASURER
E. John Wolfzorn

THE DAY PRESIDENT KENNEDY was shot John Wolfzorn was holed up in a backroom at *The Kentucky Post* wrestling with carrier returns. John was eighteen and studying accounting. He put in afternoons in *The Post* circulation office to help meet his tab at Thomas More college. It was not much shakes of a job—but it was his first connection with Scripps-Howard.

"The pay was maybe two dollars an hour," says John. "Somebody had left. After I had been there a while I knew why."

Even so John stayed a little over a year. The circulation

manager was a baseball-playing pal of John's father, who was purchasing agent for a kitchen equipment firm and ran a sandlot team.

John, obviously a dad's lad, got his first taste of accountancy at fifteen when he helped his father take inventory. "It was nuts and bolts, pretty rudimentary. But I learned something about manufacturing, and had some exposure to office types, and how they did their accounting. It was small enough that I could see everything. I would say that got me interested in business and accounting."

John was born September 8, 1945 in Newport, Kentucky. Under his father's tutelage he became a good shortstop and second-baseman—and on his own a bright student. At Covington Latin School he got a heavy dose of Latin, Greek, and another foreign language, plus heavy sprinklings of English, algebra, trigonometry, some basic calculus and chemistry. John was not quite seventeen when he finished this classics-type education.

FRIENDS ADVISED him there was big money in engineering. That sounded reasonable. John enrolled at University of Cincinnati. After a year he decided he wasn't cut out for the science load and transferred to Thomas More and into the business department. He went to summer school and made up the time lost.

In his last year at Thomas More, John married Sandra Suchanek and their first child, Angela Maria, was born in 1966 when he was graduated with his accountancy degree. He promptly joined Haskins & Sells.

He started at $600 a month as a staff accountant and made the normal type of progression. He was assistant accountant after two years, senior accountant (also known as *in-charge*) after two more years, running various "engagements"—as auditing contracts are known.

In the summer of 1973 John came to a career crossroads. Dan Castellini approached him, looking for a financial analyst for Scripps-Howard. That feeler set John thinking. He wondered if he wanted to continue at a CPA firm or get into something else. He started looking around. There were several other tempting offers. He almost took one. But finally, October 1973, he went with Scripps-Howard.

FOUR OR FIVE people from Haskins & Sells had preceded him in joining Scripps-Howard, but John was unique.

"At H&S, I had never charged an hour of time to the Concern. I knew literally nothing about it," he says.

Obviously he learned fast. In April 1975 he was promoted to assistant treasurer. On June 4, 1979 he was made treasurer.

John maintains a close relationship with his former wife (they were divorced in 1980) and his children—"a cheerleader and three great ballplayers." The sons are Jon Allen born in 1968, Michael Joseph (1969), and Bradley Ervin (1974). (The Ervin was his father's first name, and also John's.)

For hobbies John says he has "about a 13 handicap" in golf. His dad used to "drag" him around a course in Campbell County, Kentucky. He reads a lot to get away from business texts—current novels, spy and adventure stories.

One of his responsibilities is investment of the Concern's excess funds. He also handles banking relationships, lines of credit, insurance functions, and gets involved in executive compensation, some fringe benefits—"and that's about it."

Then John adds: "I've got plenty to do. I find it challenging. I'm very happy I made the decision to come over here. It couldn't have turned out better."

GENERAL BUSINESS MANAGER/NEWSPAPERS

Robert H. Hartmann

BECOMING A SCHOOL TEACHER was Bob Hartmann's college goal. He got his educational degree. Then came the shock. Teachers were then starting at $2400 a year.

"I couldn't live on that," says Bob. "I was married and we were expecting our first child."

His brother-in-law was an ad salesman on Philadelphia's spunky but struggling *Daily News*. He helped Bob get a job in the general ad department. Bob was put on food accounts. He quickly caught on, and soon caught fire.

Since then he hasn't seemed to slow down much.

His youth was a mixture of books, basketball and bayonets. He was born November 6, 1927 in Dover, New Jersey. Bob spent summers helping his father, a painting contractor, and clerking part-time in his uncle's haberdashery.

HE TURNED OUT husky, six-four, fast on his feet. He became a basketball star at Dover High. That earned him a scholarship at Seton Hall University at South Orange, New Jersey. He helped meet college expenses by "opening the gym mornings for the nuns."

In 1947, at twenty, he enlisted for a two-year Army hitch. Then on the GI Bill he finished his college work at Kutztown, Pennsylvania, State College. He got his degree in education just in time to go back into the Army for the Korean War. He served in the Far East in 1951-52.

About the first thing Bob did after he got out of khaki

General Management and Staff

was to look up Rosemary Condon of Boonton, New Jersey. They'd met at a basketball game back in high school days and dated through college. They were married in January 1953.

Not too long after that came his break at *The Philadelphia Daily News*. He was getting $65 a week; but even that was a budget pinch and Bob clerked some weekends in a haberdashery for extra income.

Scripps-Howard first came into Bob's life in 1958. *The Washington Daily News* needed a man to handle food advertising. Ray Mack asked the Concern's regional advertising offices to suggest candidates. Our Philadelphia office had Hartmann tabbed as a bright prospect.

RAY GOT BOB down to Washington to talk to *The News* ad director. Bob agreed to take the job, at $170 a week. "You'll have to pay my moving expenses," said Bob. The ad director shook his head. Only in the case of a transfer from one Scripps-Howard paper to another. Bob stood up and got his hat. "Wait a minute," said Ray Mack, who at the time was only the paper's circulation director. He took the ad director into the next room. "He's our man—we need him. If you won't pay his moving bill, I'll do it—and take the heat."

Mack thinks that turned out to be a good investment for the company. (The move cost about $400.) Bob worked hard trying to build up *The News'* food advertising. "He'd start early in the morning," Mack recalls, "and we'd be there at 10 or 11 at night analyzing accounts, records and devising strategy."

Bob's strong suit at *The News* was, in Mack's opinion, his professional approach to selling advertising. "When he made a presentation it had class. It wasn't just a bunch of figures thrown together. He got new business. I credit him with doing a lot to keep *The News* going as long as it did."

Work on the struggling *News* was back-breaking and often heart-breaking. Still Hartmann's reputation grew in the trade.

In 1969 *The Philadelphia Inquirer* sought him as ad director. It was about twice his Washington pay. Bob finally accepted the job, but Ed Estlow, then assistant general business manager, asked him to come up to New York on the next day, a Sunday, and talk about it.

Later that Saturday Bob decided he was certain about

going to *The Inquirer.* He called Ed in New York to tell him he wouldn't be coming up. But Ed didn't answer. Bob kept phoning until midnight Saturday.

He tried again Sunday morning. He didn't know Ed was away on a trip. Ed returned at 2 Sunday afternoon, and waited two hours at his PanAm building office for Bob in vain.

On Monday Bob told Ray Mack he was leaving *The News* for a better opportunity. Ray invited Bob and Rosemary—they had all become good friends—to lunch. He told Bob it was a mistake to leave if he wanted to ever become a business manager. He said he could get Estlow on the phone and get a commitment "without any time limit" that Hartmann would become a business manager. He called Estlow and came back to the table and told Bob he had a promise.

Bob and Rosemary looked at each other. "We'll stay," she said. Bob, sighing, nodded.

RAY MACK WHO by that time had become business manager made Bob his assistant and started schooling him in the art of running the business side of a newspaper. "He was a very good student," says Mack. "His strongest suit was that he was very professional in his sales approach. He did his homework, knew exactly what he was talking about. He never got tripped up. And he spoke with conviction."

After about eighteen months as assistant business manager, Bob was sent to Cleveland in September 1971 as business manager of *The Press.* In June 1976 he was appointed president and business manager of *The Pittsburgh Press.*

Bob has never been much on hobbies. His chief interests are work and his family. He and Rosemary have two sons and four daughters: Craig born in 1953, Gwen (1954) Deborah (1956), Bruce (1957), Gretchen (1959) and Rosemary (1960). Bruce is something of a chip off the old block; he is an ad salesman for the *Sun* papers in Baltimore.

While in Pittsburgh, Bob served as director or officer of the Symphony Society, Pittsburgh Opera, Carlow College, Better Business Bureau, Chamber of Commerce, Convention and Visitors Bureau, Guild for the Blind, Pennsylvania Newspaper Publishers Association, and other organizations.

When he was asked to come to Cincinnati as assistant

general business manager Bob found it a tough decision to make. "It wasn't easy," he says. "For one thing *The Pittsburgh Press* is so significant in the community. And the people there are just great."

Hartmann made the transfer to general management June 2, 1980. On the retirement of Jacques Caldwell December 31, 1980 Hartmann was appointed general business manager/newspapers.

EVERYWHERE he's been people talk about the fact that he is a serious, no-nonsense type, who is aggressive and expects his troops to be likewise. "He doesn't like people who don't know what they are doing," says Ray Mack. "Anybody who's a surface-skimmer and doesn't have the answers had better watch out. You can't con him."

Characterizing Bob's managerial style, Estlow likens him to executives in Pittsburgh. "He is just the way they are—straightforward but blunt and get right to the heart of it. I think he's a good listener, but he can be very blunt. He's physically dominating, and he doesn't make that bashful, either.

"He gets things done. He's a doer."

Being dubbed hard-nosed doesn't faze Hartmann. "The only comment I have on that is, what's right is right, and what's wrong is wrong. And if it is wrong, it has to be made right."

EDITOR-IN-CHIEF
Bernard J. Cutler

"B.J." STARTED OUT to be a mechanical engineer, but somewhere along the line decided that creating with a typewriter was considerably more to his liking than doing so with a slide rule.

Lucky for Scripps-Howard.

Bernie's predecessor as editor-in-chief, Earl Richert, believes Cutler to be one of the finest editorial craftsmen in the business and the editors of Scripps-Howard Newspapers don't disagree.

Before becoming a member of the editorial board of Scripps-Howard Newspapers in 1969, Bernie had spent a large part of his newspaper career abroad. His years of covering the world have given him a near matchless grasp of foreign affairs. But at the same time he has never lost his love of things American from good California wine to football and politics.

Bernie went to work as a cub reporter for *The Pittsburgh Press* in 1945 despite the complaints of a journalism professor at Pennsylvania State College who was outraged that an engineering graduate should get such a job over his own products.

It was paternal urging that initially got Bernie aiming for an engineering career. He was born in New York City May 26, 1924. His father owned a foundry. "He was willing to stake me to a Master's in engineering," Bernie says. "But I had become hooked on journalism. Come to think of it, I had a taste of that in the family too. My father manufactured ingots of 'white metal'—for linotypes."

After six years with *The Press*, Bernie headed for New York and the *Herald-Tribune* which soon afterward would lose one of its stars, Jack Steele, to the Scripps-Howard Bureau. After several years reporting in New York, Bernie won a coveted prize. He was named Moscow correspondent for the *Herald-Tribune*.

While in Moscow he covered Nikita Khrushchev's rise as near-dictator, his elimination of his party rivals and his secret speech to the 20th Party Congress denouncing Stalin's crimes. He reported on Russia's launching of the first Sputnik and wrote bleakly that a rocket capable of placing such a large object in orbit could also deliver a nuclear warhead to any city in America.

Bernie left Moscow in 1958 to take over the *Herald-Tribune* Paris bureau and in 1960 and 1961 successively became managing editor and editor of the European edition of the *Herald-Tribune*.

In Paris he reported on Charles de Gaulle's rise to power, his growing anti-U.S. turn, his near-sabotage of NATO, the Common Market and Britain's efforts to join the continent. Other specialities were the Algerian War, rightist military plots against the French Republic and French domestic policies which, he says, led to an interest in Byzantium.

Bernie rejoined Scripps-Howard in October 1966 as European correspondent, based of course in Paris, covering the major stories of Europe and the Middle East for three years.

His byline appeared over stories datelined from Geneva, Bonn, Athens, Brussels, Rome and London. He covered the 1967 Arab-Israeli war.

When Middle East hostilities loomed, Bernie flew from Rome where he was covering a story on the Common Market, to Jerusalem without waiting to get the proper attire. He stepped off the plane into a war zone in a fashionable blue suit and black shoes to write one of the first stories to describe the military preparations then underway. It was several days before his wife Carol could ship him khaki pants, shirts and boots. Tucked down in the parcel was a can of excellent pate.

Bernie's reports throughout the war consistently ranked among the best written and Scripps-Howard readers received a rare insight into not only the struggle but its impact on both Arabs and Jews and what it was likely to mean to the world in the years to come.

In between his "hard news" assignments, Bernie found time to file a weekly "Letter from Paris" about food, drink, mores, fashions and a host of other light subjects.

Bernie became chief editorial writer for Scripps-Howard in 1972, succeeding the late Kermit McFarland. And on January 1, 1980, he succeeded Earl Richert as editor-in-chief of Scripps-Howard Newspapers with responsibility for overseeing the production of national and foreign-policy editorials and carrying out the policies set by Scripps-Howard editors at their annual meetings.

Bernie has kept his nearly six-foot frame slim over the years despite his penchant for good wine and food. He is an acknowledged expert on both and his wife, Carol, is a widely known writer on art who also has gained a national reputation as a cookbook author. They live in the Georgetown section of Washington.

ASSISTANT GENERAL
EDITORIAL MANAGER

David Stolberg

DAVE HAS IT figured out that he is "the one in the middle" of three generations of Stolberg writers for Scripps-Howard. His father, Benjamin, was a freelance writer who did occasional pieces for Concern newspapers.

Next comes Dave, putting in time on beats and city desk in Denver and as m.e. in Washington before joining general management.

GENERAL MANAGEMENT AND STAFF 141

Third is daughter Mary, who broke in as a cub reporter in Fort Smith, Arkansas and in 1978 went to *The Pittsburgh Press.*

Dave was born in New York October 10, 1927, attended private schools there as a youngster and was graduated from Washington, D.C.'s Western High School. He attended Swarthmore College for a couple of years and broke in as a reporter in 1947 just across the Potomac on *The Arlington* (Virginia) *Daily.*

THE ARMY INTERRUPTED his career—but not completely. Dave, avoiding the draft, enlisted in a fledging PR program set up by the Army. One of the carrots was an internship (detached service, they called it) at *The Arkansas Gazette* in Little Rock.

When the Korean War erupted, he wound up with the title "Army correspondent" and was the NCO in charge of the press train at the Pan Mun Jon peace talks.

Dave has never been bashful about meeting strangers and in the war theater he looked up Jim Lucas, the famous Scripps-Howard war correspondent. It turned out to be fortuitous for Stolberg.

He came home with a recommendation from Lucas that helped land his first job with Scripps-Howard—as a reporter for *The Rocky Mountain News.* That was July 9, 1952.

For *The News,* Dave covered the police, federal and statehouse runs. He exposed nepotism in federal bankruptcy court. That won him a Denver Newspaper Guild award, and triggered national reform.

In 1960 he was appointed city editor. In his eight years in that job, Dave started a pioneer Colorado free press-fair trial committee, taught a Sunday school class, launched an Episcopal diocesan newspaper, and took up tennis. "I played lousy, but a lot." He also made two-week reporting trips to Germany, Sweden and Canada.

IN 1968 HE WENT to *The Washington Daily News* as managing editor. He put in four hard years, but there was really no hope of unlocking the economic stranglehold that was killing the paper. Dave found he had to give up tennis as a steady date, but did manage to get elected secretary of the National Press Club, sing in the church choir, build a sailing kayak in his living room, and take another brief swipe at foreign correspondence, this time in Spain and Portugal.

Then came that sad day in July 1972 when *The News* folded. "In Key West a year or two later, I overheard a man telling someone else he was the first managing editor of *The Washington Daily News*," Dave recalls ruefully. "I stuck out my hand and said, 'Meet the last.' His name was Burt Garnett and we had a lot to talk over, including the fact that Ernie Pyle came somewhere in between us. *The News* was a marvelous, vibrant paper. I miss it badly. And so does Washington."

For the next three years Dave worked out of Washington on assignments for Jack Howard. He was, as it turned out, understudying the one-and-only Jack Lockhart, assistant general editorial manager for almost three decades who virtually became a Concern "institution."

When Lockhart retired June 1, 1975, Dave succeeded him and moved to New York, with his wife, the former Anne Stewart Brand, whom he married in 1950. Mary, born in 1956, was then already in college—not actually interested in journalism, though she caught the bug a couple of years later.

In his Cincinnati office, Dave occasionally gets nostalgic about the fun of being caught up in getting out a paper. "I was a newspaperman once myself," he cracks.

BUT HIS CAREER is not all budgets, heavy travel, people management, content studies and corporate paperwork. Gordon Hanna gives him assignments that pretty much insure that Dave still is a newspaperman. He is deeply involved in product, helping to make sure the right newspaper people are in the right newspaper places, and in the midst of First Amendment battles.

No one has heard Dave complain about not having to get up anymore at 5 in the morning.

Dave points out that Gordon has sprung him free to stick with editorial challenges—and frustrations—to a far greater degree than his predecessors, as management has added experts in personnel, production, data processing, accounting and other such technical and awesome skills.

Stolberg has been a trustee of the Scripps-Howard Foundation since 1969. As a member of the American Society of Newspaper Editors since 1970 he is active on bar/press, freedom of information, minority employment and speakers committees.

Now back to that three generation angle. Suppose one day Mary has a son or daughter ... hmmm ...

PROMOTION EDITOR

James H. Wagner

JAMES H. WAGNER—the H. is for Harrison after the middle name of his father who was named for President Harrison—is The Thin Man of Central Trust Tower. Jim stretches scant one hundred thirty-five pounds over an erect five foot, ten and a half inch frame topped by sharp features; his appearance and manner might remind a chess player of the knight piece.

But as editorial promotion director of Scripps-Howard Newspapers, Jim doesn't just move—he charges his job like a quick-footed shortstop, gets a firm hold on the ball, and fires it to first in time. He doesn't muff many chances.

Jim was picked for his job by Jack Howard in 1960 after fourteen years on *The Houston Press* during which he held every editorial job from reporter to managing editor. He never worked on any other publication except for one summer on a country weekly that first interested him in newspapering.

Born in Chicago March 11, 1921, Jim majored in English

at DePauw University in Greencastle, Indiana. Graduated by DePauw in 1943, Jim promptly had greetings from the Army, and an apparent horse-lover assigned him to the cavalry.

Jim went into action as a radio operator with the First Armored Division in the critical days of the Anzio beachhead invasion in Italy. He served through the Italian campaign, then crossed the world to put in what must have been one of the shortest hitches of Japanese occupation duty on record, about two weeks. This was at Kure Base some fifty miles from Hiroshima, but Jim started home before he could get a look at where The Bomb had been. He was discharged a sergeant after two and a half years of service.

In Houston was Jim's uncle who once owned the country paper of his college summer, and Jim went to see him about fame and fortune. The uncle pointed him towards *The Houston Press* and Jim put over his first major promotion by landing a job as a reporter.

One of his first big stories was the Texas City disaster in 1947. And early in his career he was introduced to the National Spelling Bee, a program he now directs nationally, when he made three trips to Washington with Houston spellers.

After a couple of years as a reporter Jim moved to the copy desk. In 1952 he was named assistant managing editor, and in 1955 he became managing editor.

The Houston Press received numerous citations for news coverage while Jim was managing editor, and Jim is still proud of this. Perhaps the outstanding award was for coverage in 1957 of Hurricane Audrey which devastated the Louisiana fishing village of Cameron.

Nowadays Jim's duties are not quite as hectic, but cover a wider field. Recently, *Scripps-Howard News* was made a part of his operation. Yet he seldom knows what he will be doing next. Whatever it is he grabs hold and shakes. His once brown hair is non-existent, but his gray-eyed glance through hornrim glasses is just as intense as always, and he hasn't lost his command nor his big grin over success.

Jim lives in Cincinnati with the Oklahoma girl, Barbara, he married in Houston. They have three grown children, one of whom, James A., is executive sports editor of *The Albuquerque Tribune*. There is one grandchild; James R.

PRESIDENT & GENERAL MANAGER, SCRIPPS-HOWARD SUPPLY COMPANY

Homer E. Taylor Jr.

WHEN HOMER TAYLOR GOT ON as apprentice pressman at the hometown *Daily Mail* in Charleston, West Virginia he had not the slightest idea that sixteen years later he would head up one of the nation's largest agencies for buying newsprint and ink. And one of the oldest. Which is, of course, the Scripps-Howard Supply Company.

What Homer thought about most in 1961 was collecting that $44 weekly paycheck from the *Mail* cashier and keeping the wolf away from the door of his honeymoon cottage. He was newly-married to the girl who had been cheerleader when he played guard for Stonewall Jackson High, Donna Marguerite Thompson.

Her father had been pressroom foreman at the *Daily Mail*. That gave Homer a foot in the door. But on his own he had to pass a battery of tests. His good mechanical mind came up with the right answers.

Homer was born in Charleston March 3, 1942. His father was a carpenter. Homer got out of high school at seventeen. He went right to work for the state in the workman's compensation division. After a year he quit to take a football scholarship at West Virginia Institute of Technology. As a freshman, he was starting guard.

IN THE SPRING of 1960 he and Margie got married. Homer dropped out of West Virginia Tech and landed the pressroom job. He liked the work and did well. But in a few years it dawned on him it would be smart to get his electrical engineering degree. One incentive was their three children: David born in 1960, Douglas (1961), and Beth (1964).

He got back into West Virginia Tech in 1966, but kept working at the newspaper. It was a winding thirty-mile drive from the *Daily Mail* to the campus at Montgomery. He began to branch out at the newspaper, splitting his time between the pressroom and production. He learned data processing and when he got his West Virginia Tech degree in 1970 moved full time into production engineering.

It was a break for him to be on an expanding paper. He cut his engineering teeth on demolition and construction of a new production wing with a vast array of modern equipment at the *Daily Mail*. It was almost finished in June 1973 when he accepted an offer to become Ralph Eary's assistant production director in Cincinnati.

THAT PROMPTLY threw him into three years' involvement in design and construction of the new production facilities for the Memphis Publishing Company. He acted as "corporate liaison" and had a hand in decisions on the press installation and overall mechanical complex.

That was barely behind him in 1976 when he took a similar role in development of a production warehouse at the *Rocky Mountain News* in Denver.

Then came appointment as vice president and general manager of the Supply Company at the end of 1976 with promotion to president in June 1977.

The Supply Company has an intriguing history. It came into being, not to satisfy some abstract theory of newspaper publishing, but to meet a practical problem. Until shortly after the turn of the century each Scripps paper dealt directly with newsprint manufacturers and the sales agents. The situation was chaotic, both as to quality and price. Newsprint was sold under a system of so-called sidewalk delivery and in some instances payment was made only on the basis of copies printed. The manufacturer received nothing for the inevitable transit loss and pressroom waste.

A MEETING OF newsprint manufacturers was held in

General Management and Staff 147

Chicago to discuss trade abuses and try to remedy them. Willis W. Thornton, then president of the Scripps enterprises, could see that Concern managers were making unreasonable demands and had a fair chance of finding themselves without a source of supply.

He took it up with E. W. Scripps. They decided to draft Colonel William M. Day, then business manager of *The Cincinnati Post*, to organize the Newspaper Supply Company (which later became the Scripps-Howard Supply Company). That was in 1907. Its primary purpose was to buy newsprint for all the Concern papers, to collect from the individual publications and to pay the suppliers. All complaints, claims—all dealings, in fact—were to clear through Colonel Day's office.

It was a small office—the Colonel, a stenographer and a bookkeeper. In the Eighties Taylor had an equally compact shop with but six associates. The Supply Company buys a lot of rolls of photo composition film and paper, some printing presses, front end systems and processing equipment—and will rassle up a price on a secretary's chair or water cooler, if asked—but its main function still is to purchase newsprint and ink, 99 per cent of which is for the Concern.

The Supply Company moved from Cincinnati to New York in 1934, and returned to Cincinnati in 1977.

BEFORE HE LEFT West Virginia, Homer Taylor also picked up a degree from Tech in business management.

He has a wide range of hobbies. He goes hunting for goose on the eastern shore of Maryland, fishes for salmon and trout in northern Canada, and bags small game in West Virginia with his father. On the golf course he's in the low 90's. He is enamoured of old cars and tinkered with a 1946 Ford sedan until Margie made him get it out of the garage. (He gave it to Ralph Eary.)

Margie and Homer take care of maintenance and decorating around the home.

Homer can fix anything—except the refrigerator.

"I don't remember ever," he says, "having a repairman—except for the refrigerator—in any of my homes."

Now you know who to call for help.

PRODUCTION DIRECTOR
Ralph E. Eary

RALPH'S NEEDLE-POINTED pixie sense of humor prompts him to offer a headline for this profile: "Destined To Be a Printer—Always Wanted To Be a Sports Writer." Not bad, Ralph; makes you sound interesting.

And definitely he is; his life and career have taken several storybook twists and turns.

For starters: he dropped out of high school in 1945 in Charleston, West Virginia (where he was born March 3, 1929) to work in a defense plant. Then the big war ended. "My father gave me the best advice of my lifetime," says Ralph. "It was 'Go back to school!'"

Ralph did, enrolling in Dunbar High because his Stonewall Jackson classmates had already graduated. He lettered in three sports, baseball, basketball, football (co-captain). He dated the head majorette, Rea Jo Lathey. In Ralph's eyes she was "the most beautiful girl in the world."

HE WENT ON to college for a couple of years. The owner of his hometown newspaper, where Ralph had worked as a copy boy during high school, was having labor problems in the composing room. He prevailed upon Ralph to take over. This was 1949. Ralph took on the job, and at the same time married the majorette.

He ran the composing room until January 1951 when he beat the draft by joining the Air Force. Late that year Rea Jo sold their Charleston home and joined Ralph at Biggs AFB in El Paso. They moved on to Bergstrom AFB at Austin, Texas.

General Management and Staff

Ralph made military history of a sort in the 97th Aviation Squadron by becoming the U.S. Air Force's youngest first sergeant.

Almost overnight the 97th loaded up two A-bombs and relocated at Eilson AFB in Alaska. They got there just as the armistice ended the Korean war, and the troops started sitting it out. He spotted an AFR that said non-critical soldiers could go home, stamped the magic words on his papers and on Christmas Eve 1953 was back in Charleston to resume life as a civilian printer.

By the time first son Christy arrived in Coral Gables, Florida—nine months to the day of his return from Alaska— Ralph was a printer at *The Miami Herald*. He toiled in that plant 13 years, rising to assistant production manager. Knight Newspapers picked him as one of ten for a year's management training.

"Being somewhat impulsive or aggressive," Ralph says, he looked beyond Knight for a new challenge. He queried his old boss Ron White, who had become Scripps-Howard production chief. Ron put Ralph in touch with Ed Estlow in Denver—and the Earys promptly headed West to a new job.

IT WAS RALPH'S debut as production manager on a big paper. Likewise he was the first for *The Rocky Mountain News*. Estlow taught him patience. While the plant was being doubled in size, a production team was formed, with all-new presses, plate-making equipment, composing room, and engraving department.

Ralph was production manager of *The News* seven years. Then Estlow, who had joined general management in New York, tapped him to succeed Ron White as production and engineering director in January 1972. Ralph operated out of Cincinnati, where the New York officers were later transferred.

It turned out that Cincinnati is mainly a place where Ralph hangs his hat. "I spend most of my time," he says, "flying to Scripps-Howard properties on matters relating to production and engineering."

The Earys also have a daughter, Leslie Joette born in 1964. As a family they golf, bowl, and attend Mariemont Nondenominational Church in the suburban "village" where they reside.

In Miami Ralph played golf almost every day—and learned to swing a mean club. "My handicap was whatever I wanted it to be—most of the time scratch to plus one." He got a chance to play with the touring pros.

HIS BIGGEST THRILL in golf was scoring a 64 on a par 72 course, beating two "good" pros. That was his best-ever score. In that game he got a hole-in-one and also eagled a par 5 hole.

When he arrived home, beaming, he suggested to Jo that they sell out, buy a trailer and join the pro tour. She may have thought he was more than half serious. "How much money did you win shooting a 64?" she asked.

Ralph admitted he didn't win any money but said he had learned how to beat the guys who do win money.

That logic didn't exactly bowl over Jo.

"Look," she said, probably with her arms akimbo, "when you play ten sub-par rounds—*consecutively*—come talk to me about turning pro."

Ralph hasn't made it yet.

"But, listen, I've come close several times."

DIRECTOR OF
HUMAN RESOURCES

Robert E. Brophy

FOR A SPLIT SECOND, Bob Brophy, driving to a wedding, had a fleeting horrified glimpse of the giant semi swooping into his lane on the crest of a hill and screaming head-on into his little Chevy.

Bob finally woke up in the hospital. He was lucky to be alive. All he got was compound fractures, and a lot of surgery.

GENERAL MANAGEMENT AND STAFF 151

This happened in 1953. He had been out of service just nineteen days, and starting full-time in the circulation office of his hometown newspaper, the *Globe Gazette* in Mason City, Iowa (better known as River City in *The Music Man*). The tractor-trailer driver had been trying to avoid ramming a bus that was turning; he totalled Bob's Chevy.

Not much of a debut in newspapering, obviously. But it all turned out pretty good. When he was able to get around again, Bob worked part-time at the *Globe Gazette*. The next year he married his hometown sweetheart, Martha Ann Fandel, and decided to take advantage of the GI Bill to further his education.

BOB GOT INTERESTED in newspapers at age twelve, delivering the *Globe Gazette*. At fourteen he started in their mail room. He was born June 27, 1928 in Mason City, and after high school attended St. John University at Collegeville, Minnesota, majoring in history and economics. Summers and vacations he kept his hand in at the newspaper.

When he graduated from St. John the Air Force grabbed him and tossed him back in school in such places as Texas, Colorado, Florida, Georgia, Puerto Rico and England. They were trying to teach him to interpret aerial recon photos, and otherwise perform like an intelligence expert. He wore khaki three years.

Then came the untoward waltz with the semi.

To use his GI benefits, Bob and Martha went to Denver in 1955 and he enrolled in University of Denver to begin work on a master's degree in personnel and industrial relations. He got that in 1956.

Their first child, Michelle, was born in Denver in 1956. Eventually they had six more: Tom born in 1958, Maureen (1959), Jim (1961), John (1963), Mary (1966), and Mike (1968).

THERE WAS NO WAY Bob would stay away from newspapers. He joined the staff of The Register System of Newspapers, a group of weekly Catholic publications headquartered in Denver. He worked variously in personnel, labor relations and production. He took the opportunity, too, to earn another master's degree—in business from The Register College of Journalism, in Denver.

In his work he was well acquainted with personnel and production people at The *Rocky Mountain News*. When he read in 1970 about Ed Estlow being promoted to New York as assistant general business manager he promptly phoned his congratulations.

Ed told Bob that Bill Fletcher, personnel manager, was becoming his successor as The *News* business manager.

Bob called Fletcher to offer congratulations.

He was ready to go on down the line and phone congrats also to the new personnel manager.

"Who's taking your place?" he asked Fletcher. "I'd like to say hello to him."

"Darned if I know," said Fletcher. "Hey, would you be interested?"

"Well, hmm," Bob responded. "I'd sure think about it."

They danced around for a couple of weeks and then Bob was installed as The *News* new personnel director.

IN 1975 BROPHY was tapped to go to Central headquarters in Cincinnati and break ground on a new job, director of employee benefits. That meant serving in a consulting capacity for the Concern employees—nearly 12,000—in the areas of benefits, pensions and other personnel matters.

The work remained much the same but the title was changed first to Director of Personnel and finally to Director of Human Resources. Bob is vice-chairman of Media Pension Plan and has been a member of its board since 1978.

Bob carries a compact 190 pounds on a five-nine frame. His auburn hair is tinged with gray, and his complexion is ruddy. His middle name is Emmett.

In spare time he reads historical novels, plays bridge and poker. He has one other avocation, Fair weather or foul, every day Bob tries to cap lunch with a mile walk and two miles after his evening meal.

DIRECTOR OF CIRCULATION

Jimmy E. Manis Jr.

FOR A COUPLE OF YEARS Jimmy Manis regularly scouted the Pacific west of Hawaii in a Navy radar plane for signs of a possible sneak attack on America. It wasn't war, but it wasn't a piece of cake, either.

"Nothing happened to me," he says soberly. "I had a lot of friends who ditched. And a lot of friends who died."

He spent four years in the Navy as an aviation electronics technician, reaching Petty Officer 2nd class. From 1956 to 1958 he was on the assignment out of Hawaii. That wasn't all bad. He had been married about a year and was able to take his bride on a government-paid honeymoon to the land of Waikiki's golden beaches.

Then came his return to civilian life—to Miami, Florida where he wound up following his father into newspaper circulation.

JIMMY WAS BORN in Knoxville, Tennessee September 12, 1936. His father was an over-the-road truck driver. Jimmy grew up under pretty normal circumstances. At twelve he had a *Knoxville News-Sentinel* route. In high school he was in football and track, but not spectacularly—"the other guys were bigger." He worked after school and summers as a stock boy or bag boy for a supermarket. Then he became an usher at the Bijou in Knoxville. "I memorized a lot of dialogue, with my back to the screen." His shift was from right after school to near midnight.

His father decided to move to Miami when Jimmy was in

the middle of his senior year. Jimmy went, too. But he came back to Knoxville, lived with relatives, and was graduated from Fulton High in 1954. His father got into the circulation department of *The Miami Herald.*

Jimmy, just seventeen, volunteered for the Navy, and started his four year hitch. He trained at Corpus Christi, Texas; Biloxi, Mississippi; Memphis, Tennessee, then went to the early warning flight squadron in Honolulu.

IN HIS BRIEF PERIOD OF HIGH SCHOOL in Miami Jimmy met June Thompson; she was fourteen and a freshman. Jimmy couldn't get her off his mind, even while undergoing Navy training. In 1955, back home on leave, he talked her into marrying him, and they had to drive across the state line into Mississippi because at sixteen she was too young to marry in Florida. "I had her mother's permission," says Jimmy.

June finished high school in time to go with him to the Hawaiian assignment. Their son Michael was born in 1957.

His father obviously put a bug in somebody's ear at *The Miami Herald.* Jimmy was looking for a job as an electronics technician, to take advantage of his Navy training. When *The Herald* called, they told him he could work for them while he kept looking.

That seemed fair enough. He started at $40 a week as a phone clerk. He also carried a route of 300-400 papers. June gave him a hand on that, collecting. They had that route a couple of years. He forgot looking for an electronics job. They had a daughter, Valerie, in 1959. He liked circulation. He kept going up the ladder. It was exciting and a "challenge to learn." He went from bookkeeper, to district manager, to circulation controller and to office manager in ten years, supervising forty people.

When Mike Tynan resigned from *The Herald* and went to *The Pittsburgh Press* as circulation director he promptly offered Jimmy the job of circulation manager of *The Pittsburgh Post-Gazette,* part of the agency setup. Jimmy took it. He put in a lot of ten-hour days to solve problems. In 1970 he was promoted to circulation manager of *The Pittsburgh Press,* and then to assistant business manager.

JIMMY ATTENDED Miami-Dade Junior College for a while. He transferred those credits to University of Pittsburgh, and finally to Point Park College in Pittsburgh where he got a degree in business management in 1976. "It was all night school," says Jimmy. "It seemed like it took forever."

When Mike Tynan retired as circulation director, Business Manager Bob Hartmann "looked all around for a replacement—without much luck."

"Finally," says Jimmy, "I went to Bob and said, you don't really need an assistant business manager, if you want me to, I'll take over as circulation director.

"Bob gave me a big grin. He said, 'I thought you'd never ask.'"

Manis held that post two and a half years until he was promoted May, 1980 to the Cincinnati headquarters to give overall circulation direction to sixteen daily, seven Sunday and twenty-three weekly newspapers published by Scripps-Howard.

Jimmy is a fisherman—wall-eyes in Canada, once a year. He also plays golf, with a 21 handicap, "about every chance I get."

DATA PROCESSING DIRECTOR

William J. Lee

BILL LEE WAS UP against the wall. His wife's odd illness baffled doctors. Bills were piling up. He was teaching music in a public school, going to graduate school, and playing trombone in a night club till 3 in the morning. He couldn't keep it up. He told his wife Romayne he was going to look for another job.

"Bill, what could you do? All you know is music."

"I don't know. But I'll find something."

It was not easy. Bill went around Pittsburgh, trying all kinds of businesses. Everybody turned him down. "What could you possibly do for us? You are a music-maker." He heard that over and over.

By the time Bill reached IBM he was angry, so he told 'em. "Listen, I don't see much difference in programming something into one of your computers and, say, writing a symphony. And I *know* music." He explained the similarity further. The IBM fellow became interested.

"Okay, take our tests. If you pass *excellently*, we'll hire you. *Excellently*." Bill took the tests. He passed—*excellently*. He had to wait a while but eventually—this was 1960—IBM put him on.

IN THE MEANTIME, Romayne, down to sixty-five pounds, was taken to the hospital for exploratory surgery. Doctors found a rare tubal-type pregnancy, took care of it, and she began recovering.

Bill dug in on his new IBM job. He started making sales. One customer was *The Pittsburgh Press*, where he did a systems study and sold a computer. Two years later, in March 1965, *The Press* hired Bill as data processing manager.

Even as a youngster, Bill had rhythm in his soul. Born in Pittsburgh August 2, 1931, he attended Central Catholic high school, graduating in 1949 just in time to go into the Air Force. That wasn't bad. He played with Air Force bands and orchestras at Bolling Field in Washington, D.C. and Edwards AFB in California, where he was first sergeant of the 503rd AF Band.

Out of uniform toward the end of 1952, Bill became a professional musician, playing with dance bands—including Tony Pastor, Billy Butterfield, and Billy May. He also pulled gigs with night club orchestras, in theatre pits, civic light opera, and played lead trombone for the Pittsburgh Opera orchestra. He played in the band of the Barnum and Bailey Circus.

BILL ATTENDED Duquesne University, graduating in 1957 with a B.S. in music education, magna cum laude. He was married the same year. He and Romayne had met while

General Management and Staff 157

both were with a touring quartet, The Collegiates. She had been a dance band vocalist, and had performed in night clubs and on television.

Bill taught public school music, vocal and instrumental, in Owendale, Michigan and in Pittsburgh. He has a daughter, Tracey, born in 1950, who has her own modeling agency in Richmond, Virginia.

After a little more than four years at *The Pittsburgh Press*, Bill was tapped in September 1969 to transfer to Scripps-Howard headquarters in Cincinnati to become data processing director.

Actually he wears two hats. He also is vice president and general manager of Dataway Inc., a wholly-owned subsidiary, established in October 1969 to acquire and lease items of electronic equipment to affiliates of The E. W. Scripps Company.

IT WAS STRICTLY COMPUTER equipment in the beginning, but Dataway has broadened its operations to include buying and leasing presses, and in one instance, acquiring a site and putting up a building in Dallas for United Press International's computer center. Scripps-Howard Supply Company is involved in some of these deals.

Dataway also offers maintenance agreements and places engineers on site in some Concern plants.

Creation of the Scripps-Howard typesetting system was Dataway's first big project. Working with a vendor, this meant acquiring the software and hardware for six major newspapers, managing the development, assisting in installation, and providing software modifications to meet changing conditions.

Another high point was doing a classified advertising system on the same basis—to overcome the change-over from hot metal. Dataway's system lets the computer handle insertions, kills, and billing.

Dataway was the first to incorporate programmed billing as part of this electronic classified system. Dataway had the responsibility for helping the six major papers add on this to their basic typesetting system.

An example of the effectiveness of the computerized classified is that the *Rocky Mountain News* can paginate as many as 156 full pages of liners for a single edition with appropriate "holes" left to the pasteup of display ads.

"It is decidely more accurate than the old method," says Bill.

ADMINISTRATIVE PROGRAMS to handle payroll, accounts receivable, general ledger functions, budgeting and financial reporting are also devised by Dataway, mainly acting in the role of consultant.

The newest mountain for Dataway to climb is to computerize newspaper circulation. The goal is a system that starts right from the subscriber level and controls every aspect of delivery from the pressroom and mailroom through the carrier. It also will do all billing and accounting, including reports to the Audit Bureau of Circulation. It will blanket a city to such an extent that it will identify all occupied housing units, showing those which do and do not receive newspapers. This obviously is a potential marketing and promotion tool.

This will be no overnight achievement. The project started in December 1977. A task force of four Scripps-Howard circulation directors met with Ray Mack, Ralph Eary and Lee to develop the functional requirements. This took until mid-1979. Bids were then taken from competent vendors, and finally IBM was given a contract.

By August 1980 the technical requirements, the first of three phases, were developed. Then began the design of that system; targeted to end in March 1981. The final phase would be to actually write and test all the programs. A computer for that purpose was installed in the Central Trust Tower.

The original timetable called for Dataway to reach the stage of actual installation at the newspapers in late 1982 or 1983.

Some Saturday nights Bill can be found at certain Cincinnati clubs where they hold an old-timers jam session. Some orchestra leaders have asked Bill to join their band.

Bill Lee smiles and just shakes his head. He's had it with playing "Goodnight, Sweetheart" at 3 a.m. He'll stick with the challenge of data processing.

DIRECTOR OF RESEARCH
William R. Niehaus

BILL NIEHAUS HAS SO MANY hobbies you'd think he might not be hep to his work—but don't make the mistake of trying to one-up him on hypervelocity impact.

Never heard of that? Just happens to be something about at what speed outer space detritus collides with planets—and makes craters like those we have seen on the moon. Bill figured out they hit at a closing rate of about twenty thousand feet per second.

He determined that in research at NASA by building a "gun" with a barrel a thousand feet long, and shooting tiny pebbles out of it.

For relaxation, Niehaus builds sailing ship models in bottles, coaches kids baseball, flies radio-controlled planes, ties fishing flies, dabbles in politics in his Cincinnati suburb where he serves on the recreation commission, writes a little technical stuff, sometimes lectures on physics, does occasional target shooting, and used to avidly collect frontier Colts revolvers. (There may be two or three hobbies that weren't mentioned.)

THOUGH BORN in Cincinnati June 10, 1932, Bill went all around Robin Hood's barn before winding up at Scripps-Howard headquarters in December 1970 as chief research engineer. Incidentally he got his political bent from his father, who was chief of visitor security at the General Electric complex and mayor of suburban Deer Park.

Bill graduated from Cincinnati's Purcell high school in 1950. He went to Xavier University to get his physics degree. One summer he worked as an ink-splattered fly boy for a printer. He put in two summers at a paper supply house and one at General Electric.

After being graduated in 1954, he obtained a two-year fellowship at Saint Louis (Missouri) University where he got his master's in physics. Then his ROTC obligation (from Xavier) caught up with him and he put in a couple of years in the U.S. Army.

Assigned to ordnance, he went from Aberdeen Proving Grounds, Maryland, to the new National Space Agency (NASA) at Ames lab in California. That's where he did some of the initial work on hypervelocity impact and the theory of moon cratering. He was one of the youngest engineers at Ames given an independent project.

On being discharged in 1958, Bill remained with NASA a short time then returned to the East and Midwest to follow aerospace engineering. In Middletown, Ohio he headed Aeronca Manufacturing's aerothermodynamic systems group doing studies on the re-entry heat shield for the space shuttle.

He was married in 1961 to Marian Camille Martinson. They have six children: Ted born in 1962, Dave (1963), Jennifer (1965), Tom (1967), Juliet (1969) and Natalie (1977).

At Wright Field at Dayton, Ohio he was involved for four years in an Air Force foreign technology intelligence operation. Then he migrated into consulting systems engineering and management. That led to joining the research operation at Scripps-Howard.

In 1976 he was promoted to Director of Research. He and his staff have been involved in everything from readership surveys to OSHA, energy conservation and training programs. Principally he now works in the area of corporate development, looking into the crystal ball for methods of improving and expanding operations, studying trends in the media, charting demographics and their potentials. Not just keeping up with the world but trying to get ahead of it for new corporate targets.

Bill's younger brother Dan is a physician in Cincinnati. One sister is a professional dancer who appeared on the Jackie Gleason show, Broadway musicals, and in the movies.

The other is a professional organist as was his mother who also was a pianist with WLW in Cincinnati.

His interest in baseball stems from playing in the Xavier infield, beating a collegiate rival that had Sandy Koufax of later Dodger fame as pitcher. He had visions of playing pro ball himself but the Army took care of that. He was on the Xavier rifle team for three years.

Bill has been coaching baseball because of his boys' interest in the game. "They grow up fast, though," he observed. "Looks like I have maybe one more year of that."

General Counsel

Sherm Dye's Crew Handles Many Chores

Sherman Dye

THE CODE OF REGULATIONS of The E. W. Scripps Company and the various other corporations in the Concern provide that:

> The general counsel shall be the chief consulting officer of the Company in legal matters, and shall have general control of all litigation and all other matters of legal import concerning the Company.

This sterile sentence does not adequately describe the current scope of the activities of the general counsel. The legal adviser has seen its historical function expand from counseling in business, real estate and litigation matters to a role involving, among other things, that of a buffer between the manifold acts of a complex national and international operation and the functions of the several governmental levels with their various departments, agencies and commissions.

The law firm of Baker & Hostetler has been associated with Scripps-Howard over sixty years. The firm began work for E. W. Scripps in 1919 which culminated in organization of The E. W. Scripps Company in 1922. Since then it has served as general counsel for the parent company and all other Scripps-Howard corporations.

One founder of the firm was Newton D. Baker, who served as Secretary of War in the cabinet of President Wilson. Other early stalwarts included Tom Sidlo and Paul Patterson.

As Scripps-Howard has grown, so has the law firm. It now is a multi-office national law firm headquartered in Cleveland with offices in Columbus, Ohio, Washington, D. C., Denver, Colorado, and Orlando, Florida. There are now approximately 200 lawyers in the firm, and about 100 in an average year will do some Scripps-Howard work. This ranges from 90 per cent of an individual attorney's time to a few hours.

Baker & Hostetler is called on to run the entire gamut of legal services counseling in business transactions to defense of reporters jailed for contempt of court. Of particular importance are matters of taxation; labor relations; corporate housekeeping; finance and securities regulations; radio and television; libel, right of privacy and First Amendment rights; and copyright and trademark matters of all kinds from contracts to infringement litigation.

The increasing complexity of the law and the diversity of Scripps-Howard operations are responsible for the increasing number of lawyers involved.

Sherman Dye has the overall responsibility for seeing that general counsel meets its obligation to Scripps-Howard. Born in Portland, Oregon November 18, 1915, Sherm grew up in Lakewood, Ohio. He was graduated from Oberlin College in 1937 and from Western Reserve Law School in 1940. He had an early taste of printer's ink, working on the school paper in both high school and college.

After two years in Washington, Sherm joined the law firm in the fall of 1942 and immediately began working on Scripps-Howard tax matters. He continued primarily in the tax and financial fields until 1970 when he succeeded Joe Fawcett as head of the Scripps-Howard legal team. As such he directs and supervises a number of his partners and associates who bring their particular specialities to bear on Scripps-Howard problems.

These individuals include:

Corporate, Securities, Acquisitions and Special Projects

John H. Burlingame—born Milwaukee, Wisconsin, 1933; admitted to bar Ohio 1963. Preparatory education,

University of Wisconsin (B.S. 1960); legal education, University of Wisconsin (LL. B. 1963).

John L. Thomas—born Cleveland, Ohio 1941; admitted to bar Ohio 1966. Preparatory education, Yale University (B.A. 1963); legal education, Harvard Law School (J.D. 1966).

Radio and Television

John R. Baskin—born Cleveland, Ohio 1916; admitted to bar Ohio 1940. Preparatory education, Western Reserve University (A.B. 1938): legal education, Western Reserve University (LL.B. 1940).

Norman S. Jeavons—born Cleveland, Ohio 1930; admitted to bar Ohio 1958. Preparatory education, Dartmouth College (A.B. 1952); legal education, Case Western Reserve University (LL.B. 1958).

Donald P. Ziefaing—born Niagara Falls, New York, 1936; admitted to bar D.C. 1965. Preparatory education, University of Notre Dame (A.B. 1960); legal education, George Washington University (J.D. 1963); formerly senior vice-president government relations, National Association of Broadcasters.

Labor, Employee Relations, Benefits and EEOC

Victor Strimbu Jr.—born New Philadelphia, Ohio 1932; admitted to bar Ohio 1960. Preparatory education Heidelberg College (B.A. 1954); legal education Columbia University (J.D. 1960).

John F. Novatney Jr.—born Cleveland, Ohio 1930; admitted to bar Ohio 1959. Preparatory education, Brown University (B.A. 1952); legal education, University of Virginia (LL.B., J.D. 1955).

Betty Southard Murphy—born East Orange, New Jersey; admitted to bar D.C. 1959. Preparatory education, Ohio State University (B.A. 1952); legal education, American University (J.D. 1958). Former chairman, National Labor Relations Board.

Paul D. White—born LaGrange, Kentucky 1917; admitted to bar Ohio 1950. Preparatory education, Kentucky

State College (B.A. 1940); legal education, Western Reserve University (LL.B., J.D. 1950).

Richard H. Leukart II—Born Detroit, Michigan, 1942; admitted to bar Ohio 1967. Preparatory education, Dartmouth College (A.B. 1964); legal education, University of Michigan (J.D. 1967).

John H. Wilharm Jr.—born Pittsburgh, Pennsylvania 1932; admitted to bar Ohio 1960. Preparatory education, Amherst College (B.A. 1954); legal education, Case Western Reserve University (J.D. 1960).

W. James Ollinger—born Kittanning, Pennsylvania 1943; admitted to bar Ohio 1968. Preparatory education, Capital University (B.A. 1966); legal education, Case Western Reserve University (J.D. 1968).

Charles T. Price—born Lansing, Michigan 1944; admitted to bar Ohio 1969. Preparatory education, Ohio Wesleyan University (B.A. 1966); legal education, Harvard University (J.D. 1969).

Taxation

Richard R. Turney—born Oelwein, Iowa 1930; admitted to bar Ohio 1958. Preparatory education, University of Iowa (B.A. 1952); legal education, Harvard Law School (LL.B. 1957).

William M. Toomajian—born Troy, New York 1943; admitted to bar New York 1968, Ohio 1978. Preparatory education, Hamilton College (B.A. 1965); legal education, University of Michigan (J.D. 1968); New York University (LL.M. Taxation 1975).

Libel and First Amendment

Bruce W. Sanford—born Massena, New York 1945; admitted to bar New York 1970, Ohio 1971. Preparatory education, Hamilton College (A.B. 1967); legal education, New York University (J.D. 1970).

Anti-Trust, Trade Regulation and Special Litigation

Jonathan E. Thackeray—born Athens, Ohio 1936; admitted to bar Ohio 1961. Preparatory education,

Harvard College (B.A. 1958); legal education, Harvard Law School (J.D. 1961).

Copyright, Trademark and Unfair Competition

Charles H. Cleminshaw—born Cleveland, Ohio 1929; admitted to bar Ohio 1954. Preparatory education, Amherst College (B.A. 1951); legal education, University of Michigan (LL.B. 1954).

George Downing—born Girard, Pennsylvania 1934; admitted to bar Ohio 1962. Preparatory education, Gannon College (B.A. 1956); legal education, Case Western Reserve University (LL.B. 1962).

Bruce O. Baumgartner—born St. Louis, Missouri 1942; admitted to bar Ohio 1967. Preparatory education, Northwestern University (B.A. 1964); legal education, Northwestern University (J.D. 1967).

Wills, Trusts and Personal

Robert M. Brucken—born Akron, Ohio 1934; admitted to bar Ohio 1960. Preparatory education, Marietta College (A.B. 1956); legal education, University of Michigan (J.D. 1959).

Letter to a Young Man

In the late Forties when he was a student at Stanford, Ted Scripps asked John H. Sorrells about the advisability of entering a newspaper career. John, then Executive Editor of Scripps-Howard Newspapers, responded with his typical eloquence and clarity. On these two pages are excerpts from his classic letter to Ted.

On Becoming a Newspaperman

¶ ASSUMING THAT A YOUNG MAN has some reasonable assurance of the staying qualities of the newspaper business, from a material point of view, I think he should ponder the matter from a different point of view. It seems to me that the newspaper business would prove inadequate and unsatisfactory to anyone who considers it as merely the means of earning a living, because the newspaper is more than a business or a trade or a profession; it's a way of life.

One who goes into newspaper work ought to consider that he is enlisting in a cause, is dedicating his life to something. He should inquire not only about the material rewards, but also ask about the spiritual rewards.

¶ THE AMERICAN NEWSPAPER IS evolved from, and is part of, the folklore of this country. A free press, in its day-to-day performance, is the composite of a lot of little things. It is an item about a birth or death or marriage; it's a piece about the opening of a new store, or what is the price of this or that; a story about a heroic cop, or a false and malicious arrest. It is an article about health, or a bad slum condition; it's a bit of scientific information. A free press is a vast collection of items which gives a community knowledge of itself. It is an institution that enlightens, and, by virtue of that enlightment, a community is freer to know, to ponder, to appraise and to judge.

A newspaper gives cohesion and direction and purpose to community life. It agitates; it creates demands; it articulates wants and needs; it establishes and preserves standards of public morals. It is the community's physician, father confessor, and advocate.

¶ I HAVE FELT THAT TO BE A newspaperman was a post of honor; I have felt that it lifted me above and beyond the common run of men. I have felt that its obligations and responsibilities were of such character as to command something extra-ordinary in the way of human behavior. I have felt that it requires that a man not merely be honest, but that he think with integrity; I have felt that mine is a noble profession, because I feel that primarily I am serving interests other than my own.

¶ THE NEWSPAPER BUSINESS IS, in a sense, a greedy and insatiate business; it will absorb the eagerness, the vision, the energy, and the imagination of young men. It will drink thirstily of these things but it will issue a great dividend from them in public service. The newspaper business will endure so long as there are young men who are willing to subordinate themselves to the common good; who are willing to use their strength and give voice to the hopes and aims of the inarticulate. So a young man has to consider whether it's worth it.

¶ I THINK THERE WILL ALWAYS be young men with the spirit of adventure in them, young men bound by something within them to take the role of gentlemen *(of the press)* in our society. So long as there are such men, nobody has to worry much about the enduring qualities of journalism.

SECTION FIVE

Some Scripps-Howard Institutions

Including a Rundown on the Key Staffers in Our Washington Bureau, UPI, United Media, And Elsewhere

The Washington Bureau Scripps-Howard News Service

Teaming Up To Produce News and Editorials.

THE Washington Bureau of Scripps-Howard Newspapers and the Scripps-Howard News Service always have been a team operation. But that never has been more clearly defined than now as this sixty-three-year-old operation moves into the decade of the Eighties.

The two distinct functions of the bureau—producing editorials on national and international affairs and the gathering and distribution of news—have been placed under two separate heads.

B. J. Cutler, as editor-in-chief of Scripps-Howard Newspapers, supervises editorial policy, including the editorial cartoons of Gene Basset.

Dan K. Thomasson, as editor of Scripps-Howard News Service and Washington Bureau chief, is responsible for SHNS's national and international news operations.

But while their authority is separate and distinct, it does not mean that they go separate ways. In fact, in the best traditions of cooperation which always has marked the Scripps-Howard family, both Cutler and Thomasson regard their operations as complementary. Frequently, SHNS stories stimulate editorials and policy and conversely editorials frequently generate news stories.

Change is nothing new to the Scripps-Howard Washington Bureau. It was born in a period of change, World War I, and has altered considerably over the decades.

In 1917, when the United States entered "the war to end all wars," E. W. Scripps set up a headquarters in Washington to direct Scripps-Howard's support of war efforts. He put Robert P. Scripps in charge and shortly thereafter appointed him Editorial Director.

Bob ultimately set up an office in a small back room of the original *Washington Daily News* building, gathered a group of men and called it the Editorial Board. Its aim was to coordinate and express Scripps-Howard policies.

From that beginning, through various leaderships including those of G. B. "Deac" Parker, Walker Stone and Earl H. Richert grew Scripps-Howard Newspaper Alliance and then the Scripps-Howard News Service with a much greater and more diversified role.

The major change was the addition of Washington correspondents: A national staff—reporting for all of the Scripps-Howard papers—and regional correspondents reporting mainly to their own news desks. Through the years, beginning with the advent of World War II, the bureau added an international reporting responsibility.

Cutler implements the editorial policy of Scripps-Howard which is determined at the annual conference of editors, expressing those policies in the editorials distributed daily from the bureau. On occasions when an editorial policy must be determined to meet a spot situation, that determination is made in the Washington Bureau.

The news operation, under Thomasson, consists of reporting and interpreting events in the nation's capital as well as wherever else the news requires attention.

But the emphasis is not on spot news, as such, but on interpretation, enterprise, investigation, and generally anticipating the news—to come in ahead whenever possible, and not to duplicate the major wire services.

That's why the bureau sends its diplomatic correspondents worldwide to relate and interpret events and conditions abroad. And why it sends correspondents to political conventions, on presidential campaigns, and across the nation to report on the American scene.

The bureau today is organized on a beat structure. That is, the national staff is somewhat specialized along particular lines: Ted Knap for the White House and national politics; R. H. Boyce and Walter Friedenberg for State Department and foreign affairs; Don Kirkman for science, Dale McFeatters for labor and Congress.

And the scope of this specialization has been enlarged to embrace new fields: Ann McFeatters for consumer affairs; Jim Foster for energy; Gene Goldenberg for the legal beat, from the Justice Department to the U.S. Supreme Court; Stewart Lytle on military affairs, Alan Thompson on Congress.

Plus, of course, those general assignment-investigative reporters so valuable for any staff: Jim Herzog and Bill Steif.

This structure has come about gradually.

In the old days of SHNA there was a sort of star system. The No. 1 and No. 2 reporters would get the top stories, whether they involved a political campaign, a revolution in Central America, a major strike issue or the development of Alaskan oil. Now, each such assignment would be handled by a different reporter who is intimately familiar with the subject.

The bureau also gets help from the staffs of Scripps-Howard papers when it needs to gather local data for a roundup, or when a local reporter has a story worth sharing nationally. And the bureau also is now distributing, in its role as Scripps-Howard News Service, a number of special columns—religion, economy, etc.

The material is transmitted nightly via UPI's DataNews system. DataNews is available to the bureau at all times, day and night, but it mainly transmits in the late afternoon and night hours. The regional reporters make use of the system to file at any time they need to make a deadline.

Once located in *The Washington Daily News building,* the bureau moved to the Wyatt Building on 14th Street, and in late 1980 again moved—to 1110 Vermont Avenue, N.W., Washington, D. C., 20005.

EDITOR OF SHNS
Dan K. Thomasson

BEFORE Watergate, investigative reporting in Washington often amounted to keeping your ears open at Georgetown cocktail parties. But not for Dan K. Thomasson, editor of the Scripps-Howard News Service and chief of the Washington Bureau.

A native of Shelbyville, Indiana, Dan has parlayed his seemingly boundless energy, keen sense of proportion and basic Hoosier curiosity into a career that led *Washingtonian Magazine* to list him in 1973 as one of the "lean gray wolves of Washington journalism."

Even back in 1963, a year before the *Rocky Mountain News* sent him to Washington as its correspondent, Dan was smoking the rascals out. He won the Denver Newspaper Guild's award for top story of the year with his expose on Colorado officials who were converting state vehicles to their private use and feeding their families with raids on the meat lockers of state institutions.

But that was only a warm-up for Washington, where Dan dug into scandals from Watergate to ITT, from Chappaquiddick to health-care ripoffs among the elderly in Miami. He revealed John F. Kennedy's close relationship with the girlfriend of Mafia chieftains and broke the story about long-time FBI burglary teams that secretly worked national security cases.

"It got so I was spending six months of every year on one bloody scandal," Dan recalls. "I was out on so many limbs by myself that I felt like a lumberjack in a windstorm."

But everyone who knows Dan understands that he loved every minute of it. A gregarious six-footer whose once red dish-black hair is now distinctively gray, Dan was so good at his craft that he was named assistant managing editor of Scripps-Howard News Service for investigative reporting in 1974. And he was picked for the managing editor's job a year later when Milton Britten went to *The Memphis Press-Scimitar* as editor.

In January 1980 Dan took the logical next step, assuming command of the SHNS Washington news operation with the retirement of Jack Steele.

As long as Dan can remember he wanted to be a newspaperman. In Shelbyville, where he was born December 22, 1933, Dan restarted the student paper in Shelbyville High, and took to journalism so well he was editor of the campus daily at Indiana University, while stringing for the AP and *The Terre Haute Star*.

After his graduation in 1956 he worked briefly on *The Indianapolis Star* until he was drafted and sent to Fort Sill, Oklahoma where he edited the post newspaper and moonlighted a full shift as a reporter for *The Lawton Constitution*.

Somehow during those sixteen-hour, four-story days he found time to court and marry La Queta Forducey, daughter of a Lawton merchant, who was to become the mother of four little Thomassons—Scot, Lisa, Sean and Patrick—and the ever tolerant, steadying influence of Dan's life.

"She rarely squawked, even at the times when she had a right to take a ballbat to me," Dan recalls.

Out of the service in 1959, Dan decided he wanted to do his newspapering in Denver. "As a flatlander and Western history buff, I wanted to see those mountains," he explains.

"Besides, in Indiana I had grown up in 'Scripps-Howard country' with *The Indianapolis Times* and *The Evansville Press*. So I asked then Managing Editor Vince Dwyer for a job on the *Rocky Mountain News* and he gave me one."

Dan moved to Washington for the *News* in 1964 and joined the national staff of SHNS three years later.

Dan's furious digging into the seedy side of politics has still left him with many more friends than enemies. But that's not hard to understand given his basically decent approach to people, even those whose deeds he tears apart on the news pages.

Dan is a jazz buff and he and Queta enjoy entertaining in their suburban Annandale, Virginia, home that is littered with the trophies and ribbons of their athletic children. And don't ever make the mistake of talking sports unless you are ready to do serious damage to a bottle of fine bourbon while extolling the virtues of football and basketball.

Dan is a member of the prestigious Gridiron Club, a group of sixty Washington journalists who each year present a musical review that puts the great and near great into proper perspective. Those who have seen Dan perform decline comment when asked about his singing voice.

MANAGING EDITOR

Powell S. Lindsay

POWELL LINDSAY brings a genuine liking for people and a well-honed sense of outrage to his post as the minute-by-minute supervisor of one of the largest bureau staffs in Washington.

For eight years, Powell covered Congress for Scripps-Howard, developing a deep understanding of the legislative process. It was once said that he knew as much about the technicalities of legislative floor action as the parliamentarians of Congress.

A laconic six-footer with an earthy sense of humor, Powell was so married to his Tennessee mountains that he declined an Ivy League education after honors graduation from Lawrenceville School and returned to Knoxville and the University of Tennessee.

It was after U-T graduation and a stubborn refusal to enter the family milling business that he joined *The Knoxville News-Sentinel* as a copy boy in 1956. He moved into general assignment reporting for ten years, until leaving for Washington as Tennessee regional correspondent.

He was appointed to the national staff of the Washington Bureau in 1970 and eight years later began writing editorials in the terse, frequently eloquent prose that has marked him as one of the city's better writers. In early 1979 Powell joined then Managing Editor Dan Thomasson, with whom he had collaborated on a number of stories over the years, on the bureau's desk. He replaced Thomasson as managing editor on January 1, 1980.

Powell, born April 29, 1934 in Knoxville, is married to the former Malinda Midkiff of Knoxville. They have three sons, the oldest a student at Vanderbilt University in Nashville. Powell is a great sports fan and has only a couple of major problems; his inability to beat his wife on the tennis court and his refusal to admit that his alma mater is now a second-rate football power.

EDITORIAL CARTOONIST

Gene Basset

Gene BASSET insists that his formative years were largely dominated by Flash Gordon comics and Willard Mullin sports cartoons. That led him, about nine years after he was born July 24, 1927, in Brooklyn, New York, to draw his first political cartoons—on brown paper bags—about the Spanish civil war, imitating Goya's style.

His drawing talents were guided toward newspaper work when at the age of seventeen he met author Dashiell Hammett in the Aleutians while on World War II duty with the Coast Guard. He worked as editorial cartoonist for *The Indi-*

anapolis Times, The Brooklyn Eagle, The Boston Post, The Honolulu Star-Bulletin, The Cincinnati Post and then became Scripps-Howard's cartoonist in 1963.

Gene and his wife, Charlotte, have a son, Roger, who is a graduate of the Royal Academy in London; a son, Brian, who is the youngest editorial page cartoonist in the country, for *The Seattle Times,* and a daughter, Darien.

Ron Royhab

Assistant managing editor is Ron Royhab, an enthusiastic midwesterner who is always cooking up something—either in the kitchen or at the office. Ron started his career at *The Lorain Ohio Journal* and had risen to state editor when he moved on to the Scripps-Howard Ohio Bureau in Columbus in 1969. He joined *The Cincinnati Post* in 1971 and then transferred to *The Cleveland Press* in 1973. He left Cleveland to become the chief of the Ohio Bureau in 1975.

In 1978 Ron went to Washington to assume the night editor's duties and in January 1980 moved into the day editor slot. In between his reporting and editing chores, Ron has found time to serve as a board-director trustee of the Montessori School of Ohio, work with college journalism students, and aid the faculty for exceptional children at Ohio State University.

Ron was born October 6, 1942 and attended Lorain County College, Kent State University and American University where he was an American Political Science Fellow. He won seven Cleveland Newspaper Guild awards for excellence in journalism.

A confirmed jogger, Ron goes through his daily work at about the same pace. He is married to the former Roberta Libb of Canfield, Ohio and they have two sons.

Richard H. Boyce

The man who is chief diplomatic reporter for the Washington Bureau also is one of its most traveled. In fact, Dick has been called a switch-hitter for his coverage of so many foreign crises.

Some Scripps-Howard Institutions 179

Until 1964, Central and South America was his beat. Then he jetted to Africa, covering such stories as the coup in Zanzibar, the Somali-Ethiopian border clashes, and foretelling the troubles that beset Southern Rhodesia. As Scripps-Howard's European correspondent from August 1969 until 1973, he covered news in London, Paris, Algeria, Greece, Turkey, the Middle East.

Dick was born January 1, 1919, studied journalism at the University of Kansas and the University of Iowa. He began reporting for *The Kansas City Kansan* and *Kansas City Times*, served in the Navy and then went to Scripps-Howard's *Houston Press* where he was assistant managing editor before joining the Washington Bureau's national staff in 1961.

He is married, has two children who are no longer children.

Kenneth Eskey

After ten years as an editorial writer for *The Pittsburgh Press* and Scripps-Howard, Ken began covering business and economics for the bureau in March, 1978.

Born in Pittsburgh June 6, 1930, Ken earned bachelor's and master's degrees in journalism at Northwestern University, served in the Navy during the Korean war, started newspapering on the copy desk of *The Pittsburgh Press* in 1955 and went on to reporting. He left there for the Washington Bureau in 1969. He won four Golden Quill awards for education writing in Western Pennsylvania and three state-wide awards for education and editorial writing.

Ken is married, has two teenage sons and likes to play tennis—boasts of a good backhand, bad forehand—and coaches a basketball team for teenagers.

James E. Foster

Jim's specialty today is the "energy" beat, but it wasn't always so.

His first assignment for the bureau was helping to cover the Apollo 11 moon shot. Then he became Asian correspondent headquartered in Hong Kong but darting off to Cambodia and Vietnam and other places. Returning to the states in the fall of 1972, Jim worked the Latin America beat and made a number of news trips to Central and South America. He moved into the field of energy when that became a beat of its own in 1977.

Jim was born in Wellman, Iowa, June 8, 1932, attended Grinnell (Iowa) College and graduated from the University of Iowa in 1953. After two years as an Army photographer in Europe, he worked on *The Omaha World-Herald,* the *Marshalltown (Iowa) Times-Republican* and *The La Porte City (Iowa) Progress-Review.* He joined Scripps-Howard as a reporter for the *Rocky Mountain News* in 1965 and came to the bureau as correspondent for that paper in 1967.

Jim and his wife, Joanne, an ex-*News* reporter, collect Oriental, Latin American and American Southwest art.

Walter Friedenberg

A background of foreign affairs, both as reporter and editorial writer, fits Walt ideally for his role as a diplomatic correspondent for the bureau. And the fact that he is an ex-editor gives him an insight into what the editors want.

Walt, a Phi Beta Kappa graduate of Wake Forest University with a master's from Harvard, spent five years as a roving correspondent for Scripps-Howard. He roved throughout Europe, Asia, and Africa and served three tours of duty in Vietnam. After that, he spent three years writing editorials for the bureau. In 1969 he was named editor of *The Cincinnati Post* and in 1977 returned to the bureau to go abroad as European correspondent based in London. He returned to Washington in 1979.

Born in Connecticut December 22, 1928, Walt spent three years in South Asia as a Fellow of the Institute of Current World Affairs, joining Scripps-Howard on *The Pittsburgh Press* in 1960. The Friedenbergs have three children.

Gene Goldenberg

The bureau's legal affairs reporter thrives on turning legal gobbledygook into understandable English.

His beat includes the U.S. Supreme Court, Justice Department, American Bar Association and wherever else the legal process is or may be at work or not at work.

A native of New York (born March 28, 1945), Gene is a graduate of Cornell University and Northwestern's Medill Graduate School of Journalism. He spent five years as a correspondent for papers from New York to Alaska before joining Scripps-Howard's bureau in 1973 as the Southwest regional reporter. A year later he was made night editor. He moved to the legal beat in 1976.

He and his wife Jean have two children. That—and a dismal backhand—is what keeps him from deserting journalism for pro tennis, he says.

James P. Herzog

Before joining Scripps-Howard, Jim helped to bring a Pulitzer Prize to *The Akron (Ohio) Beacon Journal* for coverage of the Kent State shootings, and won an Edward J. Meeman Award of the Scripps-Howard Foundation for his reporting on the ravages of strip mining.

Jim specializes in investigative reporting and political reporting, mainly on Capitol Hill. He joined the national staff in May 1978 after less than a year as correspondent for the Scripps-Howard Ohio papers. He previously worked for *The Louisville Courier-Journal*.

Born July 23, 1943, in Stamford, Connecticut, Jim has a B.A. in history from Grinnell College and an M.S. in journalism from Columbia University. He spent two years in the Peace Corps in Tunisia, then taught journalism at Cuyahoga Community College in Cleveland before turning to newspaper work.

Jim and his wife, Margot, have three children.

Paul Hope

Paul B. Hope, an award-winning Washington newsman, is an editorial writer for Scripps-Howard News Service.

He was born January 2, 1925 in Hemlock, Ohio, where he attended public schools. After three and a half years in the

Navy during World War II, he enrolled at Ohio State University where he received a degree in journalism and won a Sigma Delta Chi award for scholastic achievement.

He began his newspaper career at *The Alexandria (Va.) Gazette* in 1950, serving as a reporter, city editor and assistant managing editor. He moved to *The Washington (D.C.) Star* in 1955. For his work on the Bobby Baker scandal in Congress, he won two top Washington Newspaper Guild awards, the Raymond Clapper and the Polk awards, and was nominated for the Pulitzer Prize.

He became chief national political writer for *The Star* in 1965 and was made an editorial writer in 1973. He joined Scripps-Howard as an editorial writer in May 1979.

Paul is married, has four sons and lives in Springfield, Virginia.

Donald C. Kirkman

Don's beat is science—everything from health to medicine through weather to space exploration. In recent years he has concentrated more on medicine, producing in early 1980 the first definitive pieces on the miracle drug, Interferon.

He covered the first landing on the moon in July 1969 and all the subsequent Apollo moon landings and has visited the South Pole.

Don was a meteorologist before getting into news work, serving as an observer for the Navy and the Weather Service. He was born in New York City April 23, 1929, and collected a degree from Kent State University, got into journalism with *The Akron Beacon Journal,* worked for Aerojet-General Corp. for a while and joined Scripps-Howard's bureau June 1, 1966. He is a lieutenant commander in the naval reserve, past president of the National Association of Science Writers.

He and his wife, Natalie, have four children.

Ted Knap

Ted, who covers the White House and national politics, has traveled to the other side of the world with three presidents and to New Hampshire with more presidential candidates than there's room for.

During his seventeen years with the bureau, he managed to go to the Bolshoi ballet with Richard Nixon, to the Great Wall of China with Gerald Ford and to Normandy Beach with Jimmy Carter. He skied in New Hampshire with George Romney, played golf in Florida with Ed Muskie and walked the beach in Oregon with Bobby Kennedy. He's written some other stories too.

Once a week Ted produces the widely used column, WHITE HOUSE WATCH, that former President Ford once conceded privately hits the mark more consistently than any of its kind.

Ted is really Thaddeus, or "Tadziu" in the diminutive form of his Polish parents' native language. Born in Milwaukee May 26, 1920, he graduated with honors from Marquette University college of journalism, spent six years with the *Waukesha (Wis.), Daily Freeman*—with four years in the Army during World War II—and joined Scripps-Howard in 1950 as a reporter for *The Indianapolis Times*. He went to Washington in 1963.

He is married to Eleanore, is a member of the prestigious Gridiron Club, and swings a mean golf club.

J. Stewart Lytle

When Stewart Lytle was sixteen he unsuccessfully begged his mother to permit him to quit school so he could devote full time to a career in tennis. He was one of the top ranked players in the South and later became nationally ranked, competing against such "patsies" as Jimmy Connors and Roscoe Tanner.

Unfortunately for Stewart, he developed shoulder problems—too much American twist serve—and devoted his time to more serious endeavors, which at the moment includes carving out a niche as a military affairs reporter of note. His stories about the illegal shipment of high-risk American technology to the Soviet Union and its satellite nations received nationwide attention.

Born in Birmingham, Alabama, April 23, 1949, Stewart won an AB degree from Princeton University—he was on the tennis team—in 1971. He was a reporter for the *Birmingham Post-Herald* from 1971 to 1974 when he left to become Washington correspondent for that paper and the *Hollywood Sun-Tattler* and *The Stuart News*. He joined the national staff of Scripps-Howard in 1979.

Stewart is married to the former Karen Stephens and they have two sons, Kim and Stephen.

Ann Carey McFeatters

Ann decided to become a news reporter when, in fifth grade in Springfield, Ohio, she read about Nellie Bly, the pen name of reporter Elizabeth Cochrane who went around the world in seventy-two days, six hours, twenty minutes and eleven seconds, and beat the fictional record of Jules Verne's Phineas Fogg.

From the age of sixteen on, she worked summers in newspaper offices including the *Springfield Suburbanite* and *The Milwaukee Journal*. She graduated from Marquette University with a degree in history and journalism and worked for *The Evansville Press*, won an Edward J. Meeman conservation award, toured Europe for six months and then joined *The Pittsburgh Press*. She went to Washington to work for *The News* and in October 1970 joined the bureau.

Ann specializes in consumer and environmental news, a beat that covers a lot of ground, and also manages to do fine personality pieces from time to time.

Ann was born June 27, 1944, in Colorado Springs, Colorado. She is married to Dale McFeatters and is the mother of Dale Carey McFeatters.

Dale McFeatters

Dale's specialty is labor and Congress, and he is on closer terms with more labor representatives than any other reporter in Washington. But in the eleven years he's been with the bureau, he has handled demonstrations, political campaigns, and in conjunction with Gene Goldenberg a series on a complicated economic fraud that won an honorable mention in the Raymond Clapper awards.

Dale, who says he decided to be a reporter at the age of five (he was born September 3, 1941) when his newsman father took him on an assignment to a fire that destroyed Pittsburgh's Wabash Station, joined the Washington Bureau in June 1969. He had been working for *The Pittsburgh Press* after a tour of Africa with the Peace Corps.

At the bureau, he was at first correspondent for the *Birmingham Post-Herald* and then in 1971 joined the national staff. He also writes the weekly Washington Calling column.

He is married to Ann and there is a little Dale, whom papa refers to as "New Lead."

Don Oakley

Don began writing editorials for Newspaper Enterprise Association and was chief editorial writer when he left in 1977 to join Scripps-Howard's Washington Bureau as editorial writer.

Don is a native of Pittsburgh, born there November 3, 1927. He graduated from Western Reserve University (now Case Western Reserve) and got his master's in history at the University of Chicago. He got into news work as a copyboy for *The Pittsburgh Press* in 1944, later going to NEA as a writer. He served with the Army's paratroop infantry in Japan.

He won the Meeman Conservation Award in 1964 and the Friends of American Writers Award, 1970, for a juvenile novel, "Two Muskets for Washington."

Don is a private pilot, having owned both an airplane and a sailplane, and doodles with electronics and television repair. He and his wife, Gertrude, have a son.

Berl Schwartz

Berl Schwartz, the night editor of the Washington Bureau, decided at an early age that he wasn't much interested in joining his father's pharmacy business in Toledo, where he was born January 24, 1947. So by the time he had graduated from the University of Pennsylvania in 1969, he was ready to prove he had made the right decision.

Berl worked for *The Philadelphia Bulletin* from 1969 through 1972 before leaving to accept a job as director of information for the Pennsylvania Insurance Department. He soon decided that newspapering was his first love and accepted an offer from *The Louisville Times* in 1973, serving as that paper's Washington correspondent from 1975 to 1979 when he joined Scripps-Howard as the bureau's congressional correspondent. He became night editor on January 1, 1980.

Married to the former Alice Lafferty, a lawyer with the U.S. Internal Revenue Service, Berl is the office baseball expert who doesn't mind traveling frequently to Baltimore to see the big league teams.

Bill Steif

Bill Steif hits the ground running, wherever in the world he may be—Thailand, Afghanistan, Pakistan, the Philippines.

A prolific writer with a rare feeling for the kind of people stories that put flesh and blood into an assignment, Bill is ready at a moment's notice to head for an overseas hotspot. In between his overseas assignments, Bill finds time to produce the popular weekly column, U.S. and YOU, and to cover more ratholes in a variety of domestic agencies than anyone in town. In gathering column material he frequently comes up with news stories, particularly on his favorite subjects of anti-billboard legislation, VA hospital extravagances and conservation.

Bill was born in Chicago, February 1, 1923, graduated from Stanford and topped that off later with a Nieman Fellowship. He served as an Air Force weatherman in the Arctic in the Second World War and began news work on *The San Francisco News* in 1946. He's been with the Washington Bureau since 1962.

From mid-1973 until late in 1976 he was European correspondent covering the Yom Kippur war and other hotspots abroad. He is married and has three daughters.

Alan R. Thompson

When Alan Thompson received his bachelor's degree in history in 1963, he vowed that there was a lot more world to see than his hometown of Chagrin Falls, Ohio, where he was born September 22, 1941.

Some Scripps-Howard Institutions

So at twenty-one, he zipped off to Latin America, hoping to eventually make his way to Europe. He spent two years teaching school in Latin America. Then he came back home and landed a job on *The Chagrin Valley Herald.*

Al joined *The Cleveland Press* in 1967 and served during his 10 years there on the police and federal beats, general assignment, and as assistant city editor. He became a Washington regional for the Scripps-Howard Ohio papers in 1977 and joined the national staff on March 1, 1980.

He is married to the former Nancy J. Barrett, whose father, Bill, has worked for *The Cleveland Press* for more than thirty years. Nancy and Al live in Arlington, Virginia.

Correspondents:

MORRIS CUNNINGHAM and
JOHN L. BENNETT
    For The Commercial Appeal

ROBERT DUKE
For The Albuquerque Tribune, the *El Paso Herald-Post and* the *Fullerton Daily News Tribune*

JOSEPH SHAPIRO
    For The Evansville Press and The Kentucky Post

JERRY CONDO
    For the Columbus Citizen-Journal and The Cincinnati Post

FRANK MORRING
For the *Birmingham Post-Herald,* the *Hollywood Sun-Tattler* and *The Stuart News*

RICHARD POWELSON
For the *Memphis Press-Scimitar and The Knoxville News-Sentinel*

ALAN GORDON
    For the *Rocky Mountain News*

DOUGLAS HARBRECHT
    For The Pittsburgh Press

HARRY TURNER
    For The San Juan Star

United Press International

Built by Sticking to
A Fundamental Ideal

UNITED PRESS INTERNATIONAL is the world's largest independent gatherer and distributor of news, newspictures and broadcast services.

Unlike other international news services which operate either as cooperatives or with government subsidies, UPI has been privately owned since 1907 when it was founded by E. W. Scripps who considered the founding as one of his most gratifying accomplishments.

"I regard my life's greatest service to the people of this country to be the creator of the U.P. . . . I have made it impossible to supress the truth or successfully disseminate falsehood," he said some years later.

Three small regional news services were merged to form The United Press Associations, which became United Press International on May 16, 1958, when its facilities were joined with those of the International News Service and International News Photos.

The United Press Associations grew up as a newspaper service, distributing its dispatches in written form to be set in type. In 1935, however, it became the first news service to make its reports available directly to radio stations. It established a radio newswire for which dispatches were written in a different style so that they could be read into the microphone—for the ear rather than the eye.

SOME SCRIPPS-HOWARD INSTITUTIONS

Since then, UPI has added other forms of service as new requirements and new methods of news dissemination have appeared. Throughout its history, it has been guided by three principles: In gathering news, to report as fairly, factually and as completely without bias as is humanly possible. In distributing news, to deliver it in forms and by methods most easily and efficiently useful to its subscribers. In marketing news, to make it available to any legitimate news disseminator who is willing and able to pay for it.

IN ITS EARLY DAYS, United Press was confronted by a cartel composed of the official and semi-official news agencies of European governments. Those "allied agencies" and the Associated Press exchanged news exclusively with each other. Further, they allotted to each member the right to distribute exclusively in certain regions of the world. Only the French agency, Havas, for example, could sell its news in South America. In the Far East, the territory of Reuters, Japanese and Chinese newspapers had to depend on the British agency for their foreign news.

In its competition with the monopolistic alliance, the United Press established two new principles in news agency operation. One was that a news organization could cover the news of the world independently. The second was that newspapers anywhere could buy this news. As a result, United Press became the first North American news agency to serve newspapers in Europe, South America and the Far East. At the same time, it established its own bureaus in those areas with correspondents instructed to report the news objectively and without government or political bias.

Its success led to an invitation in 1912 for UP to ally itself with Reuters, then the dominant European news gathering organization which Roy W. Howard, then president of the young news agency, and his board rejected. Such a move would have put United Press in alliance with agencies controlled or dominated by foreign governments, tying it in with an international news cartel which, at that time, was the foundation of AP's coverage from abroad.

IT WAS A DARING DECISION for the young agency's young president, but it proved to be the correct one. United

Press set a course of aggressive, independent coverage and broad dissemination of its services. As its foreign news resources and clientele grew, the effectiveness of the allied agencies' control gradually declined, although it was not until 1934 that they formally gave up trying to retain their particular spheres of influence.

Meanwhile, United Press continued to grow at home and abroad. Shortly after its founding, United Press began sending its news to European newspapers through Exchange Telegraph, a British agency. In 1909, United Press began a cable service to Nippon Dempo Tsushin Sha, the Japanese Telegraph News agency which later merged into Domei. This service was to continue until December 7, 1941, when the Japanese attacked Pearl Harbor.

With the outbreak of World War I, newspapers in South America began chafing under the restrictions which compelled them to get their war news from Havas. The South Americans said it was officially subsidized and covered only the Allied side of the war. To get the news of both sides, they turned to United Press which began its first news file to South America in 1915. *La Prensa*, the great Buenos Aires newspaper, started using United Press service in 1919.

Direct UP service was inaugurated to newspapers in Europe in 1921, and a year later to newspapers on the Asian mainland. In 1922, British United Press, Ltd., was organized to serve newspapers throughout the British Empire.

By 1929, United Press was serving 1,170 newspapers in 45 countries and territories.

During those years, in addition to pioneering new territories, United Press broke new ground in news agency style and method. It was the first service to emphasize the byline of the correspondent who wrote the dispatch. It introduced the big-name interview and developed the feature story as an important part of the daily news report.

United Press also moved forward in the mechanics and technology of news dissemination and development of news services.

The Morse code operators who had sent UP reports to newspapers since 1907 were replaced in 1930 by teleprinters.

Next came Teletypesetters and United Press adapted this system to its newswires in 1950. This opened the way for United Press to eliminate the tedious, slow work of setting the stock market lists in composing rooms. The computer technique made it automatic—after January, 23, 1963 when the first such electronically-calculated lists of the complete New York and American Stock Exchange quotations were transmitted by UPI to newspapers.

In 1968 UPI began restructuring its worldwide communications system to permit electronic storage, editing and distribution of news reports. Switching computers were established in New York, Brussels, and Hong Kong.

THE UPI aim was to connect its bureaus and clients—worldwide—to the editing system in New York. The first goal was reached in March 1972 when UPI put into operation the first completely electronic newsroom in the world, its New York bureau.

By July 11, 1975, all of the bureaus in the U.S. had been connected to the system and were writing, editing and transmitting copy with VDTs. Europe joined the system early in 1978 by which time more than 500 VDTs were on line in the U.S., Canada, Europe and Mexico. Planning was underway for adding Latin America and Asia.

This computer system, known as Information Storage and Retrieval (IS&R), produced new and valuable services for UPI's subscribers. One of the most successful is DataNews, which combines in a single 1200-word-per-minute channel UPI's general domestic and international news, sports, business, regional and state reports plus the services of many syndicates. It is designed for computer-to-computer delivery for subscribers' own electronic editing systems.

As communications satellites became available, UPI switched many of its overseas circuits to them.

In June 1979, UPI began moving its data processing and communications headquarters to a new $10,000,000 Technical Systems Center on the outskirts of Dallas. The move was completed the following May, tripling the system's computer capacity and preparing UPI to meet requirements for higher delivery speeds, pagination and other developments then on the horizon.

Since the Fifties, UPI has been heavily involved in news pictures.

After buying Acme Newspictures from NEA, also a Scripps-Howard property, in 1952, United Press promptly launched a program to build up its Telephoto service which then was confined to the Eastern U.S. In 1954 United Press introduced facsimile for newspapers and television, an automatic receiving system which brought wired pictures within the economic reach of the smallest newspapers and television stations. This enabled UPI to fill in quickly the great gaps in its network between the East and West coasts. Today UPI newspictures are delivered by leased line throughout the U.S. and by radio, cable and satellite to every continent.

In 1975 UPI introduced a new concept in photo-facsimile equipment using an electrostatic recording process. Called Unifax-II, the receiver is 100 percent solid state, completely automatic and delivers high quality prints on single sheets of dry paper.

UPI also has a portable telephoto transmitter, light but sturdy and reliable. It is completely automatic, will work on both international and U.S. standards.

With Fox Movietone it established a film service for television stations in 1951. Now known as UPITN, this service is jointly owned by UPI and ITN of Great Britain and delivers news for television all over the world, largely by satellite. In broadcasting, UPI augmented its broadcast newswire with an audio service begun in 1958 to deliver voice reports and the actual sounds of the news for recording on tape and use by the approximately 1,000 stations it serves.

TO HELP TAILOR its services to subscriber requirements, UPI formed a Newspaper Advisory Board in 1974. Made up of editorial and administrative executives representing three circulation levels in each of five geographical areas of the country, the board works with UPI executives in the areas of service, technology and management. The UPI Broadcast Advisory Board was organized in 1976 to perform the same function in its field. Advisory boards were established in 1980 in Europe and Latin America.

All Scripps-Howard daily and Sunday newspapers and broadcast stations are served by UPI. Many of them also are members of The Associated Press. The Scripps-Howard papers are served by UPI on identically the same basis as its approximately 5,000 other subscribers in the U.S.

Some Scripps-Howard Institutions

Rod Beaton   *H. L. Stevenson*

UPI is not influenced in its treatment of the news by the editorial policies of the wide variety of publications it serves at home and in eighty-four other countries. On the contrary, there is in UPI an enormous respect for news as such—an inflexible belief in the power and effectiveness of sheer, raw facts. It has no politics, carries no torches, conducts no crusades. It merely reports.

The first president of United Press was John Vandercook, the man who sold Scripps the idea of combining the three press associations in an effort to break the grip of the Associated Press whose bylaws at the time permitted its members to blackball Scripps's application for telegraph news service in some cities where he wanted to start newspapers.

Vandercook was only thirty-two but died six months later following an operation. The next president was Hamilton B. Clark, followed by C. D. Lee, who held the post until 1912.

During this period, Roy W. Howard, who was twenty-four years old when he was placed in charge of all news operations under Vandercook, officially was first vice president. He assumed the presidency in 1912 but retained control of the news side until he resigned in 1921 to take over business direction of the Scripps-Howard Newspapers.

Howard's successors were W. W. Hawkins 1921-'22, Karl A. Bickel 1922-'35, Hugh Baillie 1935-'55, Frank H. Bartholomew 1955-'62, A. Mims Thomason 1962-'72, and Roderick W. Beaton, the incumbent.

BEATON HAS SPENT his entire career with UPI—at home and abroad. In 1948, with a brand new journalism degree from University of California, he joined UPI in San Francisco.

He became manager of the Fresno, California bureau in 1950 and subsequently was UPI general business executive at Los Angeles. He was made southern division manager at Atlanta in 1956, central division manager at Chicago in 1958, and general business manager at New York headquarters in 1962. In June 1965 he went to London as vice president and general manager for Europe, Africa and the Mideast.

He returned to New York headquarters in 1969 to assume the post of vice president and general manager. On April 28, 1972 he was elected president and chief executive officer.

Born in Escalon, California April 16, 1923, Beaton came by his profession naturally; his late father, Philip C. Beaton, was for many years executive editor of the *Stockton (Calif.) Record*. Rod served as an enlisted Navy correspondent with the Pacific fleet during World War II. He is married to the former Evelyn Miller of Stockton, California, and they have two children.

Editor-in-chief and vice president is H. L. Stevenson, who joined UPI in 1953 in the Jackson, Mississippi bureau. Subsequently he worked as a reporter in several Southern bureaus. He was Virginia state manager at Richmond and a business rep in North Carolina.

In 1960 UPI moved him to New York as a news editor. Two years later he returned to Atlanta as southern division news editor. He came back to New York in early 1965 and was named managing editor a short time later. He became editor-in-chief and vice president in 1972. He writes the weekly UPI Reporter, a newsletter dealing with media trends and happenings.

Born November 23, 1929 in New Orleans, he grew up in Picayune, Mississippi and got his start as a reporter and sports editor of *The Picayune Item*, a weekly. He attended Pearl River College and Millsaps College in Mississippi, and later served in the U.S. Army from 1950 to 1952. Steve is married to the former LaVerne Harris of Raleigh, North Carolina, who was a reporter for *The Raleigh Times* and *The Charlotte Observer*. They have one daughter, Jennifer.

Other current vice presidents and officers are:

F. W. (Bill) Lyon, Newspictures.
Gordon Rice, Broadcast services.
Donald J. Brydon, Sales.
Lawrence A. Leser, Financial.

Some Scripps-Howard Institutions

Bill Lyon

Gordon Rice

Donald Brydon

Bob Kelly

James Darr

Grant Dillman

James F. Darr, Systems development.
Grant Dillman, Washington, D.C. news.
Claude Hippeau, International General Manager, New York.
Ray Groves, Director of Computer Services, Dallas.
Bob J. Kelly, General Manager of Communications, Dallas.
Robert P. Paffen, Personnel.
Daniel J. Castellini, Secretary and Treasurer.
Frederick J. Greene, Comptroller and Assistant Secretary.

International Division vice presidents are:
Eugene H. Blabey, Europe, Middle East and Africa, London.
Albert E. Kaff, Asia-Pacific, Hong Kong.
Julius B. Humi, senior vice president, Europe, Middle East and Africa, London.
Patrick Harden, General Manager, Canada, Toronto.

Robert Paffen

Claude Hippeau

Eugene Blabey

Ray Groves

Julius Humi

Albert Kaff

Domestic Division vice presidents are:
  Thomas J. Beatty, Southern, Atlanta.
  Kenneth J. Braddick, New England, Boston.
  Robert E. Crennen, Central, Chicago.
  Leroy A. Hamann, Rocky Mountain, Denver
  Travis M. Hughs, Southwest, Dallas.
  Richard A. Litfin, Pacific senior marketing vice president, San Francisco.
  John E. Mantle, Pacific, San Francisco.
  John W. Payne, Eastern, Pittsburgh.
  Eugene Poythress, Mid-Atlantic, Washington, D.C.
  Ian Westergren, Metropolitan, New York.
Latin American Division general managers are:
  Luiz Menezes, Brazil, Rio de Janeiro.
  Alberto J. Schazin, Southern South America, Buenos Aires.
  Pieter van Bennekom, Caribbean, San Juan, P.R.
  John F. Virtue, Northern Latin America, Mexico City.

United Media Enterprises

A Far Cry From Miss Ellen's Little 'Squibs'

SCRIPPS-HOWARD took a giant step in June 1978 to adapt to the frequent and drastic shifts in pace and direction in the newspaper syndicate and feature field. The Concern consolidated two of America's leading feature companies—United Feature Syndicate, Inc., and Newspaper Enterprise Association, Inc.

Under an umbrella company called United Media Enterprises, management and operations of the two enterprises were joined. The new name was chosen to reflect not only the great histories of two major forces in American journalism, but also because the consolidated company is more than just the world's largest newspaper syndicate and feature service.

Various United Media Enterprises divisions or companies are involved in comic section printing, book publishing and distribution, character licensing, computerized television listings, cable television, and more.

Organizations such as the Bell-McClure Syndicate, North American Newspaper Alliance, National Newspaper Syndicate, Acme Newspictures, and The World Almanac had been part of either UFS or NEA throughout the years. Thus newly-created United Media became the focal point for some of America's best known and most historic journalistic traditions.

Chosen as first United Media president and chief executive officer was Robert Roy Metz, who had been president and editor of NEA since 1972 and a vice president of United Feature Syndicate since 1976.

William C. Payette, president of UFS since 1969, became chairman of the board of UME. Payette retired in 1979.

UFS and NEA retain separate identities in the marketplace but editorial, marketing and business operations, as well as production and transmission of both companies' features, have been combined.

The companies brought together to create United Media Enterprises have colorful and dynamic histories.

IN 1923 AN AGGRESSIVE United Press organization formed a special feature syndicate division to distribute the memoirs of Lloyd George. That was the start of the United Feature Syndicate, which in later years became widely known as the most aggressive and acquisition-minded of all American syndicates.

Among its earliest acquisitions was Max Elsa's Metropolitan Group and World Features. It was Metropolitan that had started the exciting continuity comic strip "Tarzan" by Edgar Rice Burroughs in the 1920s, and United wanted it. Other early United Feature comics were "Metropolitan Movies," "Broncho Bill," "Mary Mixup," "Ella Cinders," and "The Captain and the Kids."

United's main thrust then was in distributing text specials by in-the-news personalities. In addition to David Lloyd George, special United Feature series were written by Randolph Churchill, Sinclair Lewis, Frank A. Vanderlip, Benito Mussolini, Edouard Herriot and Wilhelm Marx, among others.

Another big-name special brought to three hundred newspapers exclusively by United in 1934 was Charles Dickens's previously published book, "The Life of Our Lord." This was one of the earliest examples of newspapers getting major promotional mileage out of a book serialization. (This tradition is regularly followed today by United and NEA, with major book serializations such as "Harry S. Truman" by Margaret Truman, "Jackie Oh!" and "Star Wars.")

From the early 1930s, United Feature Syndicate officed at 220 East 42nd Street, the New York News Building, until 1977 when, in preparation for the formation of UME, it moved to large headquarters at 200 Park Avenue, the Pan Am Building.

In 1936 UFS began to distribute the popular "My Day" column by Eleanor Roosevelt, a close personal friend of George A. Carlin, the syndicate's general manager. Another spectacular UFS offering of the period was "President Roosevelt's Own Story of the New Deal," in 1938.

The mid-1930s through World War II were heydays for news syndicates, and UFS was at the head of the pack with an imposing list of columnists: Westbrook Pegler, Heywood Broun, Ray Clapper, Tom Stokes and Drew Pearson.

Comics introduced in this major growth period for UFS included Al Capp's "Li'l Abner" (1935), "Abbie & Slats" (1937), and "Fritzi Ritz," (1931).

Larry Rutman became the fourth manager of UFS in 1946 and was named the company's first president after it was spun off from UPI as a direct subsidiary of The E. W. Scripps Company.

One of United's hottest properties during the 1940 war years was the column written by Scripps-Howard's roving correspondent, Ernie Pyle. "He went down into the foxholes with the kids," Rutman recalls, "and Americans couldn't get enough of it." Pyle's column ran in some seven-hundred dailies at its peak.

Another famous newspaperman who first picked up his following during World War II was editorial cartoonist Bill Mauldin, whom Rutman discovered working for the Army newspaper "Stars and Stripes." UFS also made columnist Robert Ruark a major celebrity in post-war newspapers.

A few years after the war, Rutman met a young cartoonist whose idea for a comic, called "L'il Folks," had already been rejected by other major syndicates.

"He came in lean, tired, and hungry," recalls Rutman. "But I signed Charles Schulz. We changed the name of his strip to 'Peanuts.' "

The rest is history. "Peanuts" has become probably the most successful comic strip of all time, appearing in nearly two thousand newspapers around the world and generating thousands of "Peanuts" products ranging from games and toys to clothing and jewelry.

At the end of 1968, Bill Payette was named vice president

of United Feature Syndicate. In the decade to follow he led the company to its greatest growth and profitability.

Payette had been with UP since 1936, and in more than three decades with the wire service had held a variety of editorial and business positions.

In 1970 Payette moved to make UFS a self-contained operation, with production facilities for typesetting and printing right in the office. Shortly this led to a computerized editing and typesetting system that allowed UFS to lead the syndicate field in flexibility in delivering copy to its clients. "Our computer let us produce nine different versions of every story with one key stroke," Payette says.

In 1972 UFS acquired Bell-McClure Syndicate, which included the Jack Anderson column. In 1972 Anderson won the Pulitzer Prize for his investigative coverage the previous year of U.S. relations with India and Pakistan.

North American Newspaper Alliance (NANA) had been founded in 1922 by a group of major independent newspapers as a news cooperative to produce magazine-type features that provided an in-depth look and a special literary quality. Ernest Hemingway covered the Spanish Civil War for NANA in the Thirties. Ira Wolfert won a Pulitzer Prize for his NANA war correspondence in the Forties. Other NANA byliners included President Harry Truman, who wrote a monthly column for several years; Ring Lardner, Grantland Rice, Dorothy Thompson, Averell Harriman and Winston Churchill.

NANA's biggest single success was the syndication of the memoirs of General "Black Jack" Pershing in 1929. The purchase price was $290,000, which remained the highest price paid by a syndicate until the MacArthur memoirs thirty years later.

The Independent News Alliance (INA) was created in 1980 to provide exclusive coverage by *name* writers on spot events, and found over fifty clients.

OLDER OF THE TWO major components of UME, and one of the oldest units in the Scripps-Howard family, is Newspaper Enterprise Association. NEA's earliest roots can be traced back to 1893 when "Aunt" Ellen Scripps, sister of

E. W. Scripps, was writing feature-type "squibs" for *The Cleveland Press.* These were known as "Miss Ellen's Miscellany."

Because of the popularity of the "Miscellany," proofs were sent to *The Cincinnati Post* for its use, and later to other Scripps newspapers. An occasional matted photo and, later, a few comics filled out the early lineup.

By 1902 the service based on Miss Ellen's "Miscellany" had reached the point where it had to have a name—Newspaper Enterprise Association. Soon papers outside of the Scripps organization began to ask for the service. And so it grew.

The principle of NEA that evolved over the years is one of a carefully edited, balanced text-and-comics service for daily newspapers.

Every twenty-four months NEA takes an exhaustive feature usage survey of its more than seven hundred client newspapers. The surveys test popularity of existing features and solicit ideas for new ones. Results are analyzed by the editors and changes are planned.

Among NEA's alumni are Bruce Catton, Carl Sandburg, Jimmy Breslin, Herblock (who won his first Pulitzer Prize for an NEA cartoon), John Fischetti, Dorman Smith and J. R. Williams.

Classic comics that NEA has distributed include Williams' "Out Our Way," Merrill Blosser's "Freckles and his Friends," A. D. Condo's "Everett True," and Roy Crane's "Wash Tubbs."

In addition to distributing both daily and Sunday comic features, NEA has for decades produced readyprint Sunday comic sections for newspapers. By 1976 NEA was selling some one-hundred-thirty readyprint color comics sections. In the mid-1970s United Feature Syndicate also entered the field, and by the end of 1979 the combined UME readyprint business served nearly two hundred newspapers.

America's most popular panel cartoon, Berry's World, sits on the fence between the editorial cartoon and the gag panel. Although Berry has many imitators now, his feature was another innovation when it was launched in 1963.

Today's NEA also contains the most widely printed medical column in the world by Lawrence E. Lamb, M.D., former chief of the U.S. Air Force School of Aerospace Medicine.

NEA's chief Washington columnist since 1977 has been

Bob Walters. In 1978 Walters and his wife, Martha Angle, were named "best reporting team in Washington," by *Washington Magazine*.

Over the years NEA has been quick to alter course and move into new areas of interest to the newspaper field. One of these is a program of reader-service letters, pamphlets, and books, which are promoted and sold through editorial series or ongoing columns.

In 1966 NEA acquired *The World Almanac* when Scripps-Howard's *New York World-Telegram* was merged into the short-lived *World Journal Tribune*.

NEA developed a unique co-publishing program with more than one hundred North American newspapers, and *The World Almanac* gained its greatest prominence and its highest sales ever. *The Guinness Book of World Records* lists *The World Almanac* as the largest selling book of all times, after the Bible.

Other notable achievements include pioneering the wired picture business by developing the Telephoto transceiver in the Thirties. NEA built Acme Newspictures into a worldwide network competitive with The Associated Press and International News Pictures before turning it over, in 1951, to United Press where it lives today as UPI Newspictures.

Before becoming president and chief executive officer of United Media Enterprises, Bob Metz was president and editor of NEA. Born in Richmond Hill, New York March 23, 1929, he was educated in New York public schools and at Wesleyan University, Middletown, Connecticut, where he received a B.A. in 1950.

Metz began his newspaper career in 1951 as a copy boy at *The New York Times*. Two years later he joined International News Service and served as overnight cable editor, overnight editor and assistant feature editor until the merger of INS and United Press in 1958 when he was recruited by NEA. Metz was successively news editor, managing editor and executive editor before being named editorial director in 1968. He had been appointed a vice president in 1967.

Metz lives in New York City and has two sons, Robert Sumner born in 1957, and Christopher Roy born in 1962.

At the time of the consolidation, Metz's chief editorial lieutenant was Executive Editor David Hendin who, although then only thirty-two, already had been with NEA eight

Bob Metz *David Hendin*

years as writer, columnist and editor. At the end of 1979, he became UME editorial director, responsible for the entire editorial product.

Born in St. Louis, Missouri December 16, 1945, Hendin majored in biology and general sciences at the University of Missouri, receiving a B.S. as well as a Masters in journalism. In 1977 he received the annual Book Award of the American Medical Writers Association for his book *The Life Givers*. He is the author of nine other books including the bestseller *Death as a Fact of Life*. While in Israel teaching high school biology after the Six-Day War, Hendin married the former Sandra Levine of Oxford, England. They have two children.

EVEN WHEN THEY existed as separate companies, the top management of both UFS and NEA realized that the future of their business was going to be closely tied to production and delivery systems.

Not too many years ago, the only production and distribution necessities of a syndicate or feature service were a Ditto machine and a mailroom.

Nevertheless, from its earliest days NEA provided mats of its photos and stories for client newspapers. In fact, to speed delivery of photo mats in the 20s and 30s, NEA established stereotyping set-ups in railroad boxcars so that production could be accomplished en route to clients.

For years NEA had its own carrier pigeon coop on the roof of a New York office building. Photographers took the pigeons with them when they went down to the docks to photograph luminaries arriving from overseas. Once shot, undeveloped negatives were tied to the legs of the pigeons, which, presumably, took the fastest route to NEA's photo laboratories in midtown.

Those were the dark ages compared to the sophisticated computer system with which UME staffers now edit and transmit copy to newspapers.

Daily newspapers face the problem of taking outputs from syndicates, wires, staff writers, and other sources and putting them out in one form—the newspaper.

Syndicates, however, have the opposite problem. UFS and NEA must *produce* up to ten different outputs of each text feature—DataNews, DataFeature, three forms of camera-ready copy, two forms of scanner-ready copy, "hard" copy for manual typesetting, and paper tapes. Thus UFS and NEA text columns can be made compatible with any newspaper's production system.

I<small>N</small> 1975, UFS and NEA separately and almost simultaneously entered what was then a relatively small business, the sale to newspapers and other publications of local television listings. NEA acquired a firm in Atlanta which it renamed Tele-Log in June and UFS bought TV Data of Glens Falls, New York, the following month.

TV DATA had one-hundred-fifty clients, concentrated in the northeast. By the end of 1979, after an infusion of considerable UFS capital, TV DATA was servicing seven hundred newspapers, magazines, and cable TV stations via high-speed wires of UPI, AP and AT&T. Its clients blanket North America.

TV DATA is also a major supplier of complete weekend television magazines to daily newspapers and the only company operating in this field on a national basis.

Tele-Log, under the direction of its founder and current manager, Hal Butts, also had steady growth from the fifty clients it had in the Southeast in 1975 to more than 500 five years later.

An electronic version of TV DATA's listing is marketed to cable TV systems by another UME company, TV Watch/

Distributed Information Processing. The decision to enter this field was made in 1977 in the belief that cable would be the fastest-growing segment of the media business over the next generation. By 1980 more than eighty cable systems had signed to take the service.

TV Watch/DIP also provides TV Data listings, composition and printing services to cable systems who wish to publish their own guides for subscribers and local communities. Butts was named vice president and general manager of the company in mid-1979 and its headquarters were consolidated in Atlanta.

Berkley-Small, Inc.

Post-war Steel Tubes Launch a Big Business

Robert Hendrich

WHEN GEORGE B. MOFFETT spotted a stack of steel casings the government was selling in 1947 as war surplus an idea struck him. Moffett was a veteran newspaper circulation director. He had been in charge at *The Dallas Times-Herald, The Milwaukee Sentinel, The Atlanta Georgian, The St. Louis Times,* and *The Press Register* in Mobile, Alabama.

Moffett could see they would make excellent motor route tubes. He bought hundreds of the casings and had them painted. He laid in a supply of Japanese rubber bands. With these two items he went into business in Mobile to represent manufacturers of circulation supplies to newspapers.

In 1949 Berkley Thompson, an employe of the *Mobile Press Register*, joined the firm, known as George B. Moffett and Associates. In the early years Moffett and Thompson traveled extensively by car, with three-month trips not unusual. Many products were purchased from NBA, Newspaper Boys of America owned by James Lynch, a company that was eventually purchased by Berkley-Small.

In 1958 John Small, a nephew of Moffett's, came into the business. The next year Thompson and Small bought out Moffett and were incorporated as Berkley-Small, Inc. In December 1968 the company was purchased by Newspaper Enterprise Association and in 1976 became a separate operating division of Scripps-Howard Newspapers.

Berkley-Small continues to be based in Mobile. Robert C. Hendrich is president and general manager. The executive staff consists of Timothy G. Fink, executive vice president and business manager; Donald C. Zorker, executive vice president/finance; Robert A. Brown, vice president/marketing services; Johnie L. Huey, vice president/operations; and Charles R. Willisson, vice president/sales director.

HENDRICH SPENT twenty years in sales with NEA before joining Berkley-Small in 1969 as general manager. In 1975 he was elected president also. Bob was born November 27, 1926 in Terre Haute, Indiana. After graduating from William and Mary College in 1951, he worked at a General Motors plant on the line and in the office before joining NEA in Cleveland.

Berkley-Small has sixteen regional sales representatives and does business in fifty states, in Canada and Puerto Rico, and in several foreign countries. It is the largest firm of its type and services the majority of American daily and weekly newspapers.

Product lines include coin operated and honor newspaper racks, carrier and collection supplies, motor route tubes, rubber bands, carrier and subscriber insurance, prizes and premiums and a multitude of related products.

In addition the company publishes three idea and art services and also provides consultant services for the placement and redesign of newspaper rack units.

Scripps-Howard News

By, For, and About Folks in the Concern

THE FIRST Scripps-Howard News was issued in December 1926. It was published every month from then until 1933 when it was discontinued, partly as an economy measure during the Depression.

Its first editor was the late Negley D. Cochran, who endeavored to set its tone and spirit from the background of his many years in the Concern as an editor and close associate of E. W. Scripps. Negley had been editor of *The Toledo News-Bee* and when the first World War broke out was editor of the famous, but short-lived Scripps *Day Book* in Chicago.

The News resumed publication October 1, 1946 under the editorship of Frank Aston. Publication was resumed because of a great number of requests from people throughout the Concern.

In 1963 Aston retired and was succeeded by J. Boyd Stephens, who was succeeded on retirement in 1976 by Delbert Willis, former editor of *The Fort Worth Press*. When Willis retired at the end of 1979, he was succeeded by Sue Porter.

The purpose of the News is to keep people in the Concern informed as to the doings of personalities on the various papers, what enterprises are on foot; to publicize individual achievements by members of the various staffs, and to lend encouragement to ingenuity and resourcefulness by write-ups and personality sketches of the folks who are doing something unusual. Roy Howard once recommended to its editor that he make the magazine "the conscience of the Concern."

A major policy is to encourage young people to join the Scripps-Howard family and to encourage their progress in the Concern through recognition of their work.

The first issues of the original News were pocket size, changed to 8½ x 11 inches in 1931. When publication was resumed it was kept at that, its present size.

Editorial office of Scripps-Howard News is in the Central Trust Tower, Cincinnati, where it is part of James H. Wagner's editorial promotion office.

SUE PORTER was born on a farm twenty miles east of Defiance, Ohio, third of six children and the oldest daughter. The date was October 10, 1950.

Sue Porter

While attending Defiance College, she worked at the local newspaper, the *Defiance Crescent News*, 1968-72; first as a teletypist, and later in the editorial department where she wrote features, and at one time or another edited the editorial, farm, entertainment and women's pages. While in college she met James H. Porter, a two-scholarship athlete, football and wrestling, and in 1972 they married.

Jobs on a number of southwest Ohio weekly newspapers followed, plus additional schooling at the University of Cincinnati. In 1976, when *The Cincinnati Post* launched a weekly *Valley Post* tabloid, she was hired as its editor; at the same time working as a reporter for the metro desk. She continued as editor when in 1978 *The Valley Post* became a full-sized daily.

Sue loves to write, and for a period in 1977 she took maternity leave and wrote a column for *The Cincinnati Post*, "Watching Baby Grow." The subject, of course, was their daughter Julia Marie, born in 1977, and it became a popular Cincinnati newspaper feature.

When Gordon Hanna looked around the Concern for a young person with growth potential who could give readers of Scripps-Howard News a magazine that was sprightly and informative, Sue was the choice for editor. She is the publication's youngest.

Sue and Jim live in Milford, Ohio. Her hobbies outdoors are skiing—water and snow—and canoeing. Some day she hopes to take up where she left off with golf and flying lessons. Indoors she's a Civil War buff and has put together a library on the subject.

One hobby she no longer pursues is muzzle loading. "Some people have tattoos," she says. "My badge of honor is this." She shows a small scar on her left arm from a powder burn.

Scripps-Howard Foundation

Aids J-schools and Students, Awards Prizes for Excellence

As THE CONCERN entered the 1980s, one of its institutions registering a significant increase in influence was The Scripps-Howard Foundation.

Grants and awards to schools of journalism and to promising students in these schools had soared. In the 1970-80 decade, 541 direct grants to colleges were made, 1,234 individual students received financial help, and 108 special projects, ranging from internships to seminars to helping a university buy electronic newsroom equipment, were supported.

The number of annual competitions recognizing outstanding accomplishment by persons already in the communications field was increased from four to seven.

Annual disbursements had grown from $100,000 to nearly $500,000. And the foundation's overall worth exceeded $5,000,000. The Scripps-Howard Foundation was organized to accept and administer gifts having as their objective the improvement and advancement of journalism through education and research. It was incorporated August 15, 1962, under the laws of Ohio as a charitable, non-profit corporation.

The foundation was the outgrowth of the idea that many persons engaged or formerly engaged in newspaper news gathering or allied pursuits would welcome the opportunity to make a personal contribution in the interest of activity to which they have devoted their life effort.

The foundation also devotes its funds to such things as

research in the communications field, results to be made available to the entire communications industry, and special incentives to encourage young men and women to pursue careers in journalism.

Under a 1962 Treasury Department exemption, contributions to the foundation became deductible for purposes of income tax, and so did gifts, legacies and bequests for estate tax and gift tax purposes.

CONTRIBUTIONS MAY BE made without restriction or designation of specific purposes. In such case the foundation trustees have complete discretion within the limits of its charter. Or a donor may specify his or her wishes as to special use of the contribution, within the scope of the charitable and educational purposes of the foundation.

The foundation has received large gifts of corporate stock. Individuals have bought life insurance, naming the foundation as beneficiary. Others have named the foundation as beneficiary in their wills in various amounts.

In 1979 The E. W. Scripps Company adopted a policy of making a matching gift in the amount of a donation, except donations from the Scripps and Howard families.

The Scripps-Howard Foundation embraces The Roy W. Howard and Margaret Rhoe Howard Fund; The Roy W. Howard and Margaret Rohe Howard Memorial Fund; The Roy W. Howard Awards; The Ernie Pyle Memorial Fund; The Ernie Pyle Award; The Edward J. Meeman Awards; The Walker Stone Award; The Edward Willis Scripps Award; and The Charles M. Schulz Award.

THE ROY W. HOWARD and Margaret Rohe Howard Fund was established by Mr. and Mrs. Howard to provide journalism scholarships with preference given to students needing assistance and who are able and willing to work in order to provide part of their educational expenses.

The Roy W. Howard Awards are made to the newspaper and to the TV or radio station judged to have been outstanding in its public service efforts. It is the only award by this foundation that honors both the print and broadcast media.

SOME SCRIPPS-HOWARD INSTITUTIONS

THE ERNIE PYLE Memorial Fund was established by the Scripps-Howard Newspapers in 1952, for educational, scientific, philanthropic and public uses and to encourage other reporters to strive to attain Ernie's high craftsmanship as a "people writer." Its assets were transferred to The Scripps-Howard Foundation in 1965.

The Pyle Award is given for outstanding human interest reporting. Its first winner in 1953 was Jim G. Lucas of the Scripps-Howard Washington staff. Lucas won again in 1964. In its early years co-winners were often picked. Since its founding thirty-nine newspapermen and women have won Pyle awards.

THE MEEMAN AWARDS are for excellence in writing on the subject of conservation of natural and wildlife resources. They were established by a donation from Meeman, late editor of the *Memphis Press-Scimitar* and conservation editor of Scripps-Howard Newspapers, and have been conducted nationally since 1967. One grand prize is awarded, with other prizes distributed in two categories, newspapers with more than 100,000 circulation and those with less.

THE STONE AWARD, established in 1973, honors newspaper editorial writing. It is named for the late editor-in-chief of Scripps-Howard Newspapers and former president of The Scripps-Howard Foundation.

THE SCRIPPS AWARD, established in 1976 in honor of one of the giants of American journalism and founder of Scripps-Howard Newspapers, recognizes that newspaper which in writing, reporting, and public education, has performed the most outstanding service in the cause of the First Amendment guarantee of a free press. Winning newspapers have been *The Honolulu Advertiser; Sun Enterprise Newspapers*, Monmouth, Oregon; *Democrat and Chronicle*, Rochester, New York; and the *Norfolk* (Virginia) *Ledger-Star*.

THE SCHULZ AWARD, founded to help further the careers of promising cartoonists, was established in 1980 and

Jacques Caldwell   *Matt Meyer*

funded by United Feature Syndicate to honor Schulz on the thirtieth anniversary of his classic comic strip, *Peanuts*.

Each spring winners are presented their awards at a luncheon attended by prestigious figures from inside and outside the field of communications, many of whom have judged the contests. One such luminary was Watergate Judge John J. Sirica.

Keynote speakers on the subject of the First Amendment at these luncheons have been Leon Jaworski, Watergate special prosecutor; Keith Fuller, president, The Associated Press; Senator Daniel Patrick Moynihan (D. New York); and H. L. Stevenson, editor-in-chief, United Press International.

JACQUES A. CALDWELL, retired Scripps-Howard executive, is president of the foundation. His predecessors as president were Stone, and retired Scripps-Howard executive Matt Meyer, who served from 1971-79, and under whose stewardship the foundation came of age.

Caldwell, born in Paris April 8, 1914, grew up in South Dakota where his stepfather, who had been General Pershing's adjutant, owned two small weeklies. Jack was an apprentice pressman and then sold advertising on Chicago papers. He joined Scripps-Howard in 1944 on *The New York World Telegram*, ultimately becoming advertising director. He held that position until the ill-fated merger that became the *World Journal Tribune*.

After that paper folded, he was appointed (in 1968) president and general manager of the Evansville (Indiana) Printing Corporation. He joined General Management in 1974 as assistant general business manager. When he retired December 31, 1980, he was vice president/marketing and general business manager/newspapers.

Caldwell and his wife, Jeanne, make their home in Cincinnati. They have five sons and two daughters. When he isn't traveling abroad, Jack golfs, does woodworking, and shoots pictures.

OTHER OFFICERS are Matt Meyer, retired business manager of the *New York World Telegram and Sun*, chairman; Patrick T. Finnegan, retired budget director of Scripps-Howard Newspapers, executive vice president and chairman of distribution committee; James H. Wagner, editorial promotion director of Scripps-Howard Newspapers, vice president and chairman of publicity committee; David Stolberg, assistant general editorial manager of Scripps-Howard Newspapers, vice president; Daniel J. Castellini, vice president and controller of the E. W. Scripps Company, secretary and treasurer; Naoma Lowensohn, former assistant to Roy W. Howard, vice president and assistant secretary; and Lawrence A. Leser, vice president for finance and corporate development of Scripps-Howard, assistant secretary; W. L. Scherrer, of the treasurers office of Scripps-Howard, assistant secretary.

TRUSTEES ARE: Caldwell, Finnegan, Lowensohn, Stolberg, Meyer, Wagner, and Roderick W. Beaton, president of United Press International; William R. Burleigh, editor of *The Cincinnati Post*; Richard R. Campbell, editor of the *Columbus Citizen-Journal*; Robert D. Gordon, vice president of Scripps-Howard Broadcasting Company; Morris E. Greiner Jr., vice president of Scripps-Howard Broadcasting Company; David Hendin, vice president and executive editor of United Media Enterprises; Robert P. Scripps, vice chairman of The Edward W. Scripps Trust; and Mort C. Watters, chairman of the executive committee of Scripps-Howard Broadcasting Company.

Headquarters of the foundation is 1100 Central Trust Tower, Cincinnati, Ohio 45202.

SECTION SIX

Scripps-Howard Daily Newspapers

A Directory, With Something of Their History and Accomplishments, as Well as Personality Sketches of the Editors and Business Managers

The Albuquerque Tribune
Albuquerque, New Mexico

Founded in 1922. Purchased by Scripps-Howard in 1923 from Carl Magee to give Magee financial stability for his fight against political corruption in New Mexico. Scripps-Howard later adopted slogan "Give Light and The People Will Find Their Own Way," from *The Tribune's* masthead. Magee always attributed the quotation to Dante, although that source is uncertain. In 1933 business departments of *Tribune* and *The Albuquerque Journal* were consolidated in Albuquerque Publishing Company, a firm owned jointly by *Tribune* and *Journal*. This formed a single production-sales-and distribution unit with each paper separately owned and under separate editorial management and policy. This was the first of many joint publishing arrangements in the industry.

The Tribune sparked the investigation of Teapot Dome scandal after World War I. Won honorable mention of 1934 Pulitzer committee for editorial condemning use of National Guard in breaking coal strike. Won New Mexico Press Association community service award five consecutive years, 1960-64 and eight times since, including successively in 1977-78-79-80. Won National Headliners Award for public service in 1961 for reporting of irregularities at city hall.

Editor: WILLIAM TANNER.

THE EDITOR
William Tanner

A WRITER for a Cleveland magazine, searching for a single and meaningful phrase to describe the many talents of Bill Tanner, called him the "Lou Grant of local journalism." No one who knew Tanner disagreed.

For Bill has all the real life characteristics of craftsmanship and creativity that make Lou Grant such a television giant.

As managing editor of *The Cleveland Press*, Bill sat in the little fishbowl of an office that managing editors inhabit and directed his staff with ease and confidence. And no wonder. There was hardly a job on the payroll that he had not held himself.

He arrived at *The Press* in 1943, having secured a job as copy boy. Dashing about filling paste pots and running copy was tough and World War II intervened to offer some relief. At eighteen, Bill was shipped to France to help save Western civilization by cranking out a daily newsletter on an old mimeograph machine for his outfit—the Seventh Army Headquarters.

"I finally had become what I had always wanted to be," Bill recalls. "An ink-stained wretch. That mimeograph machine leaked all over me every time I turned the handle. I went through World War II looking like I had been fighting in a blueberry patch."

After the war, Bill returned to *The Press* and split his day between the city room and the classroom. He got his college degree from Western Reserve University in 1952. He became a financial writer, then moved on to become a general assignment reporter. A very dogged general assignment reporter. His doggedness reached a sort of climax the day he "borrowed" some evidence from a trial table to photograph it for his paper.

"When I got back to the office, the judge was already on the phone to the city editor," Bill remembers. "I caught hell for that stunt. I hate to even tell the story because I don't want to give any reporter who might work for me the idea that I condone that kind of thing."

Bill paused. "I kind of condone that kind of enthusiasm though," he said with a wink.

In 1963, Bill became an assistant city editor and took over the city desk in 1968 upon the death of Louis Clifford. He was made executive news editor of the paper in 1976 and managing editor in 1978.

"I was asked to redesign the paper," Bill says. "To change its graphics, increase its emphasis on coverage of lifestyles and develop some of the new trends toward easy-reading, interpretative coverage that the business had begun to move toward."

Bill also spearheaded campaigns, including a successful push to create a Regional Transit Authority for the Cleveland area, which became one of the best in the country.

But the people who worked for him knew, as the public couldn't know, that one of the biggest pluses of having him as a boss was his understanding and compassionate nature. As a reporter, he had been nicknamed the "fallen woman editor" because of his ability to listen to hard-luck stories from people who wandered in off the streets. He was a kind and considerate listener to the personal problems of his staff and always had time for them—even, on the busiest day.

Bill was appointed editor of *The Albuquerque Tribune* September 11, 1980, succeeding Ralph Looney who went to Denver to become editor of *The Rocky Mountain News*. Bill's office now has more wood than glass, but his door is still open to the staff and to anyone else who wants to come in for a few minutes of solace or advice.

His own personal life took a turn a few years ago. In his early days at *The Cleveland Press* the college girl writing the teen page, Rusty Brown, caught his eye. She left *The Press*, went abroad with the USIA, but rejoined the staff in 1970 as columnist and feature writer. Shortly thereafter, Bill (who could talk as well as listen) talked her into marrying him.

Bill was born in Cleveland February 22, 1925, son of a fruit merchant. In junior high school author Ben Hecht became his "hero." Bill promptly started helping put out the school newspaper, and had a fix on his career goal.

He is medium height and medium weight, which he keeps medium by playing tennis vigorously and going on long bicycle rides. He became prematurely gray at thirty—and didn't change it. He has two sons by a previous marriage, Douglas born in 1947 and Russell born in 1958, who live in Cambridge, Massachusetts.

Bill and Rusty used to live in a condominium on Lake Erie overlooking downtown Cleveland. Now they live in a home in the foothills of the Sandia mountains overlooking downtown Albuquerque. Strange way of life for a guy who says he never wanted to overlook anything.

Birmingham Post-Herald
Birmingham, Alabama

Founded January 21, 1921 by Scripps-Howard and combined in May, 1950 with the *Birmingham Age-Herald*, which dated back to 1871, to form *Post-Herald*. At that time the *Birmingham News Co.*, through a contractual arrangement with Scripps-Howard, became business agent soliciting advertising and circulation for the *Post-Herald*, which moved from the evening to the morning field. *The News* also provided housing and printing services for the *Post-Herald*. The contract was continued at the time of the acquisition of *The News* by Newhouse Corp. and now has been extended beyond its original 1980 expiration dates to December 31, 2001.

E. T. Leech was first editor of *The Birmingham Post*. The *Post* fought the Ku Klux Klan in the 1920s and the 1940s, exposed the state's convict leasing system and took a leading part in the cleanup of corruption in Phenix City in the 1950s.

During the 1960s and 1970s the *Post-Herald* played a leader's role in civil reformation of Birmingham, which moved from its world-wide image as a racially biased and backward city to one acclaimed to be an All-America municipality. The city elected a black mayor and blacks took a number of responsible positions in city government.

Editor: ANGUS McEACHRAN. Vice President: W. H. METZ.

THE EDITOR

Angus McEachran

BEFORE it really got started, Angus McEachran's career in journalism took a couple of side roads. And later when he finally got on track he came in through what he calls the "back door."

It all started in Memphis, where Angus was born August 24, 1939. In high school he was an omnivorous reader and writer, spurred on by his English teacher. But he also was a football "hero"—a nifty running back. So nifty, in fact, that he was given an athletic scholarship to Maryland University. His gridiron career ended somewhat prematurely, thanks to a hostile lick.

Angus heard that you could become an FBI agent without a law degree by enrolling in a training program that included attending George Washington University in the nation's capital. Angus signed up and was a junior G-man of sorts for two and a half years.

In the back of his mind it had finally dawned that he really wanted to get into the newspaper business, and give vent to that love of the printed word. He packed up, went home and entered Memphis State University.

He indulged himself "in a few journalism courses" and set his sights on *The Commercial Appeal*. A little knocking on the "back door" got him a job in 1960 as an ad layout man. That was a start, but Angus wanted in the editorial department. He wangled a copy boy job out of the managing editor. A few months later he got a shot as an intern, and did so well Frank Ahlgren, editor, took him on as a reporter.

One reason Angus was so happy with the solid job was that by now he had two mouths to feed; he'd courted Ann Blackwell of Memphis while she was a student at Vanderbilt University and they'd just married.

Angus seemed to be cut out for editorial work. He handled a variety of assignments—police, general assignment, education, medical, and aviation—before becoming assistant city editor in 1966. In 1968 he supervised the Martin Luther King assassination coverage, and flew to London to report the arrest and extradition of James Earl Ray.

The following year he was promoted to metropolitan editor, overseeing all local and area news except sports and the Living section. In 1970 he was again upped—to assistant managing editor.

When Angus and Ann were leaving for vacation in London in the fall of 1976, Editor Mike Grehl had the bright idea that Angus ought to drop in on Northern Ireland and write all about their trouble.

"Mike really knows how to piggy-back on a guy's vacation," says Angus. "It wouldn't have been so bad, except that I had to go off and leave Ann by herself in London." Nonetheless, Angus wrote such a nifty five-part series that many Scripps-Howard papers reprinted it, including the *Birmingham Post-Herald*.

He also traveled to Israel and wrote about its conflict with the Arab states—but Grehl didn't make him do that on vacation. His swansong in Memphis was direction of the coverage of Elvis Presley's death.

In September 1977 Angus was named executive editor of the *Birmingham Post-Herald*. Duard LeGrand, the editor, retired January 1, 1978 and Angus was appointed his successor.

Before his second year as editor was out, Angus took on a circuit judge and won. The judge had ordered a *Post-Herald* reporter to refrain from writing a story containing testimony given in a murder trial because another jury was being selected for trial of a second defendant in the case.

Angus, after consultation with legal counsel and unable to contact the judge in an effort to persuade the jurist to change his order, decided to proceed with publication of the story on the basis that the judge's action was an attempt at prior restraint and therefore unconstitutional.

The judge several days later found the reporter guilty of contempt, assessing a fine and sentencing him to jail. Angus took the ruling straightway to the Alabama Court of Appeals. This court, after hearing both sides, deliberated only thirty minutes before finding in favor of the *Post-Herald*.

Philosophically, Angus says the days he feels best are those when the phone rings off the wall with complaints from readers firing away from both sides of a story. That convinces him the paper has achieved two essentials: it has stimulated the readers to think, and it has done the job in a fair way.

Angus doesn't take himself too seriously. He enjoys puncturing pomposity. And he tries to avoid inflating himself for someone else's needle. Nevertheless, he likes a good joke—even on himself. Angus admits to "a fair hand of poker, a lousy round of golf," and says he has been introduced by people in Birmingham who've played him as "the worst racquetball player in America."

The McEachrans have a son and a daughter, Gib born in 1961, and Amanda born in 1969. Angus's favorite exercise is bass fishing, which he gives credit for keeping him in his excellent shape (burly, or more specifically about one ninety at five-ten).

VICE PRESIDENT
W. H. Metz

BILL METZ is a man with a big head of steam, a friendly, extroverted type who puts in a full day at the office then finds time for a variety of civic activities.

Bill started at the bottom in Scripps-Howard—as office boy in the advertising department of *The Indianapolis Times* in 1936. As he climbed the ladder he also covered the country, from coast to coast and practically from border to border.

He had moved through the ranks to a place on *The Times* retail advertising staff when Pearl Harbor exploded and he found himself a buck private. With the perversity traditional in the armed services, the Army took advantage of his experience in advertising and selling by singling him out for ordnance training where he won his corporal's stripes. In ordanance Officer Candidate School, his specialty was bombs and bomb fuses. Afterwards he was commissioned as a second lieutenant and promptly attached to the Air Corps. Four years later he was discharged as a major and returned to his job at *The Times*.

Next spot was the staff of Scripps-Howard's general advertising office in Detroit, then on to the same department in New York. *The San Francisco News* needed a business manager and he got the call.

In San Francisco they gave him a real West Coast welcome. He hadn't been in town a month, in early 1957, when the city was hit by the biggest earthquake since the granddaddy of them all in 1906. This one cracked plaster, shattered window panes, rocked furniture and buckled plumbing in *The News* Building.

Bill checked his first impulse to head for the airport and hurried instead to the lower floor to make sure the presses were in working order. They were and a quick extra sold more than 50,000 copies.

When *The News* and *The Call-Bulletin* were consolidated, in 1959, Bill was transferred back east—and south—to Birmingham. As co-chairman of the United Appeal (an honor seldom handed a newcomer) he helped raise a record sum in record time. Raising money for a new home for the Birmingham Girls Club was another assignment successfully concluded. In 1964 he was nominated Birmingham's Man of the Year.

He was elected president of the Alabama Press Association in 1968 and served the following year as board chairman. In May 1975 he was awarded an honorary degree of Associate in Arts in Civic Service by Marion Military Institute. Bill was general chairman when Birmingham hosted the 1978 national Sigma Delta Chi convention. SDX awarded him its "first of a kind" Certificate of Appreciation for his convention efforts.

Bill is quick and decisive in his personal mannerisms, friendly in disposition and deeply loyal in his personal friendships. He laughs easily, loud and often—even found something amusing about that San Francisco earthquake—after he made sure the press still was running.

He was born in LeFeria, Texas, January 25, 1916. He is five-eight and weighs one hundred fifty. He attended Indiana University and married Helen Cole of Marion, Indiana, August 17, 1940. They had two children, Susannah born in 1947 and Stephen born in 1952. Helen died in 1969. On January 15, 1972 Bill married Nell Sugg of Ozark, Alabama.

The Cincinnati Post
Cincinnati, Ohio

First published January 3, 1881 as the *Penny Paper*, and purchased by James E. Scripps in October of that year. E. W. Scripps assumed control from his brother on January 1, 1883 and changed the paper's name to *Penny Post*. It was E. W. Scripps's third paper. Became *The Cincinnati Post* on September 2, 1890.

On Scripps-Howard's purchase of *The Cincinnati Times-Star* in 1958, became city's only evening newspaper. From its founding a champion of civic reform, led in destroying the notorious Cox machine and in establishing city-manager form of government. Its vigilance helped Cincinnati earn reputation as best-governed city in United States.

Boasts long-standing dedication to improving public education; promoted major reforms in safety regulations for school buses; started lunch program to feed thousands of needy pupils daily. A leader in redevelopment of Cincinnati's downtown and riverfront. Persuaded doctors to inoculate 500,000 citizens with Sabin polio vaccine.

Helped rescue historic art deco murals from Cincinnati's Union Terminal. Brought about reforms in Ohio laws governing land-contract purchases.

Entered in December 1979 a joint operating agreement with *The Cincinnati Enquirer*, which now handles *Post* business affairs.

Editor: WILLIAM R. BURLEIGH. Business Manager: JOHN L. FELDMANN.

THE EDITOR
William R. Burleigh

WHEN HE WAS eight or nine years old, Bill Burleigh wrote a headline and splashed it across the front page of his Neighborhood News. It said:

KNOWLEDGE IS POWER

There was no story with it; just the headline. But what the heck, it's the thought that counts.

Ever since, William Robert Burleigh has been pursuing knowledge and, along the way, accumulating his fair share of power.

Born September 6, 1935, he grew up in Evansville, Indiana, playing baseball, fishing, goofing off along the Ohio River.

When he was six or seven, his mother went to the hospital for an operation, and he and his cousin wrote a "book" about the event, fastening illustrations on to pages with straight pins. He recalls that he enjoyed seeing the thing take shape, and that was probably when he became hooked on the printed word. His cousin happened to be secretary to the editor of *The Evansville Press*, a circumstance that proved helpful later. As Burleigh published the Neighborhood News, his sister, Charlotte Ann, corrected his English. He didn't appreciate it much then, but now he gives her belated credit. His little paper didn't last long. "We had production and delivery problems," he recalls. "Nothing's really different now."

Burleigh's father, Joseph, was a railroad man. So were Bill's grandfather and his uncle. Bill's dad offered him this advice: "Be anything but a railroader."

There was nothing to worry about. Bill didn't hanker to be a railroader. His eye was on newspapers. Through his cousin, he got favorable entree to *The Evansville Press* sports editor, Dick Anderson. Dick thought the lad pretty bright and eager for fifteen, and hired him May 22, 1951. By July 4 Bill was on Cloud Nine; he got his first byline. It was a yarn about a "plug horse derby" at the local race track.

Bill continued to work at *The Press* through high school. One of his teachers, an alumnus of Marquette University at Milwaukee, convinced him that Marquette had a good journalism program, so that's where he wound up after graduation.

Looking back, he says, "I was interested more in liberal arts, and Marquette had that, and the Jesuit tradition. My orientation has been toward liberal arts. I'm not sure I would take journalism now."

In any case, in 1957 he was graduated magna cum laude in journalism from Marquette. He was editor of the school paper and was named outstanding journalism graduate by Sigma Delta Chi.

Then came decision time. He had an offer from *The Washington Post*, and another from *The Evansville Press*.

He remembers receiving letters about this from Earl Richert, editor of *The Press*, and the late Ed Klingler, dean of Evansville reporters.

"They made the point that Scripps-Howard proceeds from no ideological point of view," he recalls. "They said you can be your own man. It offers the greatest amount of individual freedom you have in commercial life. I liked this idea. It is the single greatest attraction of Scripps-Howard."

So Washington's loss was Evansville's gain. "I've never been sorry," Burleigh says.

Another Evansville editor whom Burleigh credits with a "major influence" is Gordon Hanna, "who gives people challenging jobs and lets them rise or fall."

After starting in sports, Burleigh moved to the city and state desks, which landed him in the middle of the early school integration conflicts in the South in the late 1950s. After troops were called in to quell violence in a pair of small Kentucky towns, the commanding general went out of his way to point to Burleigh's reporting as the most accurate being produced in the crisis. That was one point of view. Some townspeople had a different slant. They chased Burleigh and an AP man out of town.

"The AP guy was driving 100 miles an hour on a country road," Bill recalls. "I held a tire tool at the ready and two carloads of unhappy coal miners were chasing us. We outran 'em."

Bill drew the first urban redevelopment assignment on *The Press*, specialized for a time in education and had a brief fling at covering the Indiana legislature. Next came assistant city editor, then city editor, managing editor and, in 1975, editor and president.

He was awarded the 1973 Byline Award by Marquette "in recognition of performance of competent journalism through the years and acceptance and fulfillment of professional responsibility." In 1979 he received an honorary Doctor of Laws degree from Indiana State University.

He won awards from the Hoosier State Press Association, United Press International and the Evansville Press Club for editorial writing. And in 1968, while he was city editor, *The Press* was honored by the Hoosier association for the best local news coverage among major Indiana dailies.

"He'll always be a city editor," says a former co-worker of *The Press*.

Another who watched him operate as city editor recalls: "He was demanding, and he had more energy than three reporters. He was the best person I ever saw at grabbing the nearest object and throwing it at the wall. It was like a volcano exploding. He said we were a daily, not a seed catalog."

When Burleigh became editor of *The Press*, he was the first native of Evansville to hold that post since the paper was started in 1906.

"I was also the shortest-lived," he adds.

He had been editor eighteen months when he was tapped to move up the river to the editorship of *The Cincinnati Post* on July 1, 1977.

Burleigh's editorship has never been of the ivory tower variety. He jumped into community and professional affairs with both feet in Evansville, and continued this in Cincinnati.

Bill now has reached that stage in life where his head is starting to push through his hair. Tall (six-four), bespectacled, he can wear a look of intense concentration one moment and then break into a broad smile. He still stalks through the newsroom with a sense of urgency. Those who have known him a long time say he has calmed down, and they attribute this to the passing years, and marriage.

It was while he was city editor in Evansville that he went on a blind date with Anne Husted, a reporter for *The Indianapolis Star*. There obviously was a little magic in the moonlight: she's now Mrs. Burleigh and there are three children: David, born in 1968; Catherine, 1972; and Margaret, 1974. Mrs. Burleigh is the author of several books.

Bill has performed just about every chore on the editorial side of a newspaper—though not all at the same time as was necessary back on his Neighborhood News.

Now he opines: "A newspaper plays perhaps the critical role in informing and forming public opinion. Informing is the heart and soul; it's what Scripps-Howard is all about."

BUSINESS MANAGER
John L. Feldmann

JOHN IS A FELLOW who strongly believes in doing his homework. As the record shows, literally.

At age fifteen, harried by the Depression, John managed to get a $5-a-week job as office boy at a new weekly starting up in his hometown, Newport, Kentucky. The paper, *The Kentucky World*, went daily, but failed after barely two years.

John had learned how to scramble. He already knew Charlie Willenborg, business manager of *The Kentucky Post*, the rival that had done in *The World*. John hurried over and offered Charlie his expertise. What went through Charlie's mind as he studied the lanky, energetic seventeen-year-old (John was born February 5, 1917) is not recorded. Charlie could have been terribly short-handed, or he detected an inner spark. At any rate, on May 24, 1934 a deal was struck; at $14.50 a week John became combination office boy and classified ad collector.

Landing his second straight newspaper job not only thrilled John, it gave him big ideas. He secretly promised himself to become business manager of *The Kentucky Post* —someday. Such ambition demanded homework aplenty. John finished high school at night, went to evening business college, and "scrounged and digested every advertising trade magazine I could lay hands on."

World War II temporarily interrupted John's climb up the ladder in *The Kentucky Post* ad department. He left his wife, the former Sarah Donelan, whom he'd married in 1940, and two boys, Dick and Don, and put on Navy blue. He saw action in the Pacific on the heavy cruiser *Salt Lake City*.

With time on his hands he tried writing a novel and airmailing it home. The fat envelope attracted the attention of the censor who read the novel and handed it over to the chaplain who ran it as a serial in the ship's newspaper. John emerged from the war intact, with the insignia of Radio Technician, 2nd class, on his sleeve.

For a couple of years, John and Sarah (known as Sally) lived in a small house they'd bought in Covington. With Dick, Don and new-addition Dave, it seemed increasingly crowded.

"Well," John told Sally, "maybe we ought to build a house. I think I can do it."

He was thirty. He bought a lot in Cold Spring, Kentucky. He read a bunch of books. He picked the brains of friendly builders. Then he started his monumental do-it-yourself venture. He got help from his brother and his dad. John hired out some of the heavy foundation work for his Cape Cod dream house. But he mainly alone did the carpentry, plumbing, wiring, installing woodwork, doors and windows. He even mixed the plaster and carried the hod for two hired plasterers. He built the fireplace.

He worked nights, weekends, during vacations. It took a year, but came the happy day in 1948 when the Feldmanns moved in. It was a darn good house.

John didn't neglect his advertising career. He kept going ahead. They also had another son, Danny. Sarah underwent an operation in November 1960 and died of complications. John tried to fill the void in his life by plunging deeper into civic and service organizations. He was a director or president of more clubs and groups in Northern Kentucky than you can count. He's pretty proud of ramrodding a couple of senior citizen apartment towers, worth $4 million.

During this period he met and married a vivacious widow, Romilda Bathalter, with two daughters, Phyllis and Tressie.

John kept his eye (and his heart) on the business manager's desk. Stanley Collins replaced Charlie Willenborg. But on January 1, 1966 John finally made it when Collins retired. Under John's direction *The Kentucky Post* started setting advertising and circulation records, and grew into what the editor called "No. 1 in everything in Northern Kentucky."

Nearly always John is on the move. He claims fishing and gardening as hobbies but those who know him say he's better with a saw and hammer. In a couple of new homes since the do-it-yourself Cape Cod, John has finished the interiors of dens, put in extra plumbing, built workshops, patios, and a lot more. He has more tools than a small Sears store.

At the drop of a hat—or less, much less—John will serve as master of ceremonies, or deliver a speech. He knows 10,000 jokes (a few of which he repeats). He is a hacker on the golf course, and there has never been a recorded match with him in which an advertiser has lost.

General management kept a sharp eye on John's skills and when the job as business manager of *The Cincinnati Post* opened up in 1977, he was the logical choice. And conveniently, he could continue to officiate as business manager of *The Kentucky Post*.

Once again John got caught up in a mess of homework. He took over in Cincinnati in the midst of protracted negotiations for creation of a joint operating agreement with *The Cincinnati Enquirer*.

Seeing his end of that through a series of court hearings and labor negotiations to a successful conclusion has been, says John, "the toughest job I ever had."

When that dust was settling, John seemed to be mumbling another secret promise to himself, something about less gardening and less woodworking, and more golf.

The Kentucky Post
Covington, Kentucky

Launched by E. W. Scripps on September 15, 1890 as Kentucky edition of *The Cincinnati Post*. Printed in *The Cincinnati Post* plant with separate editorial and business offices on the Kentucky side of the river; now produced under joint operating agreement by *The Cincinnati Enquirer*, with separate independent editorial staff.

Concluded successful campaign in the early Twenties for charter and city manager form of government in Covington and Newport. Was responsible for passage of uniform small loan law. Unearthed facts in 1938 national WPA scandal.

Organized free summer concerts in Devou Park, a natural amphitheater, that drew audiences of up to 42,000; helped bring Greater Cincinnati Airport to Boone County, Kentucky; backed reform forces that brought end of Newport "sin city" regime in late 1950s; led environmental crusade to clean up Licking River that earned a Meeman award for 1970.

Editor: PAUL F. KNUE. Business manager: JOHN L. FELDMANN.

THE EDITOR
Paul F. Knue

PAUL KNUE went to college to learn how to become an ad man.

He figured he'd need some practical experience, so he started selling ads for the newspaper at Murray State University in Kentucky. When the business manager quit to get married a few weeks later, he took her job.

"I liked advertising," Paul says, "but the people who worked on the news side of the staff had fun. They told exciting tales of the stories they covered and the people they met.

"I was missing something."

So in 1967 Paul wangled a summer job from the editor of his hometown weekly, *The Dearborn County* (Indiana) *Register*. For $60 a week, he covered the town board and Little League, sold ads, pasted up stories in the composing room, took pictures and even hauled the papers to the post office on Wednesday afternoons.

He was hooked.

College graduation and marriage were approaching, so Paul took a job as a reporter for *The Evansville (Indiana) Courier*. The pay was just a little more than he made working for a weekly, however, so he and his bride, Lissa, the former Elizabeth Anne Wegner, didn't hesitate to pack up and head for Fort Wayne when *The Journal-Gazette* offered him a job on the copy desk.

In 1970 *The Cincinnati Post* made him a better offer. He joined *The Post* as a copy editor and worked his way up.

When *The Post* decided to convert its Saturday paper from an evening to a morning edition, Paul was given the opportunity to redesign it into a modern, graphic package. The first edition of "The Weekender" rolled off the presses in January 1974.

In 1975 William Burleigh, then editor of *The Evansville Press*, asked Paul to become his managing editor. Paul spent four years at *The Press*. He helped direct award-winning coverage of major news stories that included the plane crash that wiped out the University of Evansville's basketball team and crushed a community's spirit.

While in Evansville, Paul fell in love with the outdoors. Lissa convinced him the family should get out and enjoy the fresh air, whitewater streams and sparkling lakes that abound in the area.

The Knues' outdoor adventuring began inauspiciously. They pitched their first camp at a former strip mine pit. The dirt was the hardest of hard pan. The tent stakes broke. It was cold. It rained. But they more than survived, they enjoyed themselves.

As with newspapering, Paul was hooked.

He and Lissa and their two daughters now spend blissful vacation days on a houseboat on Kentucky's Lake Barkley. Or they'll tie the canoe to the top of the station wagon and head for the rapids.

Of whitewater canoeing, Paul says: "It's kind of like baseball—short bursts of frenzied activity in between great lulls."

Sometimes he'll surrender to a contemplative mood and paddle out on a glassy lake. "There's nothing to match that feeling of serenity. To be out gliding on a lake at sunset is to feel that nothing can be wrong in the world."

That tranquil view is a contrast with Paul's opinion of a newspaper editor's proper role. "A newspaper must reflect its community. It's like holding up a mirror. We must present an accurate picture, warts and all.

"And we must reflect not only what is, but what can be. We must show a community's aspirations.

"The easiest thing to do is to go out and cover government. Reporters and editors are trained to do that. But I'd like to be smart enough to cover people and somehow in the process get all the other things, like news of government, that newspapers are supposed to cover.

"An editor needs to try to mold opinion. A newspaper

needs to be a force for good in the community. But it needs to be a mirror, too. An editor must set a tone, but he cannot allow that tone to deafen him. It's easy for an editor to curb a reporter's impulses, but who watches over the editor?

"An editor has to keep asking himself these questions: Am I being fair? Am I doing the right thing? Am I missing something?"

Paul was made editor of *The Kentucky Post* in December 1979, succeeding Vance Trimble, editor for 16 years. The appointment was something of a homecoming for the Knues.

Paul was born July 11, 1947, in Lawrenceburg, Indiana, across the Ohio River from the area served by *The Kentucky Post*. Lissa is from Cincinnati. They have two daughters, Amy born in 1971, and Kate born in 1973.

The Columbus Citizen-Journal
Columbus, Ohio

The afternoon *Columbus Citizen* was founded March 1, 1899, and was purchased by E. W. Scripps July 2, 1904. The morning *Ohio State Journal* was founded in 1811. On November 9, 1959, *The Citizen* and *The Journal* were combined into a six-day Scripps-Howard morning paper, published under a joint agreement with the afternoon *Columbus Dispatch*.

The Citizen-Journal, a state capital newspaper, has kept a sharp eye on, and provided expert coverage of, state government from the governor's office on down.

Editor: RICHARD R. CAMPBELL. Business Manager: GREGORY A. DEMBSKI.

THE EDITOR
Richard R. Campbell

ARMED WITH a fresh diploma from Ohio University in Athens, Dick Campbell in 1947 was hitchhiking across the state looking for work as a copy editor. The pickings weren't easy. In one town he was offered a sports writing berth. Dick didn't know anything about sports. A couple of towns up the road they wanted an ad man. That wasn't for Dick, either. He struck out toward Cleveland, hopes sagging, convinced that would be about the end of the line.

It was. Dick marched into *The Cleveland Press* and tackled Norman Shaw, managing editor. Two things about Dick struck Shaw. He was the first budding journalist Shaw had met who wanted to start on the copy desk. Also, Dick was young and vain enough to wear his Phi Beta Kappa key in plain sight. Both were pluses; Shaw also was Phi Beta Kappa.

"Okay," said Shaw. "I don't have a desk opening now. I can start you as a copy clerk." Shaw didn't know it but he was hiring the man who would later succeed him as associate editor. Nor was it a first for *The Cleveland Press* to snag a Phi Beta Kappa as copyboy. Dick found two fellow clerks also had that distinction. "Those were great days for hiring," Dick recalls.

Dick has held about every newsroom job at *The Cleveland Press*—except reporter. He skipped that. After six weeks as copy boy he was grabbed by the picture desk to write cutlines. Then he became assistant makeup editor, and later moved into the slot. He was news editor, assistant city editor, chief editorial writer and managing editor.

In the early Seventies his duties as m.e. got him involved in computerization of the newspaper of the future. In 1972 he was chosen as Scripps-Howard's representative to the computer development program operated by Newspaper Systems Development Group in Gaithersburg, Maryland. He was on leave of absence from *The Cleveland Press* from 1972 through 1976, living in Gaithersburg, just outside Washington, D.C.

Dick was born March 25, 1923 in Guysville, Ohio. He attended school in Pomeroy and Stewart, Ohio, and entered Ohio University in 1940, majoring in English and toying with the idea of becoming a poet. World War II rudely interrupted his college education.

In the Army, Dick met a guy who once worked for the Associated Press and the two of them began publishing a newspaper for their battalion in the Philippines. Dick reached the age of twenty-one at the same time he reached the conclusion there was very little money in poetry. But his taste of Army journalism had convinced him he still could get paid for playing with words. When he went back to Ohio University, he made sure he got into some journalism classes.

Of all his jobs at *The Cleveland Press*, Dick figures he was best at headline writing. He won two annual awards in the Cleveland Guild competition for concise, imaginative heads before his colleagues barred him from the competition.

Dick was married in 1946 to Margaret Jandes and they have a son, Christopher born in 1949, and a daughter, Constant born in 1951. When Dick took over as editor of *The Citizen-Journal* January 1, 1977, on the retirement of Chuck Egger, one grizzled staffer observed: "He's going to run a real newspaper—you can tell by the way he walks." The Campbell walk is quick, forceful and direct, even if he is only headed for the water fountain.

Dick has strong, clear ideas about what makes a newspaper good. His formula starts with believability. He is a stickler for proper spelling and good grammar. Dick likes to point out that readers are not likely to believe a news story's facts if they see the writer does not know how to spell. He also believes in good packaging. He wants readers to be able to find their regular features in the same places each morning.

And one thing is proved by the master's degree he received not long ago from Kent State University after seven years of catching classes by auto and mail. He never stops learning.

BUSINESS MANAGER
Gregory A. Dembski

THEY SAY Greg Dembski is such an ace salesman he can make you forget a morning hangover just by saying hello. And flashing his mile-wide smile he's apt to convince you that the darn hangover is good for you, anyhow.

That's doubtless a trifle strong. But there's no doubt Greg is some kind of salesman. He knows it from the bottom up. Born in Chicago March 12, 1917, he was schooled at De Paul and Northwestern Universities. He started at the bottom of the totem pole, in the merchandising department of the *Chicago Tribune* in 1939. His job was to set up advertiser displays in Chicago restaurants, taverns, and retail stores.

He was ambitious. Before long he got on in classified, and then moved up through the ranks in national and retail. He drew the attention of an outfit called Cresmer and Woodward, newspaper representatives. He spent five years with them. While the firm represented newspapers, it did not own any. Greg began to feel uncomfortable. He realized he was spending as much time "sugar-coating" publishers as he was selling for them.

So when Scripps-Howard offered him a place in the Chicago sales office in September 1949, Greg jumped at it. Now that he had only the prospective advertiser to worry about, he began making a name for himself in the eleven-state area served by Chicago. His peers took note; in 1960 Chicago's media people voted him the outstanding newspaper rep.

In 1963 he was promoted to western manager in charge of the Scripps-Howard Chicago shop.

Greg is not short on imagination. It looked like a smart move to let his salesmen represent their papers in all three classifications—classified, national and retail. He was instrumental in bringing that change about. The new system eliminated duplication of effort and provided greater "intimacy" —as Greg calls it—between salesman and customer.

He envisioned a hefty sales tool if he provided his crew with continuously updated market and newspaper data sheets. That started, his men could instantaneously provide customers a current in-depth, personalized sales pitch. That meant more time for selling.

Greg was ready for a new challenge. Scripps-Howard asked if he'd like to run the business end of *The Columbus Citizen-Journal*. Greg flashed that mile-wide grin; that would put him where the action is. He was eager. But he had a problem.

Back in his *Chicago Tribune* days, Greg had to trek up to the adjustment department on some of his accounts. There he found a bright-eyed filly named Gloni Hagenauer. They were married in 1945, and turned out a fine brood: Gregory II in 1947, Timothy in 1949, Patrick in 1951, Jeffery in 1954, and Elizabeth in 1958.

His problem was the two youngest. The oldest three were in college, but Jeff was still in high school and Liz was about to graduate from junior high. They didn't want to desert chums and move to Columbus.

"That was about the hardest sale I ever made," Greg recalls. (Gloni got in a few good licks, too). Greg took over as *Citizen-Journal* business manager April 2, 1971. "It worked out," he says. "All the kids are happy."

Greg's Columbus civic interests include serving as director and past president of the Boys Club, Blue Cross/Blue Shield director, Better Business Bureau, Chamber of Commerce, Goodwill Industries and the Heart Fund.

He plays tennis and golf, but doesn't brag about his prowess in either game.

The Rocky Mountain News
Denver, Colorado

Founded April 23, 1859 before there was a townsite or a state. Scripps-McRae founded *The Denver Express* in 1906; acquired *The News* and *The Denver Express*, 1926, consolidated into two papers—*The Rocky Mountain News*, morning and Sunday, and *The Denver Evening News*. In 1928, *The Evening News* was discontinued, coincidental with the discontinuance of *The Morning Post*. Two papers remain in the field, *The Rocky Mountain News*, morning and Sunday, *The Denver Post*, evening and Sunday.

The major growth of *The News* began with the appointment of Jack Foster as editor and William Hailey as business manager in the 1940s. They restyled the paper as a tabloid. It had a circulation of 48,179 in 1942 and twice that five years later. Today the circulation is near 300,000; advertising was 67.3 million lines in 1979, up from 24.7 million in 1960.

The paper in recent years has won numerous awards for its aggressive and thoughtful local reporting. Some major local stories have included investigations into the finances of an oil and financial leader, city financing, state government, the environment and Colorado's growth. All editorial departments have been expanded and local columnists are featured prominently.

The plant has been enlarged; the number of presses has grown from fourteen to forty since 1973. In 1977 *The News* added a new warehouse, loading dock and roll-handling equipment. Property has been purchased for further expansion.

Editor: RALPH LOONEY. Business Manager: WILLIAM W. FLETCHER.

THE EDITOR

Ralph Looney

Ralph Looney is a native of the Kentucky bluegrass who poked his nose out West and got hooked on the big sky —as well as other beauties of the great plains and the Rockies.

The move was a fortunate plus for Scripps-Howard for Ralph wound up filling the editor's chair at two of our papers —at Albuquerque and at Denver.

His Western odyssey began in 1952. On a bright fall day both Dwight Eisenhower and Looney hit Albuquerque. Ike was campaigning. Ralph, with wife Clara in tow, was vacationing. After listening to Ike's speech, Ralph dropped by *The Tribune* to talk shop with editor Dan Burrows. They didn't chat about newspapering for long. Burrows, a racing lover, discovered Ralph hailed from Lexington, Kentucky. Until dusk settled on the Sandia peak Burrows probed Ralph's abundant store of thoroughbred lore.

That, or something, impressed the New Mexico editor. Two months later back in Lexington Looney got from Burrows this laconic message: "I've got a job as reporter, if you'd like to come. Ninety a week."

That must have been more than Ralph was getting on *The Lexington Leader*. Besides the West's beauty had already captivated the Looneys. They put their house up for sale and streaked for Albuquerque. They got there a couple of weeks before Ike made it to the White House. And at *The Tribune*, except for one brief lapse, Ralph stayed nearly three decades.

Ralph was born in Lexington June 22, 1924. In junior high school he got both a camera and the journalism bug. He covered basketball and snapped pictures as a freelancer for

The Lexington Herald. By his senior year (1941) Ralph was editor of the high school paper, and evening office boy at *The Herald* at $7.65 a week.

But wanderlust overtook him after graduation. He went to Washington, D. C., as a clerk-typist in the FBI's photostat lab. That wasn't much fun; the lab was deep in the basement of the Justice Department. Ralph wangled a transfer to Louisville. There he was night clerk. In a few months he gave up on a government career and went back to Lexington to enter the University of Kentucky. He got a part-time job as proofreader at *The Lexington Leader*. There was no stopping him. He graduated to full-time photog, then sports writer and reporter. By 1944 he was so smart he made the "greatest move of my life", marrying Clarabel Richards. His A.B. came in 1948, still a *Leader* staffer, and then the January 6, 1953 move to Albuquerque.

For two years Ralph was a *Tribune* reporter. Then he got itchy feet and went to *The St. Louis Globe-Democrat*. They promoted him to the slot. But after eighteen months Dan Burrows called one midnight. Would Ralph like to come back as city editor? He would, could, and did—July 1956.

During his 13 years as city editor, *The Tribune* won more state press association public service prizes than any New Mexico paper ever did for aggressive reporting. *The Tribune* also picked up a National Headliners Award. George Carmack succeeded Burrows in 1966 and soon upped Ralph to assist m.e. When Carmack retired March 1, 1973, Ralph was named his successor.

Ralph is curious, competitive, and creative. One of his greatest ideas hit him in 1968 when New Mexico's Air National-al Guard was called to active duty in Vietnam. Ralph decided the Guardsmen ought to hear a Merry Christmas from the homefolks. *The Tribune* set up sound movie cameras and filmed messages from 269 families. That made five miles of film. Ralph bundled it up and flew to Vietnam. It took him three weeks to show his talkies to the guardsmen. He brought back a bale of his own pictures and stories. The project won *The Tribune* a raft of awards. Looney was given the New Mexico Medal of Honor.

Being editor didn't stop him from being a writer or photographer. He was usually in the office at 5:30 a.m., bustling around helping to determine the day's play, trying to do as much as he'd ask of any staffer. He has a wry sense of humor and enjoys a good laugh at his expense. But (perhaps as a hangover from his proofreader days) he agonizes over the smallest omission or blooper.

He's a mainly hard news man, and believes a newspaper's primary role is as the public's spokesman, watchdog and defender. His writing talents are redoubtable. He did a series on Navajo Indians that won the 1976 Robert F. Kennedy award. His *Tribune* columns and editorials took an unbroken string of seventeen first prizes in the E. H. Shaffer Awards (named for a former *Tribune* editor) from the state press association, plus a Freedoms Foundation George Washington Honor Medal.

Ralph's articles and pictures have appeared in many national magazines, including the *National Geographic* and *The Atlantic*. He authored a successful book on New Mexico's ghost towns, "Haunted Highways," (Hastings House, 1969).

He was a wheel in Albuquerque community affairs. He helped originate and execute New Mexico's successful drive to bring motion pictures and television production to the state.

While he was going great guns at *The Albuquerque Tribune*, Ralph was selected September 11, 1980 to go to Denver when Michael Howard resigned as editor of *The Rocky Mountain News*. The transplanted Westerner already had a good grip on the mores of Colorado. Looney had—what else?—been there on many vacations.

Anyone who knows Ralph well would not have been the least surprised that in Denver he fit right in and promptly began offering the same journalistic dividends that New Mexico got from his indomitable verve and steady effort.

BUSINESS MANAGER
William W. Fletcher

IN THE FALL of 1952 Bill Fletcher piled everything he and Sue, his bride of a year, owned ("which wasn't a lot") into their green '37 Dodge sedan and headed West. He wanted a career in advertising. An agency man back East told him to start on a Denver newspaper. That seemed like a good idea to Bill; he had spent a boyhood summer working in the Rocky Mountain National Forest and thought Denver a spiffy town.

Denver has two daily newspapers, and just by luck Bill called first at the *Rocky Mountain News*. There was no opening for an ad salesman, but the paper needed a man in the dispatch department. Bill grabbed the job, and started to hustle.

In a short time he was in the advertising department, and was catching the eye of business side higher-ups. In 1964 he was promoted to personnel director. Six years later, Bill was made business manager, which meant he was in control—except for the editorial side and its composing room—of the whole operation.

Fletcher is not the type to thump his own tub. "The paper has always grown since I've been here," he says. "There has not been a year there hasn't been an increase." Yet, compared to the two previous decades, *The News* has made elephant strides in circulation and advertising since 1970. "Well," he will finally admit, "we have accomplished an awful lot in the last four or five years."

In those four or five years *The News* steadily gained on the the rival afternoon *Post*, and finally passed the *Post* in daily advertising linage and circulation.

Tall and a trifle gaunt, Bill looks more like a former basketball player than the track man he was in high school and college. He ran the 880 and the hurdles. His outward appearance (white-haired, with penetrating eyes behind glasses) is somewhat severe. This may be uncomfortable for new employes, but they don't doubt this man is one of the bosses. In conversation, however, he is pleasant and soft-spoken, so relaxed sometimes that the unwary think he's on the verge of falling asleep. "Just when you think his mind is a thousand miles away," observes a colleague, "he'll suddenly interject a cogent thought that shows he's been right there all along!"

Born November 17, 1928 in Boston, Massachusetts, Bill served with the U.S. occupation forces in Japan, and then spent four years at Ohio Wesleyan University, majoring in economics. His more important campus achievement was meeting Sue Somerville, whom he married in 1951.

Bill doesn't try to hide from the accusation that he loves *The News*. After all, this has been his only career stop. As a result he may spend undue hours fretting about the newspaper. But he is a man who finds time to fill up a full day. He is involved in community affairs having served as director of the Chamber of Commerce and the Denver Athletic Club.

He likes the outdoors, and makes sure he gets away to the mountains to ski or hike. He was good enough to teach skiing and also race for awhile. He finds time, too, for the handball court, where he is still pretty fair.

Sue is a doer herself, especially in the YMCA. She was voted YMCA Layman of the Year (a first for a woman), and was the first woman recognized by the Y's Board of Managers.

The Fletchers have one son, John, born in 1967. The lad should be a heckuva an athlete. If not, he will for certain stay in shape. Bill and Sue will see to that.

The El Paso Herald-Post
El Paso, Texas

In 1881 B. F. Deal and James Baker hauled in a press by wagon from Colorado and, on March 27, published the first edition of the *El Paso Herald*, just a week earlier than its rival, the *El Paso Times*. The *El Paso Post* was founded by Scripps-Howard Newspapers on August 21, 1922, with Tom Sharp as its first editor. Scripps-Howard acquired *The Herald* from its then owner, Dorrance D. Roderick, April 2, 1931, to produce the consolidated *El Paso Herald-Post*. On August 31, 1936, *The Herald Post* and *The Times* formed a common publishing corporation, the Newspaper Printing Corporation, with both newspapers publishing from the same plant, with same equipment, but completely separate editorial policy and management.

The Gannett newspaper group acquired *The Times* on March 6, 1972, with the agency agreement remaining in force.

The Herald-Post has waged successful campaigns for better highways and establishment of a freeway through El Paso, expansion of the city's airport, establishment of Guadalupe National Park and diversification of farming along the Rio Grande, once almost wholly dependent on cotton. It raised money to build memorials to El Paso's World War II dead, and to those slain in the Korean and Vietnam conflicts. It helped establish El Paso's Cancer Radiation Treatment Center, and successfully campaigned for construction of a new El Paso Civic Center.

Editor: ROBERT W. LEE. President, Newspaper Printing Corporation: FRANK FEUILLE III.

THE EDITOR
Robert W. Lee

THE BIRTH CERTIFICATE of the editor of *The El Paso Herald-Post* lists him as Robert Wright Huntington, but in El Paso everyone calls him Pete Lee, as does everyone in Scripps-Howard.

He was born March 17, 1916 at Ridley Park, Pennsylvania, the second child of Earl and Edna Huntington, both stock company actors. Earl Huntington's step-father was named Lee, and that was the name he used on the stage. So Robert Huntington grew up as Robert Lee, a name he eventually adopted legally to straighten out his records before entering the Army during World War II.

If the Lee is legal, the Pete is not.

The later-to-be-editor joined the Scripps-Howard family as a copy boy on the old *San Francisco News* on September 10, 1933 and every time the city editor hollered "Bob," he jumped. Unfortunately, he wasn't always the Bob who was wanted, so the city editor kindly explained to him that his name henceforth would be Pete. And so it was. And so it is.

Pete's training for journalism consisted of travelling the country with his parents, and occasionally playing a small role on the stage in support of his father. The family eventually settled in San Francisco, where Pete graduated from Galileo high school and, jobs being scarce in the Depression year of 1933, spent the summer working at a northern California summer resort for board and keep.

Frank Clarvoe, then assistant managing editor of *The San Francisco News*, spotted him at work tearing down an old barn at the summer resort, and presumably noted that he was dumb but willing. Clarvoe offered him a $15 a week job as copy boy, a task at which Pete labored for some eighteen months. During that time he got a $1.50 weekly raise for drawing twelve cartoons a week for a short feature called "On the Sunnyside."

He also taught himself how to type, and a generous city editor allowed him to rewrite press agent handouts in order to spare the reportorial staff that chore.

Eventually Pete became a reporter, then a copy editor, then suburban editor, and assistant city editor, with occasional intervals of filling in as a drama critic and even women's page editor. As a sideline, he turned out occasional cartoons to illustrate his own stories, as well as those of others.

Came World War II and Pete entered the Army, spending a year as a radio operator and aerial gunner on a B-24 in Italy before becoming an aerial gunnery officer. He put in fifty missions over Europe before returning to the States and preparing for a tour in the Pacific—which never came about because the war ended.

Returning to *The News* after a three-year absence, he became city editor, a post he held for ten years, during which he numbered on his reportorial staff one Ted Scripps. In 1956 he became editor of the editorial page, and in 1958 was named managing editor, a post he held when, in 1960, *The News* merged with *The San Francisco Call-Bulletin* to create *The San Francisco News-Call Bulletin*. He served as a managing editor of *The News-Call Bulletin* until mid-1962, when Scripps-Howard divested itself of its interest in the newspaper, and he went home to sit and wait for his next assignment.

Pete was married on September 7, 1940 to Helen Elizabeth Garrott of Burlingame, California, and their daughter, Sandra (now Mrs. David Filleman and on the staff of El Paso's FBI office), was born on November 30, 1945.

In September 1962, the family was shipped to El Paso, where Pete became executive editor of *The Herald-Post*, taking over editorship of the newspaper on February 4, 1963 on the retirement of Ed Pooley.

As editor, he has split his time between the newspaper and community work. He has served as president of El Paso's Chamber of Commerce, president of El Paso's United Way, president of Yucca Council of the Boy Scouts, president of the Guidance Center for emotionally disturbed children, president of the Hotel Dieu (hospital) advisory board, and of the Downtown Development Assn., the Industrial Development Corporation and the National Conference of Christians and Jews. He has served, too, on the boards of a variety of other organizations, such as Goodwill Industries, the YMCA, the YWCA advisory board, and Loretto Academy, a private Catholic School (though he's a Protestant).

He holds the City of El Paso's highest civic honor, the Conquistador Award, has been named an Admiral in the El Paso Navy, and is a recipient of the National Human Relations Award of the El Paso Chapter of the National Conference of Christians and Jews.

Pete still covers an occasional civic story, edits his own editorial page, writes a thrice-weekly column called "Editor's Corner," and turns out cartoons, some for publication, some for staff amusement.

In addition to being editor, Pete is vice-president of the Newspaper Printing Corp., vice-president of The Herald-Post Publishing Co., vice-president of the Newspaper Realty Corp.

The Evansville Press
Evansville, Indiana

Founded July 2, 1906 by E. W. Scripps and his attorney, J. C. Harper; first editor, F. R. Peters. Fought successfully for toll-free bridges over the Ohio River, for good schools, better government, penal reform, better long-range financing for Hoosier roads and riverfront revitalization.

In 1938 *The Press* and *The Evansville Courier* organized a common publishing corporation to handle business affairs with each newspaper retaining separate editorial management and policy. An unusual feature of this operation is a combined *Sunday Courier and Press* with two editorial pages from the two dailies, but the Sunday newspaper has its own editorial staff.

The Press has had six editors since Peters — Frank R. Ford, Earl H. Richert, Gordon Hanna, Michael Grehl, William R. Burleigh and William W. Sorrels.

Editor: WILLIAM W. SORRELS. Editor, *The Sunday Courier and Press*: JUDITH CLABES.

THE EDITOR
William W. Sorrels

WILLIAM WRIGHT SORRELS has been the editor of *The Evansville Press* since July 1, 1977 but he's not much on formality and everyone in town calls him Bill.

On occasion Bill can shout across his Indiana newsroom and get attention. But that isn't his style. He'd rather sit down with a reporter, share cups of coffee and quietly make his point.

But he can be misread. Bill cloaks iron-ribbed determination with a soft Southern accent and a smile. He would stop a train to get a good yarn in his newspaper. In 1955 the Sunshine Special out of Kansas City jumped several coaches off the track in Marked Tree, Arkansas, killing seven passengers. A conductor let Bill aboard an undamaged coach and told him he had at least fifteen minutes to talk to survivors. When the train pulled out five minutes later, Bill bluntly told the conductor:

"Either you pull the emergency chain or I'm going to jump. I've got work to do in Marked Tree."

The conductor pulled the chain, and Bill walked a half-mile back into town.

A careful writer with an eye for detail and a lean prose style, Bill contends he came out of an excellent Memphis newspaper mold, having worked for *The Commercial Appeal* under three highly capable editors — Frank R. Ahlgren, Gordon Hanna and Mike Grehl. In Memphis, where he joined Scripps-Howard on January 15, 1954, his associates often referred to Bill as "One L" Sorrels. The late John H. Sorrells, no relation, was executive editor of Scripps-Howard Newspapers.

Born in Cordova, Tennessee, on July 28, 1924, Bill grew up in West Point, Mississippi. In high school he was on the boxing, baseball and track teams and thought more about athletics than newspapering. After Navy duty in the Southwest Pacific with the Seventh Fleet in World War II, Bill went back to Mississippi State University but discovered he liked writing better than engineering and transferred to the University of Missouri. A story he wrote at Missouri won notice in the Mahan Short Story competition, but he wanted to work as a newspaperman more than anything else.

In jobs at the *West Point* (Mississippi) *Daily Times Leader* and *The Honolulu Star-Bulletin*, he took on the toughest chores available and considered himself a good craftsman when he accepted Frank Ahlgren's offer to join *The Commercial Appeal*—at a $10 a week reduction in pay. Bill gambled on a greater opportunity on a newspaper he had read since he was six.

For the next decade Bill handled some of the top stories, performing well with the Emmett Till murder in 1955 and other racial stories until Gordon Hanna named him night city editor.

A digger with an ability to be at the right place at the right time, editors often would detach him from editing chores to cover major stories. When Dr. Martin Luther King was shot in 1968, Mike Grehl told him to leave his assistant managing editor's job to others and to concentrate on the assassination. He edited the rewrites the night of the slaying and the next day went to the scene. His word picture of the flophouse where the assassin stayed was moved around the world, and a number of editors took the time to call from as far away as Germany to compliment him.

Bill left Scripps-Howard in 1960 to start his own newspaper in Starkville, Mississippi, but lost a race with a publisher in a nearby city. Frank Ahlgren rescued him by recommending him as managing editor of *The St. Petersburg* (Florida) *Independent*. A year later, Ahlgren called Bill back to Memphis as an assistant managing editor. He became managing editor in 1969, succeeding Grehl who moved to Evansville as editor.

Bill is married to the former Cheryl Murphy. They have a daughter and two sons.

Bill doesn't do much to disabuse the idea that he's just another down-home country boy. He owns a three hundred-acre farm near West Point but he also holds a master's degree in urban history from Memphis State University. Bill also has the rights to a few palm trees on the Caribbean side of the Yucatan Peninsula, where he likes to spend his vacations. In his spare time he plays a little tennis and writes books about sports. In retrospect, Bill figures he should have been a sports editor but considers running the whole shop just as satisfying.

Sunday Courier And Press

THE EDITOR

Judith G. Clabes

JUDY CLABES became editor of the *Sunday Courier and Press* in Evansville on April 1, 1978—April Fool's Day, and she has been known to exclaim that it was an appropriate beginning.

When she moved over from *The Evansville Press*, where she was associate editor, she was told by *The Press* editor to just keep showing up every day unless "the building falls in on the first one."

It didn't.

But five days after she assumed the editorship, Judy was in an auto accident and spent the next six or seven months hobbling around with a broken leg.

Scripps-Howard Daily Newspapers 259

As an editor, she doesn't hobble. Blessed with good news judgment and a drive to succeed, she has improved an already readable and popular *Sunday Courier and Press*.

Judy Clabes speaks softly, but her staff knows where she is coming from—and responds with enthusiasm.

She is a 1967 graduate of the University of Kentucky School of Journalism. While at Lexington, she was associate editor and summer editor of the college newspaper. In her junior year at UK she was married to Gene Clabes, now a columnist for *The Press* who also calls Henderson, Kentucky his home.

Judy spent her first three years after graduation as a public school teacher, trying to drum English, journalism and assorted other subjects into high school students. After time off to have Joey, the first of two boys, she joined the Evansville Printing Corp. as its first Newspaper in the Classroom coordinator. After a year she returned to the classroom, staying there until Mike Grehl, then editor of *The Press*, spelled out the grandeur of a newsroom.

She took on the chores of editorial promotions and helping to edit the editorial page. By 1975, when she took off eight weeks to have Jake, Judy was writing a weekly column, one that attracted national attention. She also owns a Great Dane named Brandy and can tell a bay from a sorrel horse on a farm near Robards, Kentucky.

In 1977 she became associate editor of *The Evansville Press*.

Judy contends she has never burned her bra and always wears one in polite company. And, though she claims to be a feminist, she says she has never marched in a picket line. She admits to being too old for the draft, stands about five-three and says her weight is nobody's business.

She can cuss with the best editors—but seldom does. Judy Clabes handles the English language so well it's no problem.

Daily News Tribune
Fullerton, California

Founded 1891. Purchased by Scripps-Howard December 28, 1973. It began as the weekly *Fullerton Tribune* under publisher Edgar Johnson, who doubled as the city's telegraph operator and justice of the peace. In 1914 it became one of the first California weeklies to go daily, publishing six days. The semi-weekly *News* was acquired in 1926, when the paper's name was changed to its present title.

In 1939 Edgar Elfstrom, one-time secretary to E. W. Scripps, acquired the paper. The paper was in the forefront of the effort to locate a major university in Fullerton, losing the bid to get UCLA in the 1930s, but succeeding in the late 1950s with California State University, Fullerton. The *News Tribune* also led the battle to get Orange County to locate a civic center complex in the city, now the home of the north county municipal court complex.

Editor: ALFRED L. HEWITT. Vice President and Business Manager: MELVIN A. HARKAVY.

THE EDITOR
Alfred L. Hewitt

AL HEWITT doesn't know why Roy Howard fancied the bow tie but Al had a practical reason for making it his trademark. "I started back in the Fifties wearing bow ties," Al says. "I was city editor of *The Shreveport Times*. It was a crowded news room. All any reporter near the door had to tell a visitor looking for the city editor was he's the guy in the bow tie."

For a fellow born in Hartford, Connecticut (April 12, 1921), Al had meandered a fair piece down the road. He got into newspapering because of a chance remark by his seventh-grade English teacher. "You write," she observed, "like O. O. McIntyre (famous syndicated columnist of the day)." That puffed Al up so much he became editor of his high school paper.

Next thing he knew he was enrolled in University of Missouri's School of Journalism. But before he could look at the help wanted ads, the Army grabbed him (actually on the day he got his diploma). Al spent the war years training troops, winning the regimental pingpong title, and emerging as a first lieutenant.

It was time to get cranked up on newspapering, and Al spent a year as co-publisher and co-editor of a small weekly in Trenton, Missouri. By 1947 he'd had his fill of that and moved down to northwest Louisiana and *The Shreveport Times*.

In more ways than one, that was a nifty move. Al showed 'em his stuff and after being city editor was promoted in 1958 to managing editor. He filled that chair eleven years. Perhaps more importantly, he was smitten with one of *The Times'* feature writers, Louise Matthews, and talked her into sharing copypaper (as he puts it) in 1953.

The wanderlust bit again in September 1969. Al spotted a six-line classified ad about a vacancy near the shores of the Pacific. So he signed on as managing editor of the *Daily News Tribune* in northern Orange County, some twenty-five miles south of Los Angeles. Four years later Scripps-Howard bought the paper. In June 1974 Al was named editor.

Al is keenly interested in journalism education. For ten years he was a part-time communications instructor at California State University, Fullerton. He helped start an idea exchange for editors and J-school chairmen. When he retires, Al may spend more time teaching.

He's a shirtsleeves editor. He may pound out an editorial and follow it to the back shop and make up the page if a "printer" isn't handy. Louise got used to him showing up an hour late for dinner with a stack of newspapers to read under his arm. She didn't totally give up her own career; she's a telecourse editor with a community college that teaches by television.

They have two children, Steve born in 1953, a law student, and Holly born in 1955, a graduate social worker.

Al suffered a heart attack in April 1976 but it kept him off the job only a couple of months. To regain his health, he started jogging, two or three miles nearly every day. It gave him the idea for starting the *News Tribune's* ten-kilometer mini-marathon in 1978.

It's been a highly successful event, and guess who has run in it almost every year. In fact, reporters now rarely look up when a fellow in a jogging suit lopes into the news room early Saturday mornings. It's just Al stopping in to check his editorial page proofs.

BUSINESS MANAGER
Melvin A. Harkavy

NEXT TO BEING with his family, Mel Harkavy enjoys selling. In fact, he's been selling since he began pumping gas in high school at his father's service station in suburban Los Angeles.

By California standards, Mel is practically a native of the Golden State. Born in Brooklyn, New York, January 19, 1939, he came west with his parents when he was three and grew up in the small town of Tujunga in the foothills of the San Gabriel Mountains above Los Angeles.

Even while he was attending Los Angeles City College and Cal State Los Angeles, where he majored in advertising and sales, he was selling. He smiles as he recalls selling textiles out of a suitcase in Los Angeles' garment district.

He didn't set any sales records, he admits, but it was good experience for a future career as an advertising salesman. Besides, he says, it was fun watching the models.

Mel first entered the advertising field in 1961 as a sales representative for Pacific Telephone Co. where his feet did the walking, hunting ads for the yellow pages. Two years later he was selling ads for newspapers and joined the Southern California Publishing Co., a group of five community weekly newspapers in southeastern Los Angeles.

His sales experience served him well and he rose quickly through the retail and classified advertising departments. Within nine years, in 1971, he was advertising director. He was named general manager after Scripps-Howard acquired the company in 1978.

Six months later in April 1979, he was named vice president and business manager of the Fullerton Daily News Tribune. In addition, Mel oversees the operation of Southern California Publishing Co. and another Los Angeles weekly newspaper group in the Scripps-Howard family, the San Gabriel Valley Publishing Co.

He has been very visible in newspaper advertising circles, serving leadership roles in both advertising executive and publisher groups. He is a past president of the Southern California unit of the California Newspaper Publishers Association.

Responsibility for the three Scripps-Howard properties keeps Mel busy but he unabashedly admits he never neglects his family. Mel met Lynne M. Horwitz when they were students at L. A. City College. He recalls with a smile that she asked him for their first date—at a college Sadie Hawkins dance. But Mel took the lead after that and they were married at the semester break in December 1958.

With their three children, Danny born 1964, Sheryl born in 1967, and Greg born in 1968, he and Lynne treasure their weekends at home or in their motorhome exploring the mountains, beaches or deserts of California.

What success Mel has experienced in his profession and in life in general he attributes to concern for others and to a "people-oriented" business philosophy. He has a way of motivating employees and associates that works.

Hollywood Sun-Tattler
Hollywood, Florida

Founded in 1935 as the weekly *Hollywood Sun* and combined in 1942 with the *South Broward Tattler,* also a weekly. In 1951 it became a semi-weekly and in 1957 began publishing thrice weekly. In March 1959, it became a five-day, and in 1963 a six-day evening paper. Acquired by Scripps-Howard June 4, 1965. It now is the third largest p.m. daily in the state of Florida.

Early on, the newspaper was instrumental in obtaining a major hospital (Memorial) for the South Broward County area and helped knock out illegal casino gambling. More recently the newspaper revealed the existence of more than a dozen top Mafia figures living in Hollywood and surrounding communities, and exposed unscrupulous dance studio operations. Community service and extensive local coverage are the newspaper's hallmarks. In the words of the late G. W. (Bill) McCall, publisher of the Sun-Tattler for thirty five years: "If a youngster in South Broward drops a concrete block on his toe, he should be able to read about it in the Sun-Tattler." That degree of local depth no longer is possible, but it comes close.

President and Editor: EDWARD H. WENTWORTH. Business Manager: ARTHUR SEGALL Sr.

THE EDITOR

Edward H. Wentworth

ED BEGAN his career at the *Sun-Tattler* on the bottom rung, as carrier boy. This turned out to be steady work; by the time he was twenty eight in December 1966, he was editor. He was the youngest in Scripps-Howard at that time, by some eighteen years.

Getting to the top rung, Ed went from carrier to handyman in the circulation department, to university correspondent, to reporter, wire editor, city editor, and managing editor — with four years out for military service.

He attended Georgia Military College in Milledgeville (two years of high school and two years of junior college, graduating in 1959), being twice cited as distinguished military student of the year. He then entered the University of Florida where he worked afternoons in the college news bureau and evenings as a bartender. He kept the franchise as a *Sun-Tattler* staff member by sending the paper correspondence and won a first place award as outstanding correspondent for a Florida newspaper.

Graduated first in his class from the University's school of journalism and communications, he returned to Hollywood as a reporter until August, 1961, when he was called into the Army and commissioned a second lieutenant. He was shipped to Germany and became the youngest company commander in his division. Still as second lieutenant, he had charge of a combat support company, a job usually assigned to a major or senior captain.

Promoted to first lieutenant, he commanded the Davy Crockett platoon, at the time the only atomic-oriented ground unit in the Army at the troop level. This required the highest security rating possible, then called "cosmic clearance."

He got back to journalism as editor-in-chief of the Eighth Infantry Division's *Arrow*, a weekly English-language newspaper with 17,000 circulation. It was cited as the outstanding service newspaper in Europe two straight years, in competition with more than 250 publications.

Ed, born in East Orange, New Jersey, November 11, 1938, moved to Hollywood with his family when he was three. He is married to the former Elizabeth Ann Starcher of Hollywood. (His wife is the director of performing arts for the city of Hollywood.) They have two sons: Edward III, born (in Germany) in 1962, and Slade, born (in Hollywood) in 1968.

In 1967 Ed was cited as the outstanding young man in the community by the Greater Hollywood Junior Chamber of Commerce. He is an honorary trustee of Broward Community College and a director of the Greater Hollywood Chamber of Commerce.

Under his leadership the *Sun-Tattler* has undergone major changes in content and format, such as addition of a weekly entertainment section (Spotlighter), a weekly section devoted to the horse-and-saddle and upper-middle class western area (*Sun-Tattler West*). The women's section was converted into "Contemporary Living" and the sports pages and real estate section greatly expanded. Use of full color is common now—and necessary in light of the heavy competition from large newspapers to the north and south of Hollywood. But the strength of the paper remains in its heavy local coverage of the eight cities and surrounding unincorporated areas it serves.

When not concentrating on improving the product, Ed likes to fly airplanes, a hobby developed after a rather rough ride across Florida: "Hell, I can do better than that." (Ed III, who entered the United States Military Academy at West Point in 1980, also flies and soloed at age sixteen.) Other interests include skeet and trap ("although I'm not very good at it") and fishing ("damn good at that"). But mainly he enjoys just being with his family: "That's where it's at."

BUSINESS MANAGER
Arthur Segall Sr.

IN SEPTEMBER 1945 Art Segall had just registered at Northeastern University (Boston). His major area of study was journalism. A few minutes later he entered the office of the college paper. Instead of meeting the editor, he was greeted by the business manager who immediately asked if he would like to sell ads. Six months later he was named advertising manager, a position he held for three and a half years.

Art first got the idea he'd like to become a writer while attending English high school in Boston, where he was born April 21, 1928. He doubled as college correspondent for *The Boston Post* and received a degree in journalism, but somehow his urge to write waned and his urge to make things happen in a business way grew.

Following graduation in 1949, Art went to New York and accepted a job merchandising Chesterfield cigarettes on college campuses. (He was a Chesterfield representative for three years while an undergraduate, and his efforts prompted an offer after graduation.)

In 1952 he met a gal from Columbus, Ohio who was working as a dental hygienist in New York. In June of 1953 they were married, shortly after Art started (in March) on the retail staff of *The Columbus Citizen*.

The team, as they liked to call themselves, of Greta and Art produced three children. James (born 1956), Sharon (1958), and Arthur Jr. born in Washington in 1964 after the family had moved on to *The Washington Daily News*. Greta died in 1977.

It was in Washington where the retail ad salesman was provided opportunity under the demanding and guiding hands of Ray Mack and Bob Hartmann. First it was outside classified manager (48 consecutive months of gains), retail manager, national manager, and finally advertising director. He was also elected president of the Washington Advertising Club.

Memphis was the next Scripps-Howard stop for Art. As general advertising manager he was able to apply his competitive background to the Memphis Publishing Company from 1975 to 1980.

In all assignments the idea of a challenge keeps him hopping. He considers himself tough but fair, and never asks anyone to undertake something he hasn't done and/or can't do himself. In fact, he still enjoys selling ads and gets a big thrill from making a sale today as he did when he signed his first contract in Columbus. He's an early riser and has been known to open his office door at 7 a.m.

Columbus not only gave him his start with Scripps-Howard, but also made him an Ohio State fan. On any given Saturday during the fall he listens carefully to the scores to find out by how much the scarlet and grey has won. One wouldn't call him an Ohio State fanatic except he named his dog Buckeye. He also has been known to offer as much as 50 points on a particular game—and win. Among casualties of this bizarre type of wagering is Hartmann, who hasn't fully recovered from what he thought was a sure thing on at least one occasion.

In March 1980 Art came to Hollywood as business manager, to accept another challenge, another assignment and a new life. A part of this new life was Art's marriage to Patricia (Pat) Jones on September 25, 1980. In the interim, the children have also grown and developed. James will receive his law degree from Washington & Lee University Law School in May 1981. Sharon received her bachelor of science in marketing from the University of Tennessee in June 1980 and is now in graduate school at UT. Arthur Jr., is a junior in high school.

A picture of Ohio Stadium that hung in his office in Memphis is now at the *Sun-Tattler*. It's even possible that on any given Saturday afternoon in the fall some "lucky" people might be given 50 points and Ohio State's opponent.

The Knoxville News-Sentinel
Knoxville, Tennessee

Founded as The Knoxville News by Robert P. Scripps and Roy W. Howard November 22, 1921. Ed Meeman was first editor. Purchased The Knoxville Sentinel November 22, 1926, and consolidated the two as The News-Sentinel.

Took leading role in establishing Great Smokies National Park, in modernizing the State Constitution, in abolishing the justice of peace system, in getting statewide compulsory voting registration, in eliminating color bar in schools, recreation and public accommodation places, and was leading influence in getting strong shield and open meetings law passed.

Editor: RALPH L. MILLETT JR. Business Manager: ROGER A. DALEY.

THE EDITOR
Ralph L. Millett Jr.

Not SINCE THE TIME when boys started leaving the family farm have many people wound up in the place where one would expect to find them half a century later. But Ralph did.

In the late Twenties, Ralph was a blond tyke old enough (he was born in Memphis October 30, 1919) to romp into *The Memphis Press-Scimitar* office to wait for his father. After Ralph Sr., the associate editor, finished his work for the day the two would go to a ball game or something.

Ralph knew *The Press-Scimitar* like most boys know their back yards. Without conscious effort, he learned a lot about what makes a newspaper tick. He looked like a youngster who would grow up to be a newspaperman. Maybe an editor.

Things usually don't work out long range as expected, but Ralph kept generally doing the expected. He got pretty far from home base by going in 1938 to the University of Wyoming. Why? "It was high, dry, and cheap," says Ralph. "Actually I had a sinus problem."

After a couple of years out West he moved to the University of Missouri. He was, of course, working for a journalism degree. Between his junior and senior years he worked as a reporter on *The Press-Scimitar*.

When he got his degree in 1942, World War II messed up the script. Ralph had to go help out in the Pacific. He entered the Navy as a seaman, came out lieutenant, senior grade. He was in the Marshall and Palau Island campaigns, also was an instructor in the fleet radar center at Pearl Harbor. The war won, he went back to the script—graduate school and a teaching assistantship at Missouri.

Came 1947 and a time for decision. Ralph could (1) become a full-fledged university faculty member or (2) get a newspaper job. He agonized over his options. Ralph was disenchanted with Missouri's J-school philosophies. He sought *Memphis Press-Scimitar* editor Ed Meeman's counsel. "Mr. Meeman told me," Ralph recalls, "to go to Knoxville, that there was opportunity there."

Ralph took Meeman's advice. He landed a spot on the *News-Sentinel* copy desk. Six months later he moved into the slot, and in August 1948 became news editor. When Editor Loye Miller retired Ralph was named to succeed him, as of January 1, 1967.

Ralph is stocky, square-shouldered, and looks taller than his almost six-foot height. His size thirteen shoes are the biggest in the house. He's read avidly all his life and has a retentive memory that has earned him the title of "walking encyclopedia." On his list of favored literature are the dictionary, encyclopedia and World Almanac. His wife, the former Mary Virginia Smith (they were married in 1944), says he even reads while brushing his teeth.

He has strong views about the public's right to know. As chairman of the Freedom of Information committee of the Tennessee Press Association he led the drive that produced a shield law and an open meetings law. Both have been called the strongest in the country.

The Milletts have three daughters and one son, Mary Jo born in 1943, Alice Virginia born in 1948, Jan Vasco born in 1952 and Ralph Linwood III born in 1956. Ralph's hobbies center around the home—doing handyman chores, gardening, cooking. He's no dunce in whipping up a menu or a thrifty grocery list. He fancies himself as a soup chef, and often his pot holds enough to last the family for a week. He barbecues pretty good, too.

Ralph has served as chairman of the Knoxville Parking Authority. He has been a director of the Chamber of Commerce, Knoxville Tourist Bureau and the Tennessee Press Association.

He's gentle enough to like to hunt wild flowers; but at a poker table (as his fellow editors have learned in their annual confabs) he's ferocious.

BUSINESS MANAGER
Roger A. Daley

ROGER WAS BORN (December 23, 1922) and raised in the Quincy, Massachusetts area, and although he was a carrier boy at an early age, he delivered milk for the last four years he was in school. This nocturnal pursuit didn't keep him from an active sports life, particularly football and quarry diving.

His 1941 scheduled trip to Pearl Harbor as a machinist apprentice was interrupted when the Japanese got there first. So, he enlisted in the Marines, which was, at that time, the hard way to get to Hawaii.

While serving on the Marine base at Cherry Point, North Carolina, he met and married Becky (Elizabeth Beck) from New York who was a Link simulated flight training instructor. Becky had been a receptionist for J. Walter Thompson Advertising Agency in New York City. This agency handled the Marine recruiting campaign and it obviously made a big impression on her.

When Roger came home from the war he went to work for a New York department store. Becky went back to Thompson. Through her contacts, Roger got together with Frank Powers when the latter came up to Scripps-Howard headquarters. Frank had just been made advertising manager in Knoxville, and needed a good hand. He thought Roger was a bright find, and offered a job. Roger said yes, sir.

A year after going to Knoxville as a national ad salesman he was named national advertising manager. Ten years later he became advertising manager when Frank Powers was promoted to business manager. In another ten years, Roger again followed in Frank's footsteps when Powers went to New York to be Mark Ferree's right-hand man. Later Roger was also named president of The News Sentinel Co.

During these years The News-Sentinel Co. became agent for *The Knoxville Journal.* Adding of more presses (twice) and enlargement of the building (three times) plus the changeover to new processes and computers, has made The News-Sentinel Co. one of Tennessee's most progressive publishers.

If it's happening in Knoxville, Roger is probably there. He headed the Downtown Knoxville Association for four terms. He helped trigger a proposed international exposition (52 countries) officially designated "World's Fair 1982".

He was an officer of the Greater Knoxville Chamber of Commerce, and Tourist Bureau. He also was a prime mover in building a three-block downtown mall with a Hilton Hotel for the Fair, and working on a new State office building, a Federal building, plus a 20,000 seat arena. Perhaps that's why a survey by an Atlanta firm identified him as one of the area's top twenty "Prime Movers."

Roger is past president of both the Greater Knoxville Advertising Club (a recipient of the AFA Silver Medal Award) and the Sales-Marketing Executives Club of Knoxville, and is active in social and civic club work (Civitan - Cherokee Country Club). He was on the board of the Southern Newspaper Publishers Association, and chaired the personnel-labor relations committee several years.

The Daleys turned out to be an all-Marine family. They have one son, William A. (called Mac), born in 1947, who also enlisted in the Marines and was on the *Forrestal* when the aircraft carrier blew up and burned in the Vietnam action. A few years after his discharge Mac became The News-Sentinel Co. purchasing manager.

Roger and Becky have a beautiful home on a private peninsula on the Tennessee River with a boat dock. Roger is past commodore of the one hundred and fifty-boat Fort Loudoun Yacht Club. He is active in arranging multi-boat cruises, has helped friends sail their large boats between Knoxville and Florida.

It isn't hard for the Daleys to get to the University of Tennessee home football games. The stadium is on the banks of the river, twenty miles from their dock. They just hop aboard their boat and chug up.

Memphis Press-Scimitar
(Memphis Publishing Company)
Memphis, Tennessee

This newspaper dates back to 1880 when *The Scimitar* was founded. *The News* was founded in 1902 and in 1904 was consolidated with *The Scimitar* as *The News-Scimitar*. Scripps-Howard founded *The Press* in 1906. In 1926 *The Press* acquired *The News-Scimitar* and consolidated the two papers into the *Memphis Press-Scimitar*.

The *Press-Scimitar* fought for TVA; brought about establishment of the Shelby Forest State Park; led in the movement for democracy in local government; sparked permanent registration, repeal of the poll tax as voting requirement, and use of voting machines. Campaigned to maintain racial peace in Memphis and for stronger coordination of the state's institutions of higher learning.

In recent years the *Press-Scimitar* has been in the forefront of successful freedom-of-information battles to open up public records and enact a strong Sunshine Law in Tennessee. It initiated and fought for passage of a law that opened to press and public hitherto secret negotiations between local government and public employee unions. And it helped win passage of a "definition of death" bill that has become a model for other state legislatures.

Editor: MILTON R. BRITTEN.

THE EDITOR
Milton R. Britten

BRITT, LIKE HIS immediate predecessor, is a circuit rider who came full circle.

Charles H. Schneider came to the *Press-Scimitar* as an office boy in 1928 and retired as editor in 1976; Britt joined up as a green-as-grass cub reporter in 1949.

He had just been graduated from Yale with honors in English and a Phi Beta Kappa key, but the summer of 1949 was a lean one for newspaper jobs. Britt touched all bases. When he saw Jack Lockhart, then Scripps-Howard assistant general editorial manager in New York, Jack sent out a bulletin to all points saying, in effect: Britten might do—but it's your nickel.

The late Ed Meeman, then editor, figured Britt could cut it. Sight unseen he offered a six-month try-out, at $45 a week. Britt buckety-bucketed south on the Tennessean (a passenger train of fond memory) and got educated into the newspaper business.

Null Adams, an exemplar of the cigar-chomping, no-holds-barred breed of city editor, worked Britt into some semblance of shape as a reporter. After six months he was not only still on board but convinced that newspapering would be his life's work.

He began on general assignment, reviewed films and concerts, covered the social services and medical beats, reported from city hall and the federal building, worked as a rewrite man and, eventually, filled in as assistant city editor or city editor in a pinch. He also learned how to read hot-metal type upside down.

He learned a good deal, too, about political realities, for during this period E. H. (Boss) Crump was in charge. The *Press-Scimitar* fought him vigorously every step of the way and eventually loosened his grip on the state, although Crump remained in charge of Memphis until his death in 1954.

For a couple of those early years, however, Britt, born December 17, 1924, in Wilkes-Barre, Pennsylvania, remained just a displaced Yankee. He overcame that handicap in 1951 when he married the former Virginia Butler of Meridian, Mississippi, and learned to eat grits and okra like a man. The first of their four children, Ann, was born in Memphis in 1955.

The others were born in Washington, D. C.—Jonathan in 1957, Martha in 1963, and Anthony in 1965.

In 1956 Meeman and then-editor Loye Miller of the *Knoxville News-Sentinel* sent him to Washington as their regional correspondent. He'd barely found his way around the capital when he was sent to his first national political convention. The Democrats were meeting in Chicago. And three Tennesseans wanted to be the next President of the United States—Senators Estes Kefauver and Albert Gore and Governor Frank Clement, the convention keynote speaker. They were all at different hotels. It was hotter than the hinges. Days ran into nights and vice versa. And Britt—who spent three relatively congenial years in the Army during World War II—decided WW II was a piece of cake compared to covering that kind of scene.

But it was twenty years—and a bunch of conventions later—before he got the opportunity to return to Memphis. In 1963 he was named night editor of the Washington bureau. He was subsequently named assistant managing editor and then managing editor. It was on December 17, 1975, his fifty first birthday, that he got a call from Gordon Hanna offering him the chance to "go home." Britt thought long and hard for a fraction of a second and said, "Hell, yes!"

He is an editor who feels newspapers have a special obligation to tell the truth, to cherish the English language and use it with respect, force and imagination.

The paper's biggest single accomplishment since he became editor was to challenge—and eventually abolish—the practice of excluding press and public from contract negotiations between agents of the city-county governments and public employee unions.

After the costly 1978 strike by Memphis firemen, police and teachers, the *Press-Scimitar* sued for admission to the talks. The courts, all the way up to the state supreme court, ruled that the Tennessee Sunshine Law was inapplicable to labor negotiations. But that didn't stop Britt. He encouraged a state senator to introduce a bill to open up negotiations. The paper campaigned for it with strong editorials. Result: the bill passed and the governor signed it into law.

The Commercial Appeal
(Memphis Publishing Company)
Memphis, Tennessee

In 1840 when his candidate for president (Van Buren) lost to William H. Harrison, the editor of the *Memphis Advocate & Western District Intelligencer* was so upset he changed the name of his paper to the *Memphis Appeal*. As he explained, "to appeal to the sober, second thoughts" of the readers.

Two decades later *The Memphis Appeal*, on the side of the South, was forced into a hazardous three-year flight (1862-65) from Memphis, publishing on a hand press in Mississippi, Alabama and Georgia, riding flat cars and flat boats, leaving Atlanta just before Sherman rode in.

The Appeal continued publishing, even when in 1878 yellow fever swept Memphis killing thousands and bankrupting the city, and reducing its staff to only two.

The Commercial Appeal later became a regional newspaper for Mississippi, Arkansas and Tennessee and won the Pulitzer Prize in 1923 for its fight against the Ku Klux Klan. *The Commercial Appeal*'s strong regional approach is felt in two states where prison systems were overhauled after the public was told of mistreatment. A penetrating examination of the death of a young girl resulted in firmer child-abuse legislation. The paper campaigned for a riverfront rebuilding that created condominiums and smart restaurants out of falling-down warehouses.

Its "Plant to Prosper" contest for Mid-South farmers, landowners and sharecroppers encouraged better use of the soil. It led an effective battle for lower Mississippi Valley flood control; it helped improve the Port of Memphis to give the area's industry and agriculture quicker and cheaper transportation. Education was upgraded because it pushed for higher teacher pay. Fee-grabbing magistrates and quack doctors have been put out of business because of exposure.

It continues to maintain its independence from all pressures so that it can serve its readers with news and opinion based on merit not regional, political, social or economic doctrine.

Scripps-Howard purchased *The Commercial Appeal* in 1936. It and the *Press-Scimitar* operate as independent units editorially. Business offices were consolidated in 1939, and both papers are published by The Memphis Publishing Co.

Editor: MICHAEL T. GREHL.

THE EDITOR

Michael T. Grehl

"IT NEVER OCCURRED to me any time in my life," says Mike Grehl, "to be anything other than a newspaperman." Is that because he was born (December 6, 1928) in Evanston, Illinois in the shadow of Chicago's gaudy Front Page setting? "I don't understand it. Maybe, as you say, it was the hustle and bustle of Front Page City. I wish I could explain it. I don't know where it came from."

Though subsequent events that have made him virtually a legend in a number of newsrooms confirm the validity of his boyhood resolve, Mike did not plunge in head-first. He made two or three abortive false starts in other directions.

After attending public schools in Chicago and New York City, Mike entered postwar military service with the Army in Japan. When the Army discovered he didn't know how to drive, it made him an auto mechanic.

Back in Chicago, he entered a seminary, which is as close as he ever came to the Lutheran ministry. He then spent a year making lenses, which may account for his microscopic eye for style errors and grammatical transgressions.

Still dreaming of a newspaper career, Mike entered the University of Illinois and earned his degree in 1952. On the day after his last exam, he arrived in his element: He was hired as managing editor of the *Morris* (Illinois) *Daily Herald*. Four months later he moved to Carbondale, Illinois as a photographer on the staff of *The Southern Illinoisian*. Within two years he had become managing editor. A new frontier beckoned in a short time.

The frontier in those days meant Alaska, and Mike landed there in 1956 as a police reporter for *The Anchorage Times*. In Alaska he produced (1) a red beard and (2) a story about a soldier whose weekly package of Animal Crackers from his mother was laced with marijuana.

By 1957, Mike was looking for a warmer place and found one in Memphis. In May 1957 he became a reporter for *The Commercial Appeal* and was taken off the obit desk in record time after writing a creditable symphony review when there was no one else to send to the concert.

The year 1957 marked more than one milestone for Mike. In September, four months after he joined *The Commercial Appeal*, he was married to the former Audrey Ann Ewert. The marriage prospered in spite of having been performed on Friday the 13th.

Less than two years later he became night city editor, then assistant city editor, then assistant managing editor. Four years after his first obit for *The Commercial Appeal*, he was named managing editor.

On January 1, 1969, Mike became editor of *The Evansville Press*, succeeding Gordon Hanna, who had been appointed editor of *The Commercial Appeal*. For nearly seven years under Mike's guidance, *The Press* outscored all other newspapers in Indiana in gleaning Hoosier Press Association prizes for journalistic excellence. Many of those awards were for editorials and columns written by the editor—who persistently demanded the head of any deskman who played the boss's achievements above those of the staff as a whole.

In Indiana, Mike flushed political "two-per-cent clubs" into the open, attacking as "institutionalized extortion" the practice whereby political appointees had to kick back two per cent of their salaries to party bosses. A federal investigation resulted. He battled for the removal of railroad tracks that ran down the middle of one of Evansville's busiest thoroughfares. He ripped into political rakeoffs from license plate fees. And *The Evansville Press* was an early advocate of a new Ohio River port at Mount Vernon, Indiana.

Just as the port and *The Press* flourished in the seventies, so—again—did Mike's whiskers. (He had shaved his red, Alaska-cultivated beard before reporting to *The Commercial*

Appeal because he didn't know how Frank R. Ahlgren, then editor, would take to whiskers.) Now salt-and-pepper instead of red, the beard emerged anew in Evansville and today may be the most widely recognized facial growth in Dixie since Robert E. Lee's.

When Hanna became general editorial manager of Scripps-Howard Newspapers at the end of 1975, Grehl returned to Memphis, this time as editor of *The Commercial Appeal*.

He hadn't been in town long before the people knew it. He took on one of Memphis's oldest, richest and most powerful families and exposed their real estate practices, which reached into government. He took on one of the county's most well-entrenched politicians and when Mike got through with him he decided to go into the vehicle leasing business rather than run for re-election. He takes on the establishment, white, blacks—anybody he feels is acting against the best interests of the city, county, state, nation or world.

As he told a group of young people a few years ago, it will be nothing to conquer space if we "fail to conquer fear, greed, corruption, ignorance and prejudice at home." Mike is five seven and has pared his fighting weight from 185 to 144 pounds. He doesn't play golf or truly understand people who do. And although he and Audrey live in a lakeside home in Cordova, Tennessee, he doesn't fish, either. He gardens but claims his thumb is several shades shy of green, and he is a former professional photographer turned amateur. The walls of his home hang heavy with blown-up photographs from his travels.

He also is captivated by World War I aircraft, an odd fascination for a white-knuckle flyer who'd rather read about Sopwith Camels than ride in Whisper Jets.

What Mike Grehl really is is what he set out to be: a newspaperman—a working newspaperman more likely to be found near the center of action in *The Commercial Appeal* newsroom than in his office. Observed another Scripps-Howard editor who once served under him: "Despite all of the humor he cannot avoid, despite the idiosyncracies and all the rest, I've never worked with a man who was a more professional, talented, perceptive newspaperman."

Memphis Publishing Co.
Memphis, Tennessee

This company was created in 1939 to combine the business and production operations of two newspapers serving Memphis and the Mid-South—*The Commercial Appeal*, which Scripps-Howard acquired in 1936, and the already-owned *Press-Scimitar*. In 1940 the *Press-Scimitar* moved into the building which had housed *The Commercial Appeal* since 1933, a former Ford assembly plant.

Though the newspapers are published by the same company in a single plant, editorial staffs remain totally separate and competitive.

In the late 1970s Memphis Publishing Company erected a new office building and an offset printing plant at a cost of nearly $30 million on its enlarged downtown site. It is one of the most modern newspaper facilities in the United States, with an Atex editorial system, a Raycomp ad composition system, Atex classified advertising system, and one-of-a-kind computerized circulation system.

Business Manager: JOSEPH R. WILLIAMS.

BUSINESS MANAGER
Joseph R. Williams III

ON HIS WAY UP the mountain, Joe Williams has pursued many paths. Before accepting the wisdom of his grandfather and his father and following them into the newspaper business, Joe had variously been: a water skiing instructor ("the best job I ever had"), an air-cooling equipment salesman, a construction boss, an airline passenger agent, half-owner of a less-than-successful roofing firm ("we went broke") and collector for a bad-debt agency ("the worst job I ever had"). Between jobs he found time for a three-year stint in the Navy, a hitch which was memorable if not exactly distinguished.

The youthful experience with the roofing company convinced Joe to set his feet in the path of his forebears, who had published newspapers in Murfreesboro, Tennessee, Lawrenceberg, Indiana and Alexandria, Louisiana. In 1956 Joe went to work with his father, directing advertising, promotions and circulation programs for small newspapers throughout the Southeast.

He had found his field. In 1958 he became the Tennessee Press Association's first sales manager, then advertising director for *All-Florida Magazine.*

His association with Scripps-Howard began in 1961 when he joined the advertising sales staff of *The Knoxville News-Sentinel.* In ten years there he rose to general advertising manager, then advertising director. In 1971, when he was forty, he became Scripps-Howard's youngest business manager, at *The Cincinnati Post.* Four years later he was appointed business manager of Memphis Publishing Company, which produces *The Commercial Appeal* and the *Memphis Press-Scimitar.*

Joe was born (May 15, 1931) in Detroit, but is quick to point out he's "trying to live that down. My family is from the Southeast, Kentucky and Tennessee originally. They just happened to be out of pocket when I was born."

He married the former Joan Baumann of Atlanta in 1956, and they have two children, Cathy born in 1958 and Joseph IV born in 1964. The family's address—8354 Countrywood Fairway—is revealing, for Joe is an excellent golfer and it's not by chance that his home adjoins Colonial Country Club's fairways. The home was chosen, Joe explains with a characteristic grin, "so that my family could enjoy all of the facilities of a family club." One of those "facilities" is the championship course on which is played the Danny Thomas Memphis Classic. Joe goes around it with a seven handicap, but is quick to point out that when he came to Memphis the handicap was five.

He is a burly six-footer who dodges the issue of weight. "Husky," he says, "is precise enough." That "husky" frame stood him in good stead when he played quarterback on high school football teams in South Dakota and in Miami. He was skilled enough to attract several college football scholarship offers, one of them a serious look from the University of Kentucky. Says Joe, in explaining why he eventually wound up playing for Rollins College: "Bear Bryant was coaching at Kentucky then, and he had another guy he decided he'd rather have at quarterback." That other guy was Babe Parilli.

Joe had been at Rollins on a football scholarship for two years when the college dropped football. With the Korean War going on, he joined the Navy. It gave him his first real taste of Memphis, by assigning him to aviation machinists' school at the Memphis Naval Air Station. He had been in the Navy a few months when he was offered an appointment to Annapolis, and says he can't imagine why he told the admiral no thanks.

But he did apply for and win a NROTC scholarship, which took him to the University of Texas and later to the misadventure which was the highlight of his Navy career. Joe remembers:

"I fell out of the first Navy airplane I was ever in." Fortunately, it was an amphibious plane and it was taxiing across Corpus Christi Bay. "The captain told me to throw out the port sea anchor. I threw it out and tumbled right out behind it, radio earphones and all. It took them quite a while to fish me out of the bay. The captain just looked at me and shook his head. Next day I was transferred to another plane."

When the war ended, Lieutenant Williams resigned his commission and returned to college, earning his degree from the University of Miami. There he took up water skiing and became so good at it he was soon instructing others, including show business stars. His pupils included Ava Gardner, Arthur Godfrey, the singing McGuire sisters, "and a whole string of June Taylor dancers. It was the best job I ever had. The pay wasn't so hot, but the women were pretty."

Joe brought to the newspaper business the same restless energy which drove him to excel in sports. His business philosophy is simple: "Find the best people, and let them see how good they can be. All we really have is people. These new machines are magic, but they won't get the newspapers out by themselves."

He also believes in "paying your civic rent"—and he lives in the high rent district. In one year, he was on the boards of no less than twelve community organizations. It takes another page to list his professional affiliations.

The Pittsburgh Press
Pittsburgh, Pennsylvania

Founded 1884. Purchased by Scripps-Howard July 27, 1923. On November 13, 1961, a joint operating agreement was implemented under which *The Press* serves as advertising, distribution and printing agent for the morning *Post-Gazette*, which has its own editorial staff and is owned by the Block brothers.

The Press pioneered old-age pensions and mothers' assistance grants in Pennsylvania; helped upgrade coal-mine safety by exposing danger of silicosis; led campaigns for flood control and smoke control, which paved the way for Pittsburgh's Renaissance, a model of urban redevelopment; virtually wrote the Pennsylvania strip-mining law, regarded by many as a national model; championed milk pasteurization and water fluoridation; promoted conservation and recreation; campaigned for a municipal sports stadium, a civic arena, a convention center and exhibit hall.

Annually sponsors one of the most successful fund-raisers for charity in the communications industry, netting as much as $2.3 million in a single year to help defray bills of needy patients at Children's Hospital.

Editor: JOHN TROAN. Business Manager: ROBERT J. O'CONNELL.

THE EDITOR

John Troan

IT'S A CINCH BET that no other editor started his Scripps-Howard career having his name chopped in half. It happened in Pittsburgh in 1939. The legendary city editor of *The Press* was a feisty Irishman named Larry Fagan. He would take calls from beat reporters, listen to the gist of the news, then switch the call to rewrite by shouting to the switchboard operator: "Faust to Sample" or "Trosene to Anderson" or "Klein to Troanovitch."

Not long out of Penn State, John was on rewrite one day when he noticed Fagan in spirited conversation on the phone, heard him exclaim something like "Troanovitch", and slam down the receiver.

John, ready to take notes, grabbed up his phone. Nobody was on. Then it dawned on him; what Fagan had shouted was sonuvabitch, not John's real handle, Troanovitch. (His parents were immigrants from Austria-Hungary, now part of Czechoslovakia.) Fagan promptly proposed bob-tailing Troan's name. John didn't object. He had the shorter version legalized, and subsequently named his first son after Fagan.

Born August 23, 1918, John grew up in a hard coal "patch" near Scranton where his father was a miner until his death in 1933. John was then a high school sophomore, but his thrifty parents had saved enough for him to start college. John did the rest, working fifty-four-hour weeks summers on *The Scranton Tribune*, stringing on sports during the school year, and also getting paid as secretary for a semi-pro baseball league.

Years later in a Bicentennial column, John wrote: "Where else but in America could the son of an illiterate mother and immigrant coal-miner who could speak only broken English get the chance, in the brief span of half a lifetime, to become editor of one of the biggest papers in the land?"

To Troan newspapering has represented a "lifetime passport to adventure"—not even interrupted by World War II when he served as an enlisted Navy combat correspondent with the Pacific fleet. Shortly after the war he began to specialize in medical and science reporting. (The atom bomb had piqued his interest in this field.) He became a close friend of a young University of Pittsburgh scientist named Jonas Salk. Thus he was able to follow the step-by-step development of the world's first successful polio vaccine, writing numerous exclusives along the way.

In 1958 after the Soviets launched two satellites into space, John was summoned to Washington to become science writer for the Scripps-Howard bureau. For the next eight years he had a grandstand seat for some of the most exciting developments in medicine, science and technology.

He was on hand for the launch of the first U.S. satellite, the first weather satellite, the first communication satellite, and most of America's manned space flights. His scoops included licensing of the first birth-control pill, development of measles vaccine, and the first drug capable of curing a virus disease. His most *exclusive* exclusive involved the famous Surgeon General's report on smoking.

An elite committee of scientists prepared the report. The U.S. Public Health Service was fighting to prevent any leaks before a Saturday morning release. Troan went after it anyhow. The Government Printing Office was handling it like a top-secret treaty. The committee was sworn not to talk to reporters. Troan had an idea; he knew how scientists gossip with their peers. He called his friends in science all over the country. In three cities he found some researchers who'd been told parts of what the report contained. John pieced these together—and had a scoop that no one else could confirm for 72 hours. When he went to the Saturday briefing, a Public Health official joked, "Maybe Troan should give this briefing; he's already told everyone what's in it."

John returned to *The Pittsburgh Press* in 1966 as associate editor and became editor the following year. Thus he's winding up his "adventure" right where it started. And where he found his bride, the former Varcey Morrissey, whom he married in 1943 before sailing off to war while she was executive secretary to Press Editor E. T. Leech. (It was Leech who had hired John on the basis of his performance as the youngest student editor in Penn State history.)

The Troans have two sons and two daughters, Lawrence born in 1947, Judy born in 1950, Mary Lou born in 1954, and Geoffrey born in 1959. John likes to claim he started his career as "a publisher." He means that in high school he banged out on an ancient Underwood a weekly single-copy newsletter of eight pages which he passed hand to hand. That was quite a chore but even then he could type fifty words a minute with the two-finger system he still uses.

BUSINESS MANAGER
Robert J. O'Connell

"**I** HAD A POWERFUL arm, but I couldn't tell where the heck the ball was going." Bob O'Connell still shakes his head remembering his tryout with the New York Yankees.

Bob was eighteen. He had been a pitching ace since his freshman year in high school. A scout grabbed him off a Legion team.

"One trouble, I wasn't sure I wanted to be in pro baseball. I just didn't have that great desire. I'd have started in Class D. I didn't look forward to the kind of money they were paying, or the trips, or the way you had to live."

Bob's tryout was a bust. He can't remember now the name of the town in Florida where the Yankees had their spring training camp.

He was more intrigued—without really understanding why—with newspaper advertising. Bob was born in Pittsburgh October 2, 1929 and started delivering *The Press* while in high school. He threw 85 papers daily and over 100 on Sunday.

"I used to talk to the route man about how they got those ads and so forth. Then I became enamored of the whole thing."

WHEN HE STARTED attending Duquesne University in 1947 Bob heard *The Press* hired part-time workers in circulation on Friday and Saturday nights. He got a job, making $8 or $9 a weekend.

That led to a job on the circulation register desk in 1948. For $32.50 a week, he spent his days taking starts and stops, filling out trip tickets, and so forth.

A long-time associate recalls the day one of the excursion boats which travels the three rivers around Pittsburgh caught fire. "Bob and the other guy on the desk took off to see the fire and left the desk unmanned for a couple of hours. He almost got fired." But didn't.

In fact he got promoted to classified, where he put in almost a year on the front counter, getting a good look at contact with the reader and the customer. Meanwhile he transferred over to University of Pittsburgh for a night business course.

On a slow day in the summer of 1949 Bob was sharing front counter duties with a man who is now a *Press* advertising executive. In those days there was a two-story high lobby with a "Romeo and Juliet" balcony overhead. While Bob and his co-worker were playing catch with vacuum tube containers, Business Manager Frank Morrison walked in. "At least he learned our names right then," the ad exec remembers.

ONCE AGAIN Bob came out of an escapade with a promotion. He was moved to the outside classified sales staff, first on autos later on real estate.

He was drafted, at twenty, in 1951. The Army ran him through finance school and sent him to Garmisch-Partenkirchen in Germany to be a paymaster. It was a beautiful town in the Alps where the 1936 winter Olympics had been held. Bob left somewhat reluctantly and was back at *The Press* in classified in 1953.

In June 1955 he switched to retail, ten years later to general. In 1966 he was appointed assistant retail manager, retail manager in 1967, assistant advertising director in 1974, and ad director in 1975.

During this time he developed strong ties with the business community, and became known as a "spellbinder." The selling environment was a natural for him, and he could talk and sell on his feet with enthusiasm and excitement and at the same time make thorough use of all the effective research materials.

BACK IN THE EARLY DAYS in classified, there was a pretty credit clerk at the next desk, Jacqueline Lenikus. They were married in 1955 and adopted two children, Mary Ellen born in 1961, and Garrett born in 1963. They live in Scott Township, about eight miles from downtown. Bob enjoys reading history (he's going around again on Will Durant's *History of Civilization*), and occasional trips to Chartiers Country Club where he can tour the golf course in somewhere between 84 and 110.

For relaxation, he started taking guitar lessons back in the late Sixties. His teacher moved out of town, and Bob never got back to it. He can be encouraged to play and sing a bit.

Bob is a member of the Allegheny Club, Duquesne Club, and Pittsburgh Press Club, vice president and director of The Golden Triangle Association, director of the Better Business Bureau and Greater Pittsburgh Chamber of Commerce, and has been active with the International Newspaper Advertising Executives, most recently as chairman of the retail advertising relations committee.

He was appointed business manager June 2, 1980, succeeding Bob Hartmann who had moved on to Scripps-Howard headquarters.

The San Juan Star
San Juan, Puerto Rico

The San Juan Star, an English-language newspaper in a predominantly Spanish-language community, published its first newspaper on November 2, 1959. *The Star* was started by Cowles Communications, Inc., which also published Look magazine and Family Circle. Scripps-Howard bought the newspaper in August 1970. *The Star* won a Pulitzer Prize in 1961 for a series of editorials on a church-state electoral conflict in Puerto Rico.

The Star's readers are overwhelmingly Puerto Ricans who prefer it to the three Spanish newspapers being published in San Juan. They see *The Star* as somewhat of a non-partisan referee over political matters and a spokesman with a different viewpoint on island life.

Star campaigns have brought about cutbacks in the Legislature's own budget, revealed illegal practices by housing investment firms and turned a police chief out of office.

Editor: ANDREW T. VIGLUCCI. President and General Manager: JOHN A. ZERBE JR.

THE EDITOR
Andrew T. Viglucci

HIS INTRODUCTION to the newspaper game was prosaic and early. As a fifth-grader in Albany, New York (where he was born June 9, 1927), Andy started hawking *The Times Union* at the entrance of the downtown Bell Telephone Building. His "career" lasted through the sixth grade. Before graduating from high school in 1945, Andy again tested his hand —co-editor of the yearbook.

World War II was on and Andy opted for the Navy. Just about the time he was finishing boot camp at Sampson Naval Training Station near Geneva, New York, the shooting stopped. So he enrolled at Clark University in Worcester, Massachusetts.

You'd have to suspect his journalistic vibes were pretty dim because he co-majored in, of all things, pyschology and geography, the two areas for which Clark was, and still is, most noted. A vague goal must have been stirring in the inner recesses of his noggin because Andy got on the college newspaper as a sports editor.

Emerging from Clark in 1951, he sensed that journalism was beckoning and took a job as copy boy with *The Times Union* nights while working days as a welfare investigator for Albany county.

This arrangement went on for almost two years until Andy got his first reporting job with the neighboring *Schenectady Union Star* in 1956, assigned to the police and labor beats, both active in a city where gambling and General Electric were major industries. He started at $65 a week, but how could he quibble when the lady publisher allowed him to work nights on his own time developing features?

His first reward for such a feature was a hand-drawn rose, colored crayon red, on a piece of paper on which the femme honcho had printed, "Well done." Andy's shock and surprise must have mellowed into something sentimental; he still has his rose.

One particularly cruel winter in Schenectady, Andy heard about a new newspaper in a far away land of tropical enchantment called Puerto Rico. He and his friend, Bill Kennedy, applied, were accepted, and then went to the atlas to determine just where Puerto Rico fit into the Western Hemisphere.

The paper was the second *World Journal*, an English language adjunct of the principal Spanish language newspaper, *El Mundo*. The new paper lasted nine months and Andy, richer in experience, left the island for Washington, D. C. There he got his initiation into Scripps-Howard, joining the *Washington Daily News* in February 1957, to toil under the likes of John O'Rourke, Dick Hollander and Nick Blatchford. He recalls it as just about his best year in journalism, covering everything from Capitol Hill to coroner's inquests, and most of the time on deadline rush.

Even so he returned to Puerto Rico in 1958 to work for the P.R. News Service, a government outfit, and then to help organize the editorial side of *The San Juan Star* for its first edition on November 2, 1959. *The Star* was begun by Cowles Communications, Inc., publishers of Look and several daily newspapers.

Andy started as city editor and became managing editor in 1961. He again left Puerto Rico for a six-month stint back in Albany as managing editor of *The Times Union*. But in 1967 he returned to San Juan to become editor of *The Star*. He was reunited with Scripps-Howard in August 1970, when Cowles sold the paper to Scripps-Howard.

Andy likes to play tennis and keep track of his five children: Andres, born in 1959, who attended Princeton; Maria Elena born in 1963; Mariangela born in 1965; and Tina born in 1967, who was Puerto Rico's ten-year-old and twelve-year-old girls singles tennis champ; and Cara Rafaela, born in 1980, product of Andy's second marriage to Betsy Lopez.

BUSINESS MANAGER
John A. Zerbe Jr.

THE CENTRAL New Jersey town of East Orange is very important in John's life. There he was born (June 12, 1936) and married (in 1958) but he's never really lived there. He intends to steer clear of East Orange, he avers with a chuckle, lest there's another monumental happening.

When John was three, his father moved the family to the island of Puerto Rico. Zerbe Sr. was the personnel representative for "Colonel" Sostenes Behn who brought ITT to Puerto Rico.

John's association with newspapers started as a carrier boy for *The World Journal* in San Juan in the 1940s. High School summers were spent running errands for *El Mundo* and driving a delivery truck for a distributor of stateside papers. His photographic hobby led him to the college newspaper where he captured the campus pictorial news for three years and also worked on the yearbook staff.

After graduation in 1958 from the Wharton School at the University of Pennsylvania and his marriage to the former Cynthia Cummings, John's life turned away from newspapers. On a lark during his freshman year, he had joined the Navy Reserve Officers Training Corps. and was obligated to serve for three years. Assigned to Athens, Georgia for three months in the heat of summer for supply corps training school, John achieved top of his class and was eligible for one of the only shore duty assignments available—Hawaii.

There, at twenty-one, John managed the NAS Barber's Point Navy exchange complex, an $11,000,000 a year operation with three hundred employees. His bicultural background was a big asset in dealings with his Chinese, Japanese, Hawaiian and Filipino civilian personnel.

Navy life was interesting and John seriously considered making it a career. He was interviewed and selected by Admiral Rickover for the atomic energy program. Fate intervened in the form of a letter from John's father, who was in poor health, requesting that John as the oldest son think about coming back to Puerto Rico.

Trading one island for another, John returned to Puerto Rico and in January 1962 became advertising manager for *The San Juan Star*. Long hours and late nights ensued as John learned the newspaper business inside and out. He was also vitally involved with *The Star's* difficult conversion to cold type. In 1965 John was promoted to vice president and advertising director, in 1968 named vice president and general manager and in 1970 elevated to president and general manager.

Community involvement is important to John and he's always been very active. He was founding president of San Juan Toastmasters; founding director of the Advertising Federation of P. R., of the BBB of P. R. and of the Puerto Rico Pee Wee Football League. He has served on the boards of Rotary, Sales and Marketing, Variety Club, Boys Club, Salvation Army and Navy League. His association with the Young Presidents' Organization has been educational and he has served as local chapter chairman and membership chairman.

Because of a bum knee, golf has replaced tennis as John's favorite sport. He still manages to officiate Pee Wee football games and enjoys working with the eight-, nine-, and ten-year-olds. For complete relaxation John's choice is sailing in the British Virgin Islands. Traveling is also a big interest. John enjoys meeting people in other countries and learning about their way of life.

John and Cynny have two children—Jay, the football addict, born in 1962, and Christina, the ballerina/cheerleader, born in 1965. Two German Shepherds and two cats round out the family.

The Stuart News
Stuart, Florida

Founded April 18, 1913 by Will Hawley Stevens as *The Stuart Times*. Purchased April 12, 1965 by Scripps-Howard as its first weekly newspaper. Expanded to twice weekly in February 1967. On October 2, 1973 again expanded to five days a week. Now published six times a week, Monday through Friday, and Sunday. A second edition, *The Port St. Lucie News*, was launched July 17, 1978, circulating north of Stuart.

Ernest F. Lyons, who retired as editor in 1975 after forty-four years with the paper, championed conservation causes long before environmental issues were widely celebrated. He was an Edward J. Meeman Conservation Awards winner in 1965. *The News* successfully campaigned for the widening and deepening of the St. Lucie Inlet and for the purchase by the state of a three-mile wilderness beach. *The News* revealed that building departments allowed building code violations to pass unchallenged in poor neighborhoods. As a result, the city built public housing and won grants for slum renovation.

The practice of pumping untreated sewage into the St. Lucie and Indian Rivers ended after *The News* showed pollution was destroying the rivers. A series of articles that explained how the community was shortchanging education with overcrowded schools resulted in the public approving the first school bond issue in the history of Martin county. The bonds financed the construction of ninety new classrooms, five cafeterias and a new high school.

Editor: THOMAS E. WEBER JR. Business Manager: JAMES L. OVERTON.

THE EDITOR
Thomas E. Weber Jr.

IT WAS MERELY for family convenience that Tom Weber was born in Memphis January 4, 1944. His father was a World War II pilot and that meant bouncing around the country to a lot of air bases.

"The Army hospital in Memphis was convenient," explains Tom, "because my grandparents, both sides of the family, lived in Mississippi. I was only in Memphis about six weeks."

His boyhood was spent in such diverse towns as Topeka, Kansas, Wheaton, Illinois, and Fort Lauderdale, Florida. He finished high school in North Palm Beach.

It was 1966, the summer between his junior and senior years at Florida State University, when Tom showed up in Stuart, with two gleaming goals. First, to get married—and next find a job. A Stuart belle, Judith Jackson, took care of the first priority with her "I do." Tom's father gave an assist on the second objective. He spotted a help wanted ad in *Editor and Publisher* that sent Tom hurrying to the office of the editor of *The Stuart News*, the legendary Ernie Lyons.

Ernie got up from behind his typewriter. "Sit down, son," he said, "and write something about yourself. I'll be back pretty soon." Tom dutifully sat.

Twenty minutes later Lyons returned. He pulled the copy out of the typewriter, read it, and looked pleased. He put Tom on as an intern for the summer. In the fall Tom returned to FSU with his bride and completed work on a degree in English literature.

He was a member of the FSU intercollegiate wrestling team. His highwater mark in amateur athletics was taking second in the Florida AAU wrestling tournament. To help pay the bills while he was in school, Tom worked as a kitchen helper, pool hall manager, convenience store clerk, peddled commercial printing, and sold pots and pans door to door.

The money was in pots and pans. Tom sold a $360 set on credit to a young couple with two children. Walking away from their home, a rundown twenty-five-foot-trailer, Tom felt a little sick. He straightway turned in his sample kit and found another line of work.

His summer internship had given him a career goal. After he graduated, Tom hit Lyons up for a reporter's job and got it. He did well. Ernie made him assistant managing editor and in 1973 named him managing editor. Tom won a dozen awards for writing and photography from the Florida Press Association. He found time to turn out pieces on Florida fishing for national outdoor magazines. In 1972 he was president of the Stuart Chamber of Commerce.

During those years *The Stuart News* changed from hot metal to cold type, installed an offset press, and converted from a weekly to a daily with two editions.

Lyons retired in 1975 and Jack Howard appointed Tom editor.

Tom's wife, Judy, is assistant director of the Indian River Mental Health Center. They have two children, Tom born in 1969, and Jill born in 1973. The family likes to fish and skin-dive on the reefs off Stuart.

BUSINESS MANAGER
James L. Overton

WHEN JIM USED TO lean on the old saw, "I'll be there if the creek doesn't rise," he wasn't joking. He was two days late starting work at *The Stuart News* in 1963. A prodigious rain storm caused the creek between his new home and Stuart to rise, washing out the bridge.

That was not exactly the kind of weather this West Virginian and his family had been led to expect from the Sunshine State. But Florida, to be candid about it, seems to have more than made it up to him.

Jim was born April 1, 1934 in Parkersburg, West Virginia. He got out of Parkersburg High School in 1953 and attended West Virginia University and Marietta (Ohio) College. He thought the Army would be interesting. In 1956 he joined up and became a public information specialist.

He created the first base newspaper for the Nike missile installation near Milwaukee. He had fun tearing around with notebook and Speed Graphic. Circulation was 1200.

But a typical little snafu cropped up that ingrained in Jim a sympathetic appreciation of the occasional frustrations editors confront. There was this bunch of generals at a banquet. Jim shot pictures. Another Army post processed his film. Somebody looking over the developed pictures noticed the generals were all holding drinks. That photo somehow got sent to the Pentagon. Jim got a stiff letter from the Pentagon; in the future he was absolutely not to snap generals holding their whiskey. (No policy was delineated for photographing officers who could not hold their liquor.)

After a couple of years Jim had enough of the Army. He took an honorable discharge and went home to Parkersburg to try to get a job selling ads for *The News and Sentinel.* That didn't open up immediately and he spanned the gap as merchandising manager for a produce firm.

When he did get on *The News and Sentinel* retail staff his steadily-rising sales made him No. 2 man in the department. But it looked as if seniority blocked his future. Then he heard a customer talking about moving to Stuart, Florida, a small town on a big river next to the ocean. Jim was intrigued.

He hopped down to look Stuart over. *The News* was a 3000-circulation weekly, with thirty-two carriers and a staff of sixteen. Jim applied to Ernie Lyons and got hired as retail ad salesman. In less than a year (he must have been forgiven for being two days late), he was appointed advertising director. "That was no big deal," Jim chuckles. "There was only one other man in advertising."

A year later (1965) he was also named circulation director. That meant on Wednesday afternoons he would help crank up the old Duplex press and throw bundles into the company station wagon. His title was later changed to assistant business manager and in 1967 he was appointed business manager.

During the next ten years he guided *The Stuart News* through a remarkable growth period. Publication was changed from once a week to twice a week, to five times a week, and finally to six days a week with two editions. *The Stuart News* now has one hundred sixty employees and two hundred-plus carriers.

In 1979 Scripps-Howard gave Jim the added responsibility of general manager of the Jupiter Courier Highlights, a free distribution weekly with a circulation of about 20,000 in northern Palm Beach county, which the Concern purchased in 1978.

His last big lick in West Virginia was being named the state's Outstanding Jaycee in 1961. No civic grass is growing under his feet in Stuart. He has been a director and president of the Stuart Chamber of Commerce and in 1978 was president of the India-Lucie Rotary Club.

Jim has four daughters: Jenny born in 1959, Theresa born in 1962, Sabrina born in 1968, and Christina born in 1980.

His home is a working farm where he raises hogs, chickens, a small herd of cattle and produces some vegetable crops.

Now the only bridge between his home and the office is, fortunately, a high-level concrete span that is unlikely to wash out no matter how high the creek rises.

SECTION SEVEN

Other Publishing Enterprises

Cordovan's Business Journals in Nine Cities, Magazines and Books; Weeklies in California, Kentucky and Florida

Cordovan Publications

How Bob Gray's Bright
Ideas Grew and Grew and . . .

Houston WAS BOOMING and Bob Gray was not content to only report on the exciting times. He yearned to get into business for himself. Finally, in 1959, he made his decision: do it—*now!* There was a small magazine about horses for sale. Bob borrowed from relatives and took the plunge.

He was thirty-six. He had a journalism degree and ideas. He had spent four years in the Marines in World War II, and later interrupted his newsman career for two more years in Korea.

But otherwise he had pretty well swept the field in broadcast and print journalism in Houston—radio and TV reporter-photographer and news director at KPRC, KNUZ, KXYZ, and KPRC-TV, photographer and reporter at the *Citizen* newspapers, and finally on the city desk at *The Houston Post*.

Horseman Magazine was born in Bob's garage. His staff initially was his wife Nellie, their son and two daughters, and in-laws. "Everybody did something and nobody made any money," Bob remembers. "We look back and laugh, but it was pretty tough then."

THE FLEDGLING EFFORT managed to survive by a lot of seven-day weeks and late hours. In 1962 Bob moved his

Cordovan Corporation, Publishers, into rented office space and began to hire some staff.

"That's the hard way to learn publishing," says Bob, "but maybe it's the best way."

In any event *Horseman Magazine* succeeded. Cordovan branched out. It published books, both hard and soft cover. It grew. Bob got ideas for other magazines and launched them: *Jet Cargo News* (1968), *Western Outfitter* (1969), and *Texas Fisherman* (1973).

Cordovan published a highly-successful series of travel guides to Texas. Gradually its book list grew to sixty titles. Progress was steady, and then turned spectacular on another idea for Bob Gray and troops — a newspaper devoted exclusively to a city's business community.

Cordovan's debut in that field was launching *Houston Business Journal* in 1971. That weekly tabloid, which was also something of a design innovation, became the most successful paper of its type in the United States.

As founding editor of the new paper Gray recruited Mike Weingart from the business news staff of *The Houston Chronicle*. He was a newsman with precisely the right background. Born in Chicago October 3, 1941, Mike grew up in Skokie, Illinois. At fourteen he was freelancing photos to his hometown weekly newspapers.

He gravitated to the University of Houston photo-journalism course, and developed an interest in writing. Just prior to graduation, Mike joined Houston's KTRK-TV as reporter-photographer. He spent a couple of years there, with time off to join the U.S. Army Reserve as an information specialist.

Mike moved to Dallas for a few months to be a reporter for McGraw-Hill World News. Then he joined *The Houston Chronicle*, also acting as correspondent for *Wall Street Journal*, *American Banker*, and *Journal of Commerce*.

THE SUCCESS of *Houston Business Journal* set the team of Gray and Weingart on fire. They could hardly wait to branch out. "I don't think there's any question," says Gray, "but what eventually every major city in the country will have a newspaper like this. It is designed to do a very specific and specialized kind of reporting job."

Other Publishing Enterprises

Bob Gray   Mike Weingart

Cordovan expanded the local business publication concept with the opening of *Atlanta Business Journal* in 1978. Mike commuted to Atlanta, serving as interim or "start-up" editor. Besides being associate publisher of the Houston and Atlanta papers, Mike assumed that title when papers were started in Los Angeles and San Francisco in 1979.

At about this point Cordovan, needing greater capital for expansion, began negotiating to be acquired by The E. W. Scripps Company. In announcing the purchase, on February 5, 1980, Ed Estlow pointed out that the Cordovan newspapers would continue to exercise editorial independence in their handling of local business news, and that Gray would remain as president and chief executive officer until 1984.

After the acquisition by Scripps-Howard, Gray created Cordovan Business Journals, with Weingart serving as executive vice president of the division. Bob could see the possibility of starting as many as two dozen of the business tabloids.

The year 1980 was the most spectacular in Cordovan's twenty-one year growth. Four new business journals were launched and one was acquired. The acquisition, *Dallas-Fort Worth Business*, came the same day—February 1, 1980— Cordovan was purchased by Scripps-Howard.

IN SELECTING CITIES in which to start business papers, Gray and Weingart looked for strong markets where commerce is growing and business confidence is evident.

They somewhat emulated E. W. Scripps's pioneering business philosophy by launching their new papers and determining whether there would be market acceptance under actual conditions — a gamble — rather than researching the prospects for months or years.

The papers launched in 1980:

Seattle Business Journal, April 21; *San Diego Business Journal,* June 16; *Miami Business Journal,* August 18; and *Phoenix Business Journal,* October 20.

The year not only more than doubled the number of business papers, but increased the Cordovan staff from 100 to 200 employes, and almost doubled the gross volume of sales.

The Gray family members who helped Bob pioneer Cordovan continue as part of the operation. Son Bobby is distribution manager of Cordovan. Daughter Ruth Ellen (Sommy) is vice-president/administration of Cordovan Business Journals. Wife Nell is personnel manager.

Bob is a native Texan, born in Beaumont October 6, 1923. He attended high school in Hot Springs, Arkansas then went to the University of Arkansas. He attended Millsaps College in Mississippi, Miami University of Ohio, and the University of Houston where he received his journalism degree.

MOST OF BOB'S TIME is spent on recruiting, organization, administration and "start-ups." This involves a lot of travel around the country. Bob misses writing. Several times a year he will come across a marketing or a travel subject and whip out a piece for one of the Cordovan publications.

"Eventually, like most of us in this business, I want to do more writing," says Bob. "I don't believe any of us ever really finish the job of self-training that a good reporter ought to do on himself.

"Occasionally I remind myself that I'm supposed to be a writer. So, I write."

Southern California Publishing Company

14 Community Weeklies Around Los Angeles

Gordon Crawford

THIS GROUP OF FOURTEEN community weekly newspapers in the Los Angeles area came under the Scripps-Howard banner in October 1978.

At the time of acquisition they comprised three separate groups, San Gabriel Valley Publications, Southern California Publishing Company, and Pico Press, Inc. The controlled and free distribution newspapers had a combined circulation of more than 140,000. A number of them publish twice weekly. One of the papers was founded in 1897; the newest was launched in 1971.

The newspapers are:

The Monterey Park Progress, Alahambra Post Advocate, San Gabriel Progress, East Los Angeles/Montebello Progress, South San Gabriel/Rosemead Progress, Montebello News, East Los Angeles Tribune, Monterey Park Californian, East Los Angeles Gazette, Commerce Tribune, Rosemead/South San Gabriel Californian, the *Pico Rivera News, Sante Fe Springs News,* and *West Whittier Independent.*

Since January 1980 all have been operated as the Southern California Publishing Company.

General manager is Gordon Crawford who had been a stockholder and general manager of San Gabriel Valley Publications. Born in Chicago April 5, 1936, Gordon migrated to Laguna Beach, California as a child and was graduated from high school there. He attended Orange Coast College two years and in 1956 went into the Army for two years.

After five years as assistant manager of a grocery store in Laguna Beach, he got in newspapering on the ad staff of the *South Coast News* in Laguna Beach. He worked for two other weeklies and 1965 became assistant advertising manager of the *Orange Coast Daily Pilot*. He joined San Gabriel Valley Publications in 1970, becoming general manager in 1972. He was put in charge of all fourteen papers after Scripps-Howard bought them.

Gordon is married, has three children, and plays golf.

The newspapers are set and printed in Scripps-Howard's *Daily News Tribune* plant in Fullerton, where new presses were installed to accommodate the increased output.

Grant County News
Williamstown, Kentucky

Campbell County News
Alexandria, Kentucky

An Old-timer (1906)
And a 1978 Start-up

Susan Arena

THE GRANT COUNTY NEWS was founded in 1906 when Williamstown was a small rural Kentucky town barely fifty miles south of Cincinnati. It was *the* hometown newspaper with a loyal circulation. As the area developed William Matthews bought the paper in September 1975. In May 1977 he sold it to Scripps-Howard Newspapers along with *The Leader*,

OTHER PUBLISHING ENTERPRISES 313

of Boone County, another weekly he founded in November 1976. (*The Leader* later was discontinued.)

Under the new ownership, Matthews continued to operate the properties as vice president and general manager. He also founded for Scripps-Howard The *Campbell County News*, a weekly headquartered in Alexandria, in July 1978.

Matthews now directs the subsequently-acquired Scripps-Howard weekly newspaper and printing plant operations in Louisville.

Editor and general manager of both the *Grant County News* and *Campbell County News* is Susan P. Arena.

Though born (March 25, 1943) in Akron, Ohio, Susan grew up in Dallas and Lexington, Kentucky, where she was graduated from Lafayette High in 1961. She was editor of her high school paper and worked on a Lexington weekly to pay her way through the University of Kentucky.

Did she study journalism? No. She was graduated in 1965 with a degree in education of the mentally retarded and obtained a master's degree in 1967 in psychiatric counseling. For two years she worked for a Frankfort, Kentucky Comprehensive Care center.

But the newspaper bug was still biting. In 1970 she started as ad salesman and part-time writer for the *Madison County* (Kentucky) *News*, a weekly. She transferred to the Shelbyville offices of the parent company, Newspapers Incorporated, and a year later was director of advertising and promotion.

In 1975 she became publisher of the *Grant County News* and after the Scripps-Howard purchase spent a year and a half as promotion director of *The Cincinnati Post*. She returned to Kentucky in July 1979 in her present capacity.

Susan spent a lot of hours renovating her home, a 1860 Victorian farm house, a dozen miles from her office. She has a daughter, Paige, born in 1968. A prolific gardener, she canned so many vegetables in the fall of 1980 "the darn house is busting at the seams." Her hobbies are ceramics, reading, and working with miniature doll houses.

SHP, Inc.
(Scripps-Howard Press, Inc.)
Saint Matthews, Kentucky

Scripps-Howard Web Press Company
Louisville, Kentucky

In Louisville, a Daily King and Six Weeklies

William Matthews

THE FIRST ACQUISITION by Scripps-Howard in its move into the community newspaper arena in Louisville was an active modern printing plant. It was conveniently located in the Louisville Air Park and had an eight-unit Daily King web offset press capable of turning out 32-page papers at the rate of 20,000 an hour.

The company was purchased in November 1978, and William E. Matthews was named president. Bill was then publisher of Scripps-Howard's northern Kentucky weeklies.

The web press company was offering full service commercial publishing—composition, plate-making, and printing—to a variety of newspapers, such as *The Catholic Record, Louisville Defender, Action in Kentucky,* etc.

Next was the purchase March 1, 1979 of the three principal suburban weeklies in the Louisville area, the *Jeffersonian, The Voice,* and the *Reporter.* Matthews was named also as editor and publisher of SHP. The *Highland Herald* was started and in March 1980 the *Southwest Advertiser* was acquired and the name changed to *Southwest News.* The sixth of the group of weeklies is *The Mirror.* Their territory forms a crescent around Louisville, but does not extend beyond the Ohio river into Indiana.

Matthews is a native Kentuckian, born April 30, 1930 in Shelbyville. His mother noticed when he was a fifth grader he turned out a fine essay and encouraged him to seek a career in journalism. He was graduated from University of Michigan in 1952 with a journalism degree, but after ROTC service in the Army was "selected out" by the Central Intelligence Agency.

For nine years he served in the CIA in Washington and Austria, where he directed monitoring of Russian radio broadcasts to determine what the Soviet bloc was saying to its people so American forces could develop counter-propaganda.

When he left the CIA in 1962 he bought his hometown weekly, the *Shelbyville Sentinel* and ran it until 1966 when eight Kentucky publishers formed a co-op. Matthews was the manager of this operation and it had grown to five plants and twenty-three papers when it was sold in 1973 to Landmark. Bill stayed on with Landmark until 1975 when he decided to start over and bought the *Grant County News* which eventually led him to Scripps-Howard.

Bill is married to the former Else Joregensen, and they have four children. He claims no hobbies.

Kentucky Standard
Bardstown, Kentucky

**It Adds Something
To a Famous Heritage**

George Trotter

STEPHEN FOSTER made Bardstown famous with his song "My Old Kentucky Home." The town's weekly newspaper, *Kentucky Standard*, established in 1900, gained a measure of renown too by becoming one of the largest weeklies in Kentucky, with a circulation of 9500.

Alfred Wathen Sr. helped found the newspaper and later

acquired ownership. When purchased by Scripps-Howard Newspapers in November 1979 it was still in the Wathen family. Alfred Jr. was publisher, his brother B.J. was business manager, and their sister Elizabeth Spalding was editor.

A weekly shopper is published in conjunction with the *Standard*. The company also does commercial printing and sells office supplies. Bardstown is thirty-five miles south of Louisville.

George Trotter, former executive of Landmark Community Newspapers, became general manager and editor of the *Standard* as soon as Scripps-Howard assumed control.

Born in Campbellsville, Kentucky February 20, 1927, George got his baptism in newspapering at fourteen as a flyboy on the hometown weekly *News-Journal*. He spent two years in the Navy, came back to the University of Kentucky to get his journalism degree in 1950. He stepped right in as editor of the Campbellsville *News-Record* "at the princely sum of $35 a week." He stayed five years and bought the nearby *Lebanon Enterprise*.

He melded that into a co-op known as Newspapers, Inc. and after it was purchased by Landmark he joined that company to supervise fifteen newspapers in five states.

George is married and has five children. He is author of a chapter on marketing in a Prentice-Hall textbook, the first on all aspects of community newspaper publishing.

The Courier-Highlights
Jupiter, Florida

Serving a 22-Mile Stretch of The Atlantic Coast

THIS NEWSPAPER serves northeast Palm Beach County and southeast Martin County, including the towns of Jupiter Island, Hobe Sound, Jupiter Inlet Colony, Tequesta, Jupiter and Juno Beach, as well as portions of Palm Beach Gardens and North Palm Beach.

Scripps-Howard purchased the newspaper, which was established in 1958, in February 1978.

The Courier-Highlights initially was published as a tabloid on Thursdays. Since acquisition it has been converted to a full size newspaper and published twice a week, Thursdays and Sundays.

It is delivered to every occupied dwelling along twenty-two miles of the Atlantic Coast in the rapidly-growing Jupiter area. Circulation figures are audited by the Certified Audits and Circulations. The *Courier-Highlights* was the first free newspaper to be accepted for audit in Florida.

Advertising is sold also in combination with Scripps-Howard's nearby *Stuart News*, and Jim Overton, the business manager of *The Stuart News*, also serves as general manager of the Jupiter papers.

SECTION EIGHT

Scripps-Howard Broadcasting Company

How It Started in 1935, and Where It Stands Today; With Profiles of The Officials And Managers

Scripps-Howard Broadcasting Company

From Small Beginning in 1935 It Has Grown Large

SCRIPPS-HOWARD Broadcasting has been on the air for almost a half a century.

It moved from the crystal set and headphones era to the day of earth stations receiving television programs from 23,000 miles in outer space.

As far back as 1935, when radio and Jack Howard both were young, Scripps-Howard people realized that print had some sprightly competition. The organization decided to look into it and the result was what is known today as Scripps-Howard Broadcasting, a leader in television news and one of the most respected companies in broadcasting.

Scripps-Howard Broadcasting is constantly changing and has always been an industry leader. It has added UHF, FM, mini-cams, action cam vans and helicopter transmission, and earth stations to its communications arsenal. It is in the CATV business. Its latest venture is participation in one of the nation's largest earth station networks for computer to computer transmission of business data.

SCRIPPS-HOWARD Broadcasting Company is a public corporation, with approximately one-fourth of the total outstanding shares of the company owned by the public and by the employees and officers of the company. Majority shareholder is The E. W. Scripps Company, parent company of Scripps-Howard Newspapers.

Scripps-Howard Broadcasting Company owns and operates six television stations: five VHF, in Cleveland, Memphis, Cincinnati, Palm Beach and Tulsa, plus a UHF in Kansas City. It also has six radio stations—AM stations in Knoxville, Memphis and Phoenix, and FM stations in Baltimore, Phoenix and Memphis.

Scripps-Howard Broadcasting was conceived by men who feel there is a logical and natural relationship between newspapers and radio and television, in the field of public service. It began "marvelously unloved and suspected by all," to quote its organizer.

At the start it was known as Continental Radio Company, incorporated in Ohio, August 24, 1935. To those who promoted it, this company seemed the inevitable answer of Scripps-Howard to the invasion of the news distribution field by radio. This view was formalized when the United Press pioneered in serving broadcasting stations.

THE MAN WHO inspired and nursed to reality this idea of a Scripps-Howard radio company was the dynamic Karl A. Bickel. Bickel had relinquished the presidency of the United Press at the end of 1934 and retired to Florida. However, at the urging of Roy W. Howard and W. W. Hawkins, then chairman and vice chairman of the board respectively, of Scripps-Howard Newspapers, he was back in the saddle in May 1935 putting together a radio organization, and eyeing the field for the purchase or establishment of Scripps-Howard stations.

Shortly after the incorporation of Continental Radio, the late James C. Hanrahan joined the company. Hanrahan was equipped with nine years of experience in the editorial department of the *Des Moines Register and Tribune*, and four years in the management of several radio stations which the Cowles newspapers had acquired in Iowa. He brought a newspaper approach to radio broadcasting.

Bickel's "organization" consisted of himself, his secretary, John P. Smith who later became station director of WCPO,

SCRIPPS-HOWARD BROADCASTING COMPANY

Cincinnati, and Jim Hanrahan. For a while various hotel rooms around the country provided Bickel's offices; suitcases held his files.

The next step, obviously, was acquisition of some properties.

AS A RESULT OF A survey of purchase opportunities, Continental Radio bought WFBE in Cincinnati, and Federal Communications Commission approval of the transfer of the license to the Scripps-Howard subsidiary was obtained September 24, 1935. At that time the station was a 100-watter, operating on 1200 kilocycles. The call letters were changed to WCPO to signify the relationship to The Cincinnati Post, a Scripps-Howard newspaper.

Next WNOX in Knoxville was purchased, and approval of the transfer of its license was obtained from the FCC November 19, 1935. It was operating with 1000 watts on 1010 kilocycles, and on clear winter nights could be picked up as far away as New York City, so uncluttered were radio frequencies of those days. The existing call letters seemed appropriate for a station with ties to *The Knoxville News-Sentinel*, another Scripps-Howard newspaper.

Both stations were under the active supervision of Karl Bickel and James C. Hanrahan. Richard B. Westergaard, who had joined Scripps-Howard in November 1935, was commercial manager of WNOX.

WITH OWNERSHIP of WCPO and WNOX completed, Continental Radio had something to operate, even though the situations for operating radio stations in the two cities were totally different.

In Cincinnati the community was already being serviced by three or four bigger stations of greater power, including WLW—the Crosley station—at that time the most powerful in the U.S., operating with 50,000 watts.

The Scripps-Howard station emphasized news coverage, local service and performance, and found an eager and loyal audience to that concept of radio. This policy was continued in Cincinnati, under the guidance of Mortimer C. Watters, who went on to serve as a general manager, executive vice president, chairman of the executive committee and as a director of Scripps-Howard Broadcasting.

Watters came to Scripps-Howard in January 1938. He had been in the radio advertising agency business, had worked at the Gannett station WHEC in Rochester, N.Y., and had been general manager of the West Virginia Network, a group of newspaper-owned stations.

In Knoxville, WNOX was dominant in its field. The basic policy of concentration on news and local public service was also applied.

Both stations earned their right to economic survival and growth. Both developed into major community assets. Both demonstrated the positive—even imperative—part radio takes in the responsibility of serving a community with news and advertising.

IN APRIL 1936, Jack R. Howard was attracted to radio and joined up. He went to Knoxville and became associated with WNOX. He went through the mill, familarizing himself with all aspects of broadcasting, from programming to sales. After Knoxville, he spent a period in Washington studying the general broadcasting picture, and its relationship with the Federal Communications Commission, before moving his office to New York.

In March 1937 Jack Howard was elected president of Continental Radio Company.

In May 1937 the name of the company was changed to Scripps-Howard Radio, Inc. The change of the corporate name symbolized the end of an exploratory period and the beginning of Scripps-Howard's active and admitted interest in the field of radio broadcasting.

IN JULY 1937 WNBR in Memphis was acquired by The *Memphis Press-Scimitar*, a Scripps-Howard paper. This resulted from the fact that with the purchase of *The Commercial Appeal*, Memphis's morning newspaper, Scripps-Howard had come into possession of two radio stations, WMC and WNBR. Legal obstacles made it appear inadvisable for Radio, Inc. to take over these stations. However, since WNBR had been identified with *The Press-Scimitar*, and WMC long identified with *The Commercial Appeal*, the operation of WNBR was entrusted to Radio, Inc. and the call letters changed to WMPS, to indicate affiliation with The *Press-Scimitar*.

THE TASK OF overhauling WMPS, weakest of four stations in the market, fell to Jack Howard and Jim Hanrahan. They applied the basic Scripps-Howard Radio policy of emphasizing news and local coverage. Under the handicap of inferior facilities and the inheritance of a burdensome contract which monopolized prime time, the station was making considerable progress, measured by public acceptance. It was then that the FCC adopted its rule against multiple ownership in one area. Scripps-Howard could not retain both WMC and WMPS and the choice of which to dispose of was the more recent acquisition. Approval of transfer of WMPS to Plough, Inc. of Memphis, was granted by the FCC March 5, 1945.

World War II brought many changes to Scripps-Howard Radio. Jack Howard went on active duty with the Navy; Hanrahan and Westergaard on active duty with the Army. To Mort Watters fell the burden of general supervision of the stations, with John Smith backing him up in Cincinnati and O. L. Smith in Knoxville.

Both stations devoted time, programs, and the energies of their managers to assisting their communities in the war effort. Thousands of hours were donated to the armed forces, to government agencies and private organizations engaged in war work.

WNOX brought Sgt. Alvin C. York, of World War I fame, out of semi-retirement to broadcast; it was the only station allowed inside the gates of Oak Ridge—where the atom bomb was developed—for the purpose of broadcasting special war bond rallies. It was the first station to broadcast the news of the atom bomb explosions from Oak Ridge itself. WCPO was no less active in its community during this period.

WITH WORLD WAR II ended, the question before Scripps-Howard Radio, Inc. was: "Where do we go from here?"

By early 1946 Howard, Hanrahan, and Westergaard, were all back from service. Joseph B. Epperson, Scripps-Howard

Radio chief engineer, had done special unpublicized work in electronics with the War Department, and Glenn Davis, associate chief engineer, had done similar work in the Navy. Both engineers were thinking of frequency modulation and television, and both had learned considerable during the war in connection with these developments.

Radio, Inc. had proceeded with preliminary applications for frequency modulation filed in 1944 and with the conditional FM grant which had been received in December 1945 by WCPO in Cincinnati. In addition it was decided to pursue an application for a TV station in Cleveland, Ohio.

On July 18, 1946, Scripps-Howard received a construction permit for a TV station in Cleveland. The station took the call letters WEWS (TV) in honor of E. W. Scripps who founded the Scripps-Howard concern in Cleveland.

SUBSEQUENTLY a site for a transmitter and tower was obtained at Parma, Ohio, and space in a building in Cleveland was leased for ten years to provide studios for TV, FM and AM, should the latter develop.

WEWS went on the air December 17, 1947.

The station guaranteed "good coverage" over a land area 40 to 50 miles of Parma. Best reception was obtained in Cleveland, all of Sandusky, most of Akron, and its programs were picked up irregularly in Toledo, 80 miles west, and Warren, 115 miles east.

In launching their new "baby", the men of WEWS said: "We're starting in the dark. We're feeling our way. But we're going to find out . . ."

In their pioneering first, it wasn't long before they did find out. It was a historic event for Greater Cleveland, and the guiding genius again was Jim Hanrahan.

Hanrahan carried into television the basic philosophy manifested in his radio practices. He thought the neighbors viewing his effort would like a generous portion of it to be local; and while it was being local it should also be of service to the community as often as possible.

WEWS grew and so did the concept of its coverage. Newsmen from the station didn't wait for networks or free lance reporters to cover the world for them. They got the news themselves.

In 1957 WEWS moved into a new home on Euclid Avenue at 30th Street. It was elegance the original quarters on E. 13th never knew.

BUT THIS IS getting ahead of the story.

Another city, meanwhile, was preparing its own TV breakthrough. The city was Memphis, where on December 11, 1948, first pictures were flashed over *The Commercial Appeal's* station WMCT (TV).

A test run had been made a few weeks earlier when the Tennessee-Mississippi football game was televised. The station's tower stood a few miles east of Memphis. General manager of both WMC and WMCT was H. W. Slavick.

Mort Watters, in the meantime, was building fires under the situation at WCPO in Cincinnati. The big day was July 26, 1949 when WCPO-TV went into operation. Using the WCPO staff as a nucleus, and adding a batch of television technical experts, Watters led the charge into the dark valley of TV. The experts shook their heads. WCPO-TV began operation from 75 to 80 hours a week.

"Unheard of!" cried those who presumed to know better. "It'll be the death of you!" they said.

They hoped. But it wasn't. By some coincidence the opposition stations began lengthening their schedules, operating from 11 to 11 at a time when most TV stations in the country were telecasting from four to six hours per day, and some of that devoted to test patterns.

WCPO-TV's experience was an almost exact duplicate of the standard broadcast station's story ten years earlier; success over a rugged obstacle course.

NOW AND THEN things would settle down to a dull roar, but no one was very comfortable that way. The rough and ready spirit of the station has carried over to the present. Spirit and leadership, of course, have been the prime ingredients. Some years ago it was written:

"At WCPO one of the surest ways of seeing a new--not invariably successful—but a new, different idea put into operation is to step into the general manager's office and say: " 'But Mort, you can't do that!' "

To the south, in Memphis, where WMCT had been in operation since December 1948, a new development was afoot.

On March 1, 1950 WMCT hooked up with the coaxial cable. The device was extended down from Saint Louis, so that Memphis might have the joys and inspiration of shows originating in Chicago and the East. Inasmuch as WMCT was then the only TV outlet in Memphis, Hank Slavick played host to all the hookups, NBC, CBS, ABC, and DuMont. On January 1, 1967 the call letters of WMCT and WMCF were changed to WMC-FM and WMC-TV. Today WMC-TV is an NBC affiliate. In 1959 the WMC stations moved into their present home, ultra-modern, beautiful fully equipped offices and studios at 1960 Union Avenue, Memphis.

IN THE DECADE, 1950-1960, Scripps-Howard Radio, Inc. grew and prospered—alert all the while to expansion possibilities. Expansion came September 5, 1961, when Radio, Inc., filed an application with the FCC for transfer of the license of station WPTV (TV) West Palm Beach, Florida. An NBC affiliate, the station was purchased from John H. Phipps of West Palm Beach and Tallahassee.

On December 27, the FCC approved the purchase of WPTV by Scripps-Howard Radio, Inc.

Two other major developments marked the closing days of 1961 for Scripps-Howard interests in the radio and television field.

On December 31 WMC Broadcasting Company, owner and licensee of stations WMC, WMC-FM, and WMCT in Memphis, was merged into Scripps-Howard Radio, Inc.

At the same time the name Scripps-Howard Radio, Inc. was changed to Scripps-Howard Broadcasting Company.

On March 20, 1963 another significant development in the history of Scripps-Howard Broadcasting occurred. The Broadcasting Company announced the first public offering of its common stock. Three hundred seventy-five thousand shares were sold by four individual shareholders and the E. W. Scripps Company. Jack Howard said that one of the major considerations for going public was establishment of a market value for the company's stock.

In October 1965, Scripps-Howard Broadcasting officials signed a contract for the land on which to build a new studio, housing color equipment and offices, for WCPO-TV in Cincinnati at an estimated cost of $2 million. A new tower also figured in this expansion.

THAT SAME MONTH Scripps-Howard Broadcasting Company announced the sale of WCPO-AM and FM in Cincinnati to the Seattle-Portland-Spokane Radio Company. Control was transferred January 15, 1966.

In April 1980 Scripps-Howard Broadcasting purchased WITH-FM from Reeves Telecom Corporation in Baltimore, Maryland. The call letters were changed to WBSB, Baltimore.

In June 1980 the broadcasting company purchased KMEO-AM and FM in Phoenix, Arizona. This brought the number of radio stations in the group to six.

Scripps-Howard Broadcasting Company at this time is licensee of radio stations WMC and WMC-FM in Memphis, WNOX in Knoxville, and through a wholly-owned subsidiary is the owner of WBSB-FM in Baltimore, and KMEO-AM and FM in Phoenix. It is a licensee of television stations WCPO-TV in Cincinnati, WEWS in Cleveland, WMCT in Memphis, WPTV in Palm Beach, KBMA in Kansas City and KJRH, Tulsa. KJRH are new call letters for the Tulsa station which previously was KTEW. The new call letters are in honor of Scripps-Howard Broadcasting chairman Jack R. Howard.

PRESENT GENERAL MANAGERS of Scripps-Howard Broadcasting are: Morris E. Greiner Jr., Memphis; Edward D. Cervenak, Cleveland; Robert D. Gordon, Cincinnati; Robert R. Regalbuto, Palm Beach; F. Ben Hevel, Tulsa; Bob J. Wormington, Kansas City.

The managers of the radio stations are Christopher T. Gallu, Knoxville; Dean L. Osmundson, WMC-AM in Memphis; Donald W. Meyers, WMC-FM in Memphis; James P. Fox, WBSB, Baltimore; and Steve Wrath, KMEO-AM and FM in Phoenix.

Michael W. Callaghan is assistant to the president; James

E. Smith is vice-president, sales; and Richard J. Janssen is the assistant to the president for radio.

Directors of Scripps-Howard Broadcasting Company are: Jack R. Howard, Donald L. Perris, Mortimer C. Watters, Robert D. Gordon, Morris E. Greiner Jr., Edward W. Estlow and Philomene A. Gates.

Officers of the Broadcasting Company are: Jack R. Howard, chairman; Donald L. Perris, president and C.E.O.; Mortimer C. Watters, chairman of the executive committee; Robert D. Gordon, Morris E. Greiner Jr., James E. Smith, Edward D. Cervenak, F. Ben Hevel, and Robert Regalbuto vice-presidents; James E. Bloyd is vice president, engineering; Albert J. Schottelkotte, vice president, news; Lawrence A. Leser, treasurer; Daniel J. Castellini, secretary and assistant treasurer, and John Baskin, assistant secretary.

The stations licensed to Scripps-Howard Broadcasting Company are not directly connected with the Scripps-Howard newspapers. While there is mutual respect and friendliness they have remained over the years essentially competitors.

PRESIDENT

Donald L. Perris

D ON PERRIS GOT his first job with Scripps-Howard in a scene right out of a B movie on the late, late show.

Working Saturdays in a delicatessen, he was in the process of delivering a tuna on white to Louis Clifford, then the city editor of *The Cleveland Press*, when a runaway horse dragged the streetcar it was pulling through the front window of a tavern. In the confusion, Clifford mistook Perris for a newly-hired cub reporter. "Get out there and get the story," he told Perris.

Twenty minutes later, Perris was back with the facts and a picture scoop—three 8x10 glass-plate negatives, made by a passing photographer.

Don was hired as a copy boy—the first of nearly a dozen jobs he has held with Scripps-Howard—first with *The Cleveland Press*, then with Scripps-Howard Broadcasting.

BORN IN CLEVELAND June 9, 1923, Perris was just out of high school when he got *The Press* copy boy job and it wasn't long before he took notice of the attractive general assignment reporter whose desk was near the drinking fountain. Don and Barbara Fisher were married shortly thereafter.

In that original job at *The Press*, Perris worked a remarkable schedule: five shifts in three days. "I worked from 4 in the afternoon to 8 the next morning, came back at 4 the same afternoon and worked til midnight, which came to five shifts in three days. I was getting four days off every week and my starting salary was 20 bucks a week!"

Many years later, Perris was testifying before a Congressional communications subcommittee. Lionel Van Deerlin asked Perris about his first job. When he heard about the $20 a week, the Congressman made Perris feel a lot better when he commented that his first job also was with Scripps-Howard (in San Diego) "and I only made $18 a week!"

Drafted in 1943, Perris ended up at a Japanese language school and was sent to Japan. However, by then the war was over. With no urgent need for interpreters, Perris became an Armed Forces Radio newscaster.

"It wasn't a totally wasted effort, however," Perris says. "While I never got the opportunity to interpret the Japanese language in the army, over thirty years later the skill came in very handy: I was able to watch the movie *Shogun* every single night without any need for subtitles!"

NO JOB WAS WAITING when he came home from the Army. So he found newspaper jobs first at *The Dover Daily News* and then at *The Springfield Daily News*.

In 1947 Perris heard from a friend that a TV station was starting up in Cleveland, so he hopped a train from Springfield, but was never able to get an interview. He did sit in the waiting room continuously, however, for two days. Eventually, without an interview, he was told that someone would be in touch. Sure enough, two days later he received a call to start work as a newsreel writer.

The station was located in an old abandoned dance hall. Perris sat in the basement all day long doing, not so surprisingly, two things at once: writing his newsreel script and tending the furnace.

After a week the original job was abandoned and Perris worked into publicity. Then eventually he became announcer, cameraman, newscaster, interviewer, film editor, traffic manager, stagehand, salesman, station manager and executive.

His sharpest memories are the many assignments he undertook when WEWS, which pioneered local news department involvement with major news stories, wherever they were happening, sent its staff members all over the world. These assignments included the takeover of the Suez Canal by the Egyptians, and coverage of other breaking stories in Cyprus, Israel, Egypt, England, and France.

TODAY, AS THEN, Perris still feels that getting the story and pictures is what the business is all about.

"We may be using helicopters, minicams and satellites," he says, "but the idea is still the same: to present information so people want to watch."

A drop-out from Ohio State University, from Antioch College, from the University of Minnesota and from Western Reserve University, Perris still hopes to go back to school some day. He'd also like to spend more time on his hobbies —photography, jogging, and a small but growing collection of whale and dolphin recordings.

But there is much to be done in the broadcasting company. Don says that this includes "expansion in CATV and radio and developing a whole new generation of news and information programming."

Don and Barbara are the parents of three children: Katherine born in 1947, David (1950), and Barbara Anne (1953). They also have two grandchildren.

EXECUTIVE COMMITTEE CHAIRMAN

Mortimer C. Watters

MORT WATTERS is known for making waves—as a broadcast innovator or a powerboat skipper.

Often that has occurred with his cabin cruiser off Palm Beach or along the Ohio River—but mostly in his colorful distinguished and long career with Cincinnati's WCPO/TV.

Mortimer Charles Watters was born June 8, 1909 at Rochester, New York. After high school, he moved to Washington, D.C., where he was graduated from Georgetown University in 1932 with a Bachelor of Philosophy degree. He stayed in Washington for a year as radio director of Ryan Advertising Agency, then went back to Rochester to become sales manager of radio station WHEC.

Three years later, at twenty-five, Watters became head of a chain of three radio stations in West Virginia—and thus America's youngest general manager of a broadcasting organization.

TWO YEARS after that, in 1938, Mort joined Scripps-Howard Broadcasting—which was then radio only. Scripps-Howard had just bought WFBE, promptly changed its call letters to WCPO, and summoned Watters to Cincinnati to take charge and make something out of the station.

Take charge is an apt expression. That's exactly how Watters has operated in his many years with Scripps-Howard.

Scripps-Howard Broadcasting Company

He made plenty of waves in radio broadcasting. WCPO was a 250 watt station, then the least powerful of Cincinnati's five radio stations. Within a year, Watters had WCPO attracting both listeners and sponsors in numbers it hadn't known before.

Mort was willing to innovate, break tradition, attempt new approaches. He emphasized local news coverage; WCPO was the first Cincinnati station to broadcast news hourly with headlines on the half hour.

WCPO FORMED close ties with Scripps-Howard's *Cincinnati Post* (which had been the source of the WCPO call letters). Watters moved his radio news staff right into the newspaper's city room, with all WCPO newscasts emanating from there.

In 1940 Watters was named a vice president of Scripps-Howard Broadcasting; a year later he became a director; and in 1974 he was named chairman of the executive committee.

While he had great success with WCPO Radio, Mort hit his most spectacular licks in television. In 1949 Scripps-Howard opened WCPO/TV and, to no one's surprise, Watters brought along the same enthusiasm and flair he had used in radio. For starters Mort hired the first TV disc jockey. The deejay, already spinning records on WCPO radio, simply took a stack of records in front of the camera and made clever remarks between records while the camera took some wild and zany shots.

This was far from television's finest hour. But the informality and unpredictability of the disc jockey program caught the fancy of Cincinnati viewers.

The idea soon evolved into a series of production numbers in which the deejay and some pretty girl assistants pantomimed the songs. The imaginative show became so unusual that it "went network," picked up by DuMont Television Network which up until then had originated programs only in New York or Chicago.

WATTERS EXTENDED WCPO/TV's air time to twelve hours. Rival stations had much shorter broadcast days. But soon they followed Watters's lead.

Whenever Mort's name comes up, broadcast people are likely to recall how he handled talent by promising that he would not interfere with their creativity and then keeping a close eye on their progress urging them to be down to earth and innovative at every opportunity. The result was that WCPO/TV's daytime programming was a smash hit in the early days of local TV with most of Cincinnati's top air personalities developed at the station.

Among them was the station's art director, Al Lewis, who found himself pressed into service with a show called "Al Lewis' Drug Store." He soon became "Uncle Al." And "The Uncle Al Show" in the summer of 1980 celebrated its thirtieth consecutive year on television. It has been on the air five days a week, an hour a day, for all those years, making it without question the longest running children's television program anywhere.

MORT'S PERCEPTION of news as being where television had tremendous growth possibilities led him to hire Cincinnati Enquirer columnist Al Schottelkotte as news director. WCPO/TV news ratings have led all competition in virtually every rating book for the last two decades and the WCPO/TV news department is acknowledged to be one of the most respected in all of local television. With WCPO/TV's day to day operations under the firm guidance of Bob Gordon, in recent years Watters has divided his time about equally between Cincinnati and Palm Beach, and he boats enthusiastically in both places.

Mort and his wife, Paula Jane are the parents of Victoria Anne (born 1966). Mort has two other children, Mary Ellen (born 1939) and Rosemary (born 1948).

VICE PRESIDENT, ENGINEERING
James E. Bloyd

WHEN HE WAS going to high school in Bedford, Indiana, softball—not engineering—was on Jim Bloyd's mind.

Jim was a key man on the high school softball team, and his daily paper route helped him get extra copies of the paper's ballot for the high school "All Star" softball team.

"Enough extra copies, in fact," he says, "that it helped me make the All Star team!"

It was only after graduation and stints at a local dairy and as a hod carrier in the Bedford limestone area, that Jim discovered the technical interest that was to shape his career.

And it happened a long way from Bedford (where he was born February 27, 1921).

First, he joined the Navy in October 1942 and was eventually assigned to the Northwestern University Naval Training Center to study radio. Next came an assignment to a sub chaser. "We were supposed to chase submarines and drop depth charges on them," Jim says, "but it was discovered later that subs could outrun the sub chasers."

HIS SUB CHASER was USSC 697, a 110-foot round bottom boat—and one of Jim's more vivid memories of the boat was a twenty-one day trip, along with twenty-three other Navymen, in the boat across the ocean to an assignment in North Africa. "I was sick for the whole trip and a week later I was *still* sick," he says. "All I could eat for that whole time was tomato soup."

He continued to learn about radio and engineering, as his group patrolled in the Mediterranean, and participated in landings at Salerno and Sicily. At the landing at Anzio, he was with the group that led the landing craft into the shore.

Seven months before his thirty-month overseas duty was to end, the government turned his sub chaser over to the French Navy, and Jim was assigned to U.S. Naval headquarters in Algeria, then to Leghorn, Italy, still heavily into radio operating procedures.

WHEN HE RETURNED to Bedford after his Navy service, in 1945, he enrolled in nearby Valparaiso Technical Institute to learn still more about radio.

While he was going to school, he and his wife lived in a trailer. He and Jean Birdwell had met at a Halloween party in Jim's senior high school year and were married in December 1941.

The first Bloyd child, Terry (born 1946) arrived during those trailer years.

Through his connections at the Valparaiso school, Jim had a chance to work with Magnavox in Fort Wayne. His job was the testing of components. "The problem was that apartments were impossible to get at that time," Jim says, "so we had a really unsatisfactory set-up. Jean and Terry were in the trailer in Bedford and I was in Fort Wayne. After four months, I just quit."

A chance visit to Cleveland to see some relatives during that down time in his working career, proved a turning point for the Bloyds. "I heard about this TV station (WEWS) that was to be going on the air. They weren't hiring, but they were taking applications, so I left my resume," he says.

After the Cleveland trip, Jim and family returned to Bedford. He eventually found a job in broadcasting as a transmitter engineer at WSUA, an AM daytime radio station in Bloomington, Indiana.

EVENTUALLY a call came from Cleveland, and in January 1947, he joined WEWS as a studio engineer. He moved up to studio supervisor, eventually chief engineer for the station and in June 1975 was named vice president, engineering for all of Scripps-Howard Broadcasting.

Jim is active in a variety of engineering groups, including the Institute of Electrical and Electronic Engineers, the professional group of broadcasting, the Society of Motion Picture and Television Engineers and he's a senior member of the Society of Broadcast Engineers.

In addition to son Terry, the Bloyds also have a daughter Deborah (born 1952).

One of the things Jim likes to engineer most is a golf ball around a golf course. He's a die-hard, year 'round golfer. "Sure, I play all winter long," he says, "all you have to do is dye the ball red. When the snow falls, it's easy to see the red ball and unless the snow gets ridiculously deep, I'll be out there, hitting the ball, and then trying to find it!"

VICE PRESIDENT, NEWS

Albert J. Schottelkotte

AT SIXTEEN Al Schottelkotte grabbed the bottom rung of the ladder that made him the Cincinnati version of Walter Cronkite.

The year was 1943 and Al was bored with high school and toying with the idea of dropping out. He talked to his dad, a hardware wholesaler. "I'd like to try working for awhile," Al suggested. The father thought the change might do Al good.

Al grabbed the want ads and saw that *The Cincinnati Enquirer* needed a copy boy. Al, wearing neatly slicked back hair and an eager smile, hustled down to the paper. The city editor was not impressed that Al was cutting out on St.

Xavier High. "He sort of bawled me out," Al recalls. "I slunk out, figuring he didn't want me."

The city editor had second thoughts. He phoned Al at home later that night. And young Schottelkotte became a copy boy at $15 a week. Al had plenty of brass, vigor and ambition. He jumped around the newspaper plant like a small tornado. The city editor and the paper's top columnist "adopted" Al and schooled him in the intricacies of the Fourth Estate.

AL CAUGHT ON FAST. That was lucky for him. The war had more or less decimated most news rooms and *The Enquirer* was short of reporters. The city editor decided to take a chance on the new kid. So within three months Al became a cub reporter at $30 a week, probably the youngest on any U.S. metropolitan paper, certainly the happiest, and perhaps the workingest.

Schottelkotte cut his teeth on a lot of crime news across the river in Kentucky, and soon held his own with the old pros.

The Korean war found Al in the Army at Fort Knox, and as a twenty-two-year-old high school dropout, assigned as an Education Specialist. "I had to give lectures on current affairs," Al says. "Like NATO, Greece, and so forth. I really had to study hard. It was fortunate because I completed high school work in the Army and finally 'graduated.'"

In 1952 Al was back on *The Enquirer*, assigned to write his own *Talk of the Town* column. That gave him license to roam the city, unearthing news, doing commentary, stirring things up generally—and in the process—becoming a Cincinnati media celebrity. He won a "Big Story" award for helping clean up the murder of two cab drivers in Northern Kentucky.

FROM THE COLUMNIST who had befriended him as a kid Al inherited a 6 p.m. newscast on WSAI radio. He did that for a while and caught the eye of Mort Watters, who was pioneering television news on WCPO. Mort made several overtures and finally one afternoon in May 1959 Al agreed to become a newscaster on the WCPO/TV 11 p.m. news.

"I asked Mort," Al says, "when he wanted me to start. He said, 'Why, tonight, of course!' "

Al was in front of the Channel 9 camera that night—and hasn't been far from it since. For a couple of years he continued doing his *Talk of the Town* column as well as broadcasting.

Then in February 1961 he was appointed WCPO director of news and special events, and gave up newspapering. He has tried new ideas in television news, launching an hour-long Noon Report, the first of its type in the country. He still puts in a long day in the news room, anchoring both the 6 and 11 o'clock news.

In 1969 Schottelkotte was given the added duty of general manager of Scripps-Howard Broadcasting's newly-established News Division. Two years later he was made vice president/news for the entire company.

Al was Cincinnati's first newscaster to use regular mobile reports and taped interviews. He also broke new ground with live coverage of spot news, using remote vans, and eventually added a jet helicopter called "Newsbird" to his operation.

AL HAS BEEN a golfer for 25 years—and in 1980 shot his first hole-in-one, a 175-yarder. That same week his son Matt, a member of the University of Cincinnati golf team, topped the old man, with a rarer double eagle-2 on a 485-yard par 5 hole.

Al and his wife, Virginia Gleason whom he married in 1951, have an even dozen children. Besides Matt (born 1960) they are: Paul (born 1952), Carol (born 1953), Linda (born 1955), Joseph (born 1958), Louis (born 1961), Martha (born 1962), Amy (born 1963), Mary Jo (born 1965), Ellen (born 1968), and twins William and Michael (born 1973).

VICE PRESIDENT, SALES
James E. Smith

WHEN JIM SMITH took a sales job with WEWS in Cleveland in February 1958 he lived in the Akron area.

The average person might have moved to Cleveland at that point, but Jim chose to commute from Akron. "The kids were entrenched, the schools were right, and my wife was busy doing her thing—so I commuted," he says.

Over two decades later, he's still commuting!

"The roads kept getting better and the time kept shortening up," he says. "What started out as about an hour drive in 1958 is a simple thirty-minute run today. And there's only one traffic light the whole trip!"

THERE ARE FEW gray areas in Jim Smith. Whether it's shunning the obvious and *not* moving to Cleveland, or developing and implementing sales policy, Jim's position about things is always crystal clear.

That's how it was when he graduated from McKinley high school in Canton (where he was born November 2, 1929). He knew he did *not* want to go into the grocery business.

He had helped out in his parents' mom and pop grocery store all through school, doing lots of home deliveries and learning about retailing, but he had no intention of staying in that business.

He chose to go to nearby Kent State University, though not sure exactly what he did want at that point. He had a chance to take journalism but didn't know much about it. He asked his counselor for advice and promptly got sold.

Scripps-Howard Broadcasting Company 343

BY HIS SENIOR year he was editor-in-chief of the university paper. He fondly remembers one incident under his leadership: "The paper had always sponsored a Rowboat Regatta, but the school refused to underwrite costs due to too much beer drinking by the fraternities and sororities," he says, "so the paper decided to go out and get its own advertising, without any help from the school. We got enough advertising, and then some, put on the Rowboat Regatta on our own—and everybody STILL drank too much beer!"

With his Kent State Journalism degree in 1950, he married the girl he had courted from his sophomore days in high school, Nancy McDevitt. She had majored in dramatics at Oxford University.

Before graduation, Jim picked up a job at a new Akron radio station, WCUE. It meant skipping some 4 o'clock classes but it gave him a chance to work in radio news, and learn to write and prepare copy.

In 1953 he became news editor at the station and soon went on to WKBN in Youngstown. At that combination AM/FM and UHF station he quickly became involved in sales promotion, publicity and merchandising. His major assignment was to build a UHF TV market, and get it out from "under the gun" of the powerful VHF stations in Cleveland (which included WEWS).

AFTER TWO YEARS, he moved into sales exclusively. He also moonlighted as a teacher at Youngstown University business school. He was asked to teach an evening course on salesmanship. Jim allowed that he didn't know that much about sales. He was prevailed upon to take over the course, anyway. "I can almost say that my sales strength had its base right then," he says. "I had to keep two chapters ahead of the class at all times, so I forced myself to absorb every aspect of selling, to ask my own questions and to become an instant expert."

In 1956 he returned to Akron and WCUE, this time as a salesman. He made significant favorable impressions on the Cleveland business community and in 1958 the offer came to join WEWS in Cleveland. He spent eleven years in local sales. He was general sales manager 1969-1977, and assistant to president for sales, 1976 to May 1979 and was elected vice president, sales, in May 1979.

When he isn't selling, Jim is doing landscaping at his almost two acres of rolling country just outside of Akron. "The property consists of pines, about 70 tons of rocks and ground cover," he says, "but you won't find a blade of grass, because I just don't like to mow."

HE AND NANCY built the house in 1975 and it took him five painstaking years to complete the landscaping—all by himself. "I've got the blisters to prove it."

There are two Smith children: Douglas (born 1952) is a planning supervisor at J. Walter Thompson in New York, and daughter Terri (born 1954) is married and living in Washington, D.C.

VICE PRESIDENT, RADIO

Richard J. Janssen

AN OFF-HAND conversation with a radio station salesman at a party turned Dick Janssen's life around.

He had gone into business, fresh out of high school, operating two meat vendor stands at Cleveland's Central Market. That was not surprising since his parents were in the meat business. Dick grew up with a night-and-day education in the vendors' lore.

Dick, born in Cleveland May 19, 1936, enjoyed the "wheeling and dealing" at Central Market. "It was," he says, "a

SCRIPPS-HOWARD BROADCASTING COMPANY 345

great introduction to selling, managing, and administering—all in one. I'm not sure how polished I was, but I sure learned how to move the product and people."

His success led to being chosen by Sugardale Provision Company to open the Cleveland territory for their meats.

Then came the casual chat with the radio time salesman. Both exchanged shop talk about their careers. The more Dick heard about broadcasting, the more fascinated he became. He promptly decided to check out selling jobs in radio.

THIS WAS IN 1959—and the next week he was knocking on all radio station doors in Cleveland, asking for a job. Nothing happened at once. But within a couple of months he landed a local sales job with WHK Radio in Cleveland. He became top local salesman in two years. This led to a job with Metromedia, the parent company of WHK, which was starting its own national rep company. Dick was sent to Detroit in his new national rep role and soon was representing both radio and TV stations. His impressive performance brought him back to WHK in 1965 as sales manager. Three years later he became vice president and general manager of WHK. He also had responsibility for WMMS, the company's FM station in Cleveland, which was just getting started.

WMMS was the first of two radio stations which Dick put on the air, the other being KMET in Los Angeles. He had transferred to L.A. in 1968, as VP and GM of Metromedia's KLAC-AM and the brand new KMET-FM.

In 1970 he was approached by Nationwide Communications at WGAR in Cleveland, and joined that group. Two years later he became general manager. In 1975 he transferred to Nationwide's home office in Columbus, as vice president, operations, in charge of seven radio stations and three TV stations.

In July 1978 Dick joined Scripps-Howard Broadcasting as assistant to the president for radio.

AT THAT TIME, the Scripps-Howard Radio stations were WMC AM/FM in Memphis and WNOX/AM in Knoxville. Since then, both WMC/FM and WNOX/AM have been completely reprogrammed, and Scripps-Howard has acquired

WITH-FM in Baltimore (where the call letters were change to WBSB), and KMEO AM and FM in Phoenix.

Way back in high school, when Dick was learning all about selling and marketing (via the meat business), he met the girl he would eventually marry. Marilyn Spak and Dick have been married since 1955, when both were just two weeks out of high school. They have one daughter, Lynn (born 1960), a major in journalism and, not so surprisingly, in marketing, at Ohio State University.

ASSISTANT TO THE PRESIDENT

Michael W. Callaghan

IN BELLEVUE, OHIO, the *Bellevue Gazette* has been in the Callaghan family for over 110 years.

One of the many Callaghans to take a turn at running that highly successful business was Michael W. Callaghan.

Mike, who was born in Bellevue on March 19, 1947, graduated from the University of Notre Dame in 1969. His father, who had been publisher of the family's newspaper, had recently died and Mike was the logical family member to take over the business.

Up until that time his exposure to the running of the newspaper had been limited: "I had been a newspaper carrier as a kid," Mike says, "Otherwise the *Gazette* was a place where I spent a lot of time during my summers, but I couldn't say I had a lot of in-depth newspaper experience."

Scripps-Howard Broadcasting Company

HIS MARKETING MAJOR at Notre Dame (where he graduated maxima cum laude) was a big help in preparing him for the transition to the newspaper business. For two years, he was general manager of the *Gazette*, the only family member who was active at that time in the business.

He wanted something else, however. And the experience in running the paper for two years turned out to be the prelude to a whole new management career.

He went to Ohio State University in 1971 and 1972 and picked up his MBA, made arrangements for the *Gazette* to have someone other than a family member run it on a day to day basis, and connected himself with NEA as assistant to the general manager. There his many assignments included assistant publisher of the *World Almanac*.

Based at the Cleveland office, Mike moved through the organization to be vice president by 1978 when—by another shift of gears—he joined Don Perris at Scripps-Howard Broadcasting. His first assignment was as controller, then in 1979 he was named assistant to the president.

Mike's wife Kay also is a Bellevue native and has a shrewd business head of her own, with a position at a small CPA firm in Cleveland. Around the house, Kay does most of the fix up—Mike prefers to spend his spare time with tennis, racquetball, sailing, and he's a familiar figure jogging around his suburban Cleveland neighborhood most any night of the year.

MIKE IS AS QUICK to talk about the "down" time in his career as the "up" ones. For example: He flunked his first computer course—but not too many years after that he felt a lot better about computers when he became involved, at NEA, with the first computerized crossword puzzle production.

Then there was the time when he acted as publisher of a *Woman's Almanac*, too. "It bombed," he says. "Maybe it was a click or two ahead of it's time!"

WEWS
Cleveland, Ohio

Sign-On: Went on the air December 17, 1947 and became Ohio's first television station. Named for E. W. Scripps.

Highlights: Early programming, though rough around edges (Paul Hodges interviewing people at bus station, Gene Carroll conducting "Ring Around the Rosie" for kids on "Uncle Jake's House"), drew fascinated audiences.

First major program was *Cleveland Press Christmas Show*, m.c.'d by James Stewart live from Public Hall. One station stalwart is Dorothy Fuldheim, who became America's first female news commentator thirty years ago, and still does fifteen regular weekly telecasts.

Other firsts: Cleveland's first televised baseball game and America's first televised college credit courses. First local television station to receive the distinguished George Foster Peabody Award for local public service.

VICE PRESIDENT & GENERAL MANAGER

Edward D. Cervenak

FROM HIS BOY SCOUT days young Ed Cervenak was fascinated by radios—especially fixing them. Nine out of ten nights he'd be at some neighbor's house repairing a balky set.

A lifelong Clevelander, born May 24, 1925, Ed took his interest to West Technical High School, where he majored in electricity. When he joined the Navy in 1943, and was assigned to Wright Junior College radar school, he had his first real exposure to television.

"Our instructor was Captain Eddy, but he definitely was not a kiddie personality," Ed says. "He was in charge of the radar school and a pioneer in experimental television broadcasting."

To demonstrate how TV worked, Captain Eddy would set up a camera, point it out the window as the students watched the moving traffic on the monitor.

"I was fascinated," Ed says, "and right then and there—at all of 17—I knew that television was the career I wanted."

CAPTAIN EDDY encouraged Ed to learn everything he could about this burgeoning new medium and to this day Ed speaks of the Captain's enthusiasm in grateful terms.

Ed's television career had to wait. He had Navy service to complete, which he did as a radar technician, first class, in the Pacific. The Navy experience over, he set about to find a school where he could learn more about television.

It wasn't easy.

The year was 1946 and television was simply not on the curriculum of many schools. But he did eventually find the American Television Institute in Chicago, which offered accelerated electronics courses with emphasis on television.

He signed up, made living arrangements at a co-ed "Y" and started studying. There was that strikingly attractive girl named Marge Downing who lived in the same facility, though. She did a lot of listening to Ed's excited conversations about television and in 1947 they were married.

THE TIME CAME for Ed to find a job in the industry that Captain Eddy had pointed him toward. He heard about a television station that was going on the air in Cleveland, so he shot an application eastward. The station was WEWS and soon Ed received a telegram from Joe Epperson, the chief engineer at WEWS.

In May 1948 Cervenak joined the staff as an engineer. The station had been on the air only five months and there was a lot to learn.

His WEWS assignments ranged from field supervisor responsible for remote telecasts originating in the Cleveland area for local and network distribution, to producer/director of studio and remote programs; network coordinator for national syndicated "Upbeat" program. In 1961 he was named assistant operations director, the director of news operations in 1968.

Under his direction, the TV 5 "Eyewitness News" won consistent recognition as Cleveland's outstanding news program.

In 1973 he became assistant general manager in charge of programming and news and in 1975 took over as general manager. He was named vice president of Scripps-Howard Broadcasting in 1979.

Ed has never stopped learning. He has kept abreast of the constantly changing business he's in by attending Case Western Reserve University in Cleveland, Columbia University and Harvard Business School.

MARGE AND ED have four children. Three are grown and pursuing their own careers now. Sandra was born in 1948, James in 1950, Charles in 1954; at home is Steven born in 1967.

When he can find some spare time, Ed likes boating and golfing. But his neighbors in Cleveland's Seven Hills will also be happy to tell you they're lucky to have a handy guy like Ed around—whenever anything goes wrong with their radios or TV sets.

SCRIPPS-HOWARD BROADCASTING COMPANY 351

WCPO-TV
Cincinnati, Ohio

Sign On: Began broadcasting July 26, 1949.

Highlights: Station's call letters originally were assigned to the Scripps-Howard radio station in Cincinnati. The radio station was on the air from 1938 through 1965, at which time it was sold off and Scripps-Howard put all of its broadcast energies into the television facility.

Pioneered local live television and currently airs world's longest running live children's TV program, The Uncle Al Show. That program premiered in 1950 and is still a daily, five day a week, live feature on the station.

WCPO-TV News department consistently in forefront of local television news facilities, with live Instant Cam Network an innovator in news gathering techniques and concepts for local television stations.

VICE PRESIDENT & GENERAL MANAGER
Robert D. Gordon

As A YOUNGSTER Bob Gordon had some romantic notion about becoming a G-man. After he finished high school in his home town of Colorado City, Texas and worked in a hitch in the Navy V-5 program at Tulane University, and some time at McMurry College, he headed for Washington, D.C. That was 1948, and Bob was just about 21, having been born October 15, 1927. The FBI took him on. A year later he married his Texas sweetheart, Jeanne Stokes.

As appealing as the FBI job turned out to be, Bob soon developed a new interest—the broadcast business. He looked around and landed a job down on the Texas Gulf coast. The ex-FBI man became Bob Gordon, disc jockey, at KUNO radio, Corpus Christi. It turned out to be exactly the right move.

"The first day I was a disc jockey," Bob says, "I knew what I really wanted—to be a broadcast manager."

By 1951 Bob had been promoted to KUNO program director, and then his career was detoured with a stint in the U.S. Army. His ability to get ahead was amply displayed there. From artillery officer in the 45th Division in Korea he became officer-in-charge of programming for the Armed Forces Korean Network and manager of the network's key station.

OUT OF THE ARMY in 1955, Bob returned to broadcasting as announcer-director at WHEN-TV, Syracuse, New York. His own words, "I want to be a manager" kept ringing in his ears and in 1956 he became part owner and program manager of station WTMV-TV in Tupelo, Mississippi.

He quickly developed a managerial style that combined "strong gentleness" with a shrewd, even canny, entrepreneurial personality.

From Tupelo, Gordon moved to Tulsa, Oklahoma, as operations manager at KTUL-TV, then local-regional sales manager. In 1960 he heard about an opening at WCPO/TV in Cincinnati. He got the job, beginning his association with Scripps-Howard. From WCPO's local sales manager he soon advanced to assistant general manager, and in 1964 was named general manager. Two years later, he became a Scripps-Howard Broadcasting vice president and in 1971 was elected to the board.

BOB HAS BEEN first and foremost a family man, devoted to his Jeanne and their three sons, Bob Jr. (born 1953), Jeff (born 1959), and Gus (born 1965). And his lifelong strong family emotions have been translated into his feeling of responsibility as a broadcaster.

His approach to television has continued to be that it's a visitor in the home and he will do all within his ability to keep that visitor friendly, warm and genuine—not one who is offensive. He has been dubbed "Mr. Clean" for this attitude, but he has stuck to his principles, from refusing to air Cher in an early evening time slot on a Sunday night because he found the program unsuitable for family audiences, to refusing to carry programs and films scheduled by his affiliate network (CBS-TV), because he finds them offensive to family viewing.

Bob has brought this strong conviction to a number of nationally prominent broadcast industry posts. In March 1973 he was elected to the Television Board of Directors of the National Association of Broadcasters, then was re-elected for another two-year term in 1975. In January 1976, he was elected chairman of the Television Board of the NAB.

Gordon believes Cincinnati is a conservative community that wants more traditional values than New York or Los Angeles, and he runs his station with that constantly in mind.

HIS CAREER has brought him a host of honors, including an honorary Doctor of Laws degree from Edgecliff College in Cincinnati, and the establishment of a Robert D. Gordon Medical Research Fellowship at the City of Hope Medical Center in California. He has a leadership role in a wide range of health, education, civic, and business activities in Cincinnati. These include: member of the Edgecliff College Board of Trustees; associate of the University of Cincinnati College Conservatory of Music; general chairman of the United Appeal campaigns and of a United Negro College Fund campaign. He is a trustee of the Scripps-Howard Foundation.

Bob does find time to relax and his Texan origins probably are the source for his most passionate hobby—raising and showing of quarterhorses. Jeanne shares her husband's enthusiasm for quarterhorses and they have traveled around the country with the equine members of their family. On many weekends they are off pulling their horse trailer to the nearest registered quarterhorse show.

Bob has had great success with his hobby. In 1976 his frequent trips to the winner's circle qualified him for the amateur western pleasure class at a world championship show. In that same year, he topped 50 points in AQHA's highly-prized amateur western pleasure class and received his Superior Award. He then topped that by finishing third in the entire nation in junior amateur western pleasure division.

What's remarkable about that is that only two years before he had never been in a show ring! But then, after all, his associates know that when Bob Gordon sets his mind to something...

WMC-TV
Memphis, Tennessee

Sign-On: Began as WMCT on December 11, 1948, as youngest of three WMC stations in a pioneer family, and one of the earliest TV affiliates of NBC.

Highlights: First Memphis television station. Remained that for five years while FCC froze license applications and tried to figure how many VHF signals could be accommodated with minimal interference.

In early 1950's, WMCT gave a community group most of what was needed to start an educational or "public" station in Memphis: new transmitter, tower, building, and other equipment.

Call letters changed to WMC-TV on January 1, 1967 to avoid confusion with the other stations designated as WMC and WMC-FM. Since mid-60's, emphasis on local news and informational broadcasts, producing outstanding ratings locally and regional or national awards for excellence.

VICE PRESIDENT & GENERAL MANAGER
Morris E. Greiner Jr.

IN WORLD WAR II Mori Greiner was assigned to a destroyer-escort still being built. It was designated the DE-37. That didn't seem like much of a name to write home about. But the vessel turned into something of a Jonah, made Mori the butt of countless jokes—and wishing he had another name.

He did his best to get off the DE-37, but you know the Navy. He had to stick it out.

When the vessel was launched it was named for the first American to be killed in an enemy bombing of U.S. soil—Frederick Greiner of Minnesota.

Frequent jokes about the name similarity bugged Mori so much he asked for a transfer. And asked, and asked. No dice.

So Mori was not only officer of the deck when the *Greiner* was commissioned, but was commanding officer when she was put in mothballs four years later.

"In between," says Mori, "I was seasick."

THOUGH BORN IN Minneapolis (November 7, 1920), Mori grew up in Chicago and Kansas City. In high school he was very much in full view. "They said," Mori recalls, "that I was involved in more extracurricular activities than any other student up to that time."

He was president of the Literary Society, head of student council, captain of the crack drill team and ROTC cadet major. He was an Eagle Scout and camp counselor. He was chief feature editor and gossip columnist for the high school paper. He even found time to date the editor of the paper, Dorothy Jean Carter.

After high school graduation, Mori enrolled at Washington and Jefferson College to major in English literature. Disaster overtook him before he could finish his freshman year.

Mori and a couple of his buddies decided they were against compulsory religion. The three students tied a cow to the pulpit in the university chapel. The prank got a big play in the Pittsburgh papers.

Says Mori, "The cow wore a sign reading 'We don't like religious chapel—this is no bull!' And just to make sure we were noticed, we fed the cow a pretty hefty meal of bran before we took her inside."

As might be expected, Mori and his student pals were expelled. His buddies turned out to be sons of college trustees. So a little later the three were readmitted to Washington and Jefferson.

MORI TRANSFERRED eventually to Duke, where he was graduated in 1942. Then came his Navy duty. All along he had kept in touch with that high school editor and in 1946 he and Dorothy were married.

Seeking fame and fortune in the Kansas City broadcast world, he took a job at WHB radio as director of plans and promotion, writing continuity. After four years, he moved to an advertising agency as copy chief.

"I really didn't want to leave the station, but felt I had gone as far as I could go. They had no TV license and my ambition at that point was to become a TV program director. So when I saw this opportunity to make more money and gain different experience, I went to the agency."

Mori, however, had an understanding with the radio station he would come back when the TV license came through. In 1953 it happened. Mori got a call on a Friday, was offered the job of station manager, and the following Monday the station was on the air.

"It was touch and go. I was writing copy during programs that went on at the next break."

ELEVEN YEARS LATER Mori was hired as manager of WMCT in Memphis. He was elected a vice president of Scripps-Howard Broadcasting Company in 1967 and a director in 1972.

Dorothy and Mori were once designated by the American Boxer Club as "Boxer Breeders of The Year." They also raised miniature schnauzers and their dogs won best-of-show honors at dozens of national shows. One of their dogs, Barrage of Quality Hill, was the first dog to make the cover of *Sports Illustrated*.

Later they exhibited horses and won the Southern three-gaited championship.

Mori has been both president and chairman of United Way of Greater Memphis, president of the Red Balloon Players, Greater Memphis State, Memphis Speech and Hearing Center. He serves as a trustee of Scripps-Howard Foundation, as vice chairman of Memphis Academy of Arts (a four-year college), as a member of advisory council or trustee of two other colleges and two universities.

He is general chairman of the NAACP Freedom Fund dinner in Memphis and a national advisor to ACT-SO, the achievement program NAACP sponsors for teens. He is a director of Mid-South Fair.

Mori and Dorothy have one son, Derek, born in 1947.

SCRIPPS-HOWARD BROADCASTING COMPANY

WPTV
West Palm Beach, Florida

Sign On: Went on air on August 22, 1954, as WJNO-TV, operating from a former greenhouse, converted into a theater and adapted into a studio. Original owners William Cook and Theodore Granik.

Highlights: In 1956 station purchased by John Phipps interest and call letters changed to WPTV. Scripps-Howard Broadcasting acquired station December 27, 1961. One of first in Florida to go color. After Scripps-Howard purchase, public service and marketing procedures beefed up and station rapidly dominated market.

In 1971 the facility relocated beside intracoastal waterway in West Palm Beach. Initiated South Florida's first hour evening newscast. Public service and public affairs committment one of strongest in southeastern Florida.

VICE PRESIDENT & GENERAL MANAGER
Robert R. Regalbuto

THERE ARE MOVIE buffs—and there is Bob Regalbuto.

Bob's intense interest in movies—which goes back to seeing Marlene Dietrich in *Golden Earrings* in 1948 when he was only five—is insatiable, and has had a major impact in his career direction.

His fascination for film and arts-related areas literally mushroomed after seeing that first movie. "I can see a film over and over again, and still get something from it," Bob says, "and those special moments, like Bogart giving the o.k. to play the Marseillaise in *Casablanca* still are thrilling to me, even though I've seen them many times."

Regalbuto amazes colleagues with his knowledge in many aspects of the movies, of the theater, and the arts in general.

Not so unexpectedly, after LaSalle and Peekskill Military Academies, when this third generation New Yorker (born in New York City July 4, 1943), started his college education, he made a hasty switch from pre-law courses to the arts—graduating with a Bachelor of Arts degree, and eventually a Master of Arts.

THIS WAS NOT at one of the arts-oriented schools in New York, however, but at the University of Mississippi. While he had been accepted at a number of northeastern colleges, he chose to go south for his education.

"I had a desire for a totally new environment," he says, "so the University of Mississippi became a good choice for me, much to the chagrin of my parents and advisors!"

As a drama major, he was active in fifty to sixty campus productions. Some of his favorite dramatic roles were in *"Look Back in Anger," "The Zoo Story"* and *"The Caretaker."* He turned out to be adept at light comedy as well. His favorites there were in *"Love in E Flat"* and in *"Barefoot in the Park."* ("I played the Redford role in that one," he smiles.)

The timing and delivery that he perfected on the stage were also put to use elsewhere during his college days. "I operated my own advertising agency on campus and delivered timely messages on match books, pens, and balloons—as well as on the only radio station in town."

THE COMBINATION of theater and sales activities provided the framework for his eventual full-scale move into broadcasting.

Before that, though, after his formal education, he had applied at one of Wall Street's top brokerage houses. He scored in the top percentile in his employment exam, but was told that twenty-two was too young to be a stockbroker.

"The cashier's cage held no charm for me," Bob says, "so I decided at that point that I should try to combine my interest in financial affairs with my flair for communications."

The decision made, he walked into the studios of WPTV and got a job. His very first assignment was to develop the

Fort Lauderdale area which was a brand new sales market for the station.

Along the way, he met his future wife, Marlena Gallo. It came as a blind date, arranged by his host to even out a dinner party.

"I wouldn't say our romance was remembered as 'love at first sight' ", Bob says, "Rather more like *The Night of January 16th.*' "

That's a play title and both Bob and Marlena had major roles, in a community theater production of the play. Bob was cast as the prosecutor and Marlena as the victim's wife.

"During our rehearsals together, I ad libbed a marriage proposal," Bob says, "but it was three years—and a batch of acting roles—later, before we were married."

MEANWHILE BOB moved through the ranks at WPTV. In twelve years he went from local sales manager to regional sales manager to general sales manager and then general manager and eventually a vice president of Scripps-Howard Broadcasting.

Bob is a lifetime trustee of the United Way, a member of the Economic Council of the Palm Beaches, a board member of the Palm Beach and West Palm Beach Chambers of Commerce, a member of the board of the Palm Beach Civic Opera, and a member of the management board of the Flagler National Bank.

Bob and Marlena make their home in a Spanish style house in West Palm Beach, where Marlena's creativity and love for antiques are much in evidence.

When they speak of their creativity, however, Bob and Marlena point most proudly to the three Regalbuto children: Jason (born 1972), Mark (born 1974) and Lauren (born 1977).

KJRH
Tulsa, Oklahoma

Sign On: Went on the air on December 5, 1954, became part of Scripps-Howard Broadcasting January 1, 1971.

Highlights: Impressive list of "firsts" in Tulsa TV: first color studio cameras, first color station, first to broadcast a remote television news story with live ENG unit, first two-inch VTR cartridge machine, first woman news director (Susan Silver).

KJRH is NBC/TV affiliate, serving 600,000 homes in 32 counties; carried by fifty-seven cable systems in Missouri, Kansas, Arkansas and Oklahoma.

Until fall of 1980, had been KTEW. Adopted new call letters to honor Jack R. Howard, Chairman of Scripps-Howard Broadcasting.

VICE PRESIDENT & GENERAL MANAGER
F. Ben Hevel

LONG BEFORE *astronaut* and *aeronautical engineer* became everyday words, Ben Hevel thought they represented what he wanted. "I didn't know what the right words were, but I wanted to work on some project that would take people to the moon," Ben says.

That was back in the Forties and space travel was a thing mostly of fiction, but Ben was intrigued with the idea throughout high school in Oswego, Kansas.

His family had moved from Henryetta, Oklahoma (where he was born April 14, 1930), when his father bought a meat market and grocery store in Oswego.

Ben got a football scholarship to Coffeyville Junior College, but still dreamed about aeronautical engineering. "But they talked me out of it at Coffeyville," Ben says. "They told me aeronautical engineers were a dime a dozen. I should put my energies elsewhere."

So Ben took general courses at the two-year junior college. About then the Korean war broke out and, still harboring dreams of an aeronautical career, he joined the Air Force.

"Not only did I never get to be a pilot," Ben groans, "but the only time I flew in the Air Force was on a commercial air liner from San Antonio, Texas to Biloxi, Mississippi!"

He was en route to radio school in Biloxi. Ben ended up in the top five percent of the class and was promptly shipped to Nagasaki, Japan.

"The only problem was that when we got to Japan they told us that they didn't need *radio* operators, they needed *radar* operators." So he quickly learned radar and spent the balance of his eighteen months in Japan.

After discharge in 1954, he went to Wichita University in Kansas, majoring in speech, with emphasis on radio and television.

HIS FIRST TV JOB came when he called KAKE Wichita to say hello to the sports director whom he'd known at Coffeyville Junior College. The friend mentioned an opening, and Ben started out as a cameraman at the Wichita station.

During his two years at KAKE, Ben worked into directing. One of his prime projects was a live thirty-minute drama. Though originally assigned only as director, he eventually ended up also as the show's writer, producer, set designer and builder.

In 1957 came an opportunity to be a senior director and an assistant to the program director at KETV, Omaha. Ben grabbed it. His responsibilities included designing, building and formating all live shows for the new station, including news programs.

He rose to executive producer and then in 1959 moved to KTUL in Tulsa as program director and operations manager. During his seven years there, he began a friendship with Bob Gordon (who was the KTUL local-regional manager then) which was to involve some career intertwining for several years. They worked together on a variety of projects at KTUL but Ben's most vivid memory was the Cherokee Strip Land Rush. "It was a station promotion where we buried $10,000 worth of certificates in tin cans on forty acres of land surrounding the station and people were urged to stake claims all over town to find the certificates. It tore the town up in more ways than one," Ben remembers, "but we sure got our viewers' attention!"

Bob Gordon had moved on to WCPO/TV in Cincinnati as Ben continued at KTUL. Then in April 1966 Gordon called Ben and offered him the job of director of operations at the Cincinnati station.

Ben welcomed the opportunity to join his old friend and for twelve years this Cincinnati team flourished, with Hevel serving as assistant general manager for the last seven years of that time. Then in 1978 the call came to return to Tulsa —this time as general manager at KTEW, now KJRH.

In the spring of 1980, Ben was named a vice president of Scripps-Howard Broadcasting.

Ben and his wife Marlynn have three children, Mark (born 1955), Mike (born 1956) and Nancy (born 1959).

SCRIPPS-HOWARD BROADCASTING COMPANY 363

KBMA-TV
Kansas City, Missouri

Sign-On: As Channel 41, went on air September 28, 1970, nation's first computer automated television station.

Highlights: In early days, originated virtually all local programs on remote location. In first two years station crews originated 500 remote telecasts from sites around Kansas City from a Winnebago motor home converted to a mobile television unit.

Entered satellite era in 1976, second broadcast station in the U.S. to have its own earth station. Originates nearly 100 annual sports events, seen in Kansas City or distributed nationally.

Acquired by Scripps-Howard Broadcasting September 1977. Has since expanded local news coverage, broken ground for a 44,000 square foot production/television office building. In mid-1980 joined twenty-nine other stations in launching first satellite-delivered nightly network newscast on Independent News Network.

GENERAL MANAGER
Bob J. Wormington

BOB WORMINGTON, just out of the Air Force went to college in 1945 to become an aeronautical engineer but his twin brother Bill got a better idea. Bill suggested they study journalism and buy a small town newspaper.

The idea appealed to Bob. They went to the University of Kansas and got master's degrees in journalism. Their newspaper dream never materialized. But the career shift led Bob into television—as a writer, director, producer and executive.

Bob feels he has always had writing in his blood. "Good writing," he says, "is the real base of any mass communication. Unfortunately it has always been in short supply."

In the Fifties Bob was getting writer credits on such

programs as NBC's Matinee Theater. For several summers he taught television writing at the Midwest Writer's Clinic at the University of Kansas. He still feels there is a "book or two" in his head he ought to put on paper—someday.

THE WORMINGTON TWINS were born on October 17, 1926 at home, in Dodge City, Kansas. After leaving the University of Kansas (where Bob wrote his master's thesis on television production), they went their separate ways.

Bob got his first television job in 1950 at the *Kansas City Star* station WDAF/TV. Not as a writer, however. He sold ads daytime and worked on TV production at night.

One year later he was recalled by the Air Force. That looked like an unpleasant crimp in his newly-launched career. Instead it was a spectacular boon. For after a stint in the Strategic Air Command, he went to the West Coast where his group established the first Air Force television unit.

Their function was to produce low-cost training films. That gave Bob an undreamed of opportunity. "I was assigned to work with the networks in special training on television production," Bob says, "so there I was on the set of a whole slew of West Coast-originated television programs, like the Colgate Comedy Hour, the Red Skelton Show and Your Show of Shows. I was ecstatic!"

When the military service ended, Bob returned to WDAF/TV with some eminent qualifications as a television director. He moved through the ranks to become general manager, ultimately leaving the station in 1968 to form a color production company and in 1970 he started KBMA/TV, where he has been its only general manager.

BOB HAS A RAFT of production credits. He directed over one hundred different shows that were carried by the NBC network and was responsible for Midwest directing of the NBC election returns, which started the era of computers predicting elections. He recalls directing a live telecast when the remote truck caught fire and the crew hung in until the end of the show, stamping out sparks with their feet. That experience was topped by an even hotter on-scene event. Bob was directing live coverage of a gasoline fire in Kansas City when storage tanks exploded engulfing one hundred firemen in flames. That coverage won significant national attention and Bob says: "I still get chills when I listen to the replay of that event."

Bob has blazed new trails with KBMA/TV.

The station was the first in the United States to use a satellite for point-to-point program transmission, and was the country's second broadcast station to have its own earth station.

KBMA/TV ALSO ORIGINATED the first cable television network, separate from its over-the-air programming. It was called Target Network Television and it still lives on as the satellite programming service on Southern Satellite.

Bob and his wife Kareen are Irish through and through. His distant family is from Dublin and Belfast and hers (O' Connor) from County Kerry. "Our families," says Bob "grew up throwing rocks at each other."

There are six Wormington children; Nancy (born 1954), Pat (born 1956), Cathy (born 1958), Mary (born 1959), Ann (born 1964) and Joe (born 1972).

WMC and WMC-FM
Memphis, Tennessee

Sign-On: WMC born in 1923 in era of homemade crystal set receivers and earphones. Four years later became a member of newly-organized NBC Network and became only the sixteenth station in the country to offer the new programming service.

Highlights: In 1947 WMC-FM was added. Went to 300,000 watts becoming one of the most powerful radio stations in nation. With advent of WMC-TV in 1948, WMC-FM existed in background for twenty years, broadcasting classical and background music. In February 1967 underwent major format change to rock and roll. In 1973 WMC-AM switched to an all country format. Both stations switched network affiliations in 1979. After fifty-two years with NBC, both switched to ABC ... FM to ABC Contemporary Network and AM to the ABC Information Network.

Stations currently operate separately, each directed by its own management and personnel. Both dominant in Memphis market, serving different audiences.

GENERAL MANAGER
WMC-FM

Donald Meyers

"I HAVE A LADY in the balcony, Doctor!" The man behind the voice that radio nostalgia buffs instantly will recall was Don Meyers.

As a student at the College of Music in Cincinnati, majoring in radio and television and with a big, booming voice that went very nicely with his six-four, 220 pound frame he found lots of opportunities to use that voice. The nationally popular Dr. I.Q. radio show was one of them.

The show frequently originated in Cincinnati and Meyers's lady-in-the-balcony role was such an integral part of the show that he often traveled beyond Cincinnati—school permitting—with the program.

Born in Cincinnati December 28, 1928, Don received most of his education in Cincinnati, even though his engineering father moved the family around the Midwest during Don's years at Purcell High school. School rallies almost always found Don on stage as the emcee, and he also was called on to represent the school whenever they needed a "big" voice.

"I decided right then and there that if I could be successful talking in high school, I just might be able to make a living at it later on," Don says. In addition to his Dr. I.Q. stints during college, he also appeared in a wide variety of radio dramas over WLW which at the time was originating live dramas for the NBC Radio network.

AFTER GRADUATING from college in 1949, he worked at radio stations in Canton, Findlay and Toledo. While at WSPD Radio in Toledo he was chosen as one of the top 50 personalities in the country.

In 1956 he moved to Atlanta as a morning disc jockey and program director, and quickly became the voice of Delta Airlines in the area. He also picked up an award for narrating an industrial film for Lockheed Airways, and taught a course in radio/TV at night at a broadcast school there.

"I had gone a long way, using my voice," Meyers says, "But I realized that I needed a broader work background if I was going to move up in broadcasting."

As a result in 1962 Don accepted a job as a salesman for LIN Broadcasting's WAKY in Louisville. He soon became sales manager and in 1967 was named president and general manager.

IT WAS AT WAKY that Don began to acquire his formidable reputation as a "radio doctor" which had nothing to do with ladies in balconies, but rather indicated his ability to take radio station formats which had decided "lemon" aspects to them and turn them into highly successful "lemonade"!

WAKY was his first successful effort of that kind. Don continued to function as a radio doctor and was named a corporate vice president of LIN in 1973 with the charge to practice his healing arts on other LIN stations.

How did he do? "All of the patients recovered, nicely," Don says.

In 1978 Don joined Scripps-Howard as general manager of WMC-FM.

He lives on an eight-acre mini-farm just outside of Memphis with wife Pat and three children—Lorre (born 1965), Stephanie (1967) and Darren (1969)—along with two horses (hunter/jumpers) and three dogs as well as "a constantly varying number of cats."

GENERAL MANAGER
WMC

Dean L. Osmundson

"THE GREATEST hazard of life is to risk nothing." That excerpt from a speech by Dean L. Osmundson, general manager of WMC Radio, Memphis, is not just throw-away wisdom—it reflects his career philosophy.

Osmundson has taken a lot of chores and made several job changes in his broadcasting career, but he has known since the fourth grade what he wanted in life.

"My music teacher in elementary school had 'Broadcast Day' every Friday. She used a simulated microphone, and volunteers stood in front of the class and made speeches over the mike. I volunteered every Friday," Osmundson recalls. "That's when I fell in love with broadcasting, and I still love it."

Osmundson was born in Radcliffe, Iowa (population 627) May 9, 1925. In high school and college he took a wide variety of speaking and drama courses, and went on to earn his degree in broadcasting in June 1950 from the Brown Institute of Broadcasting in Minneapolis.

HE LANDED HIS first job as an announcer at WLCX Radio, LaCrosse, Wisconsin on August 1, 1950. That's when the risks began.

"I'll never forget my first day at WLCX. I was told that one of the sponsors of my 10 o'clock newscast always listened to make sure the announcer advertised his company well. I was also informed that the last two announcers had failed to satisfy him. I was scared to death, but I guess I satisfied the sponsor."

Osmundson has worked in almost every phase of broadcasting. He was program director for WLCX and WBIZ Radio in Eau Claire, Wisconsin, and a television newscaster, weather reporter and program moderator on KTVO-TV, Ottumwa, Iowa.

He first joined WMC in 1958 as a sales representative but was made program director after five months. Six years later, he returned to sales as WMC's sales manager and became general manager in 1966.

OSMUNDSON'S MANAGEMENT philosophy is that basic integrity is the primary qualification for success and that people are the competitive difference in every company or organization. "I have a strong belief that management should be communicative, beginning with emotion and feeling, not just words." Osmundson says, "I am of the management school that strives to persuade, educate and train, but never simply to order people to do their jobs."

Osmundson is very active in both Memphis Area Broadcasters Association and Tennessee Association of Broadcasters. He is also past president of both the Memphis and International Sales and Marketing Executives chapters. Osmundson is also former president of Ascension Towers, Inc., a 195-unit high-rise for the elderly, and is the Mid-South Fair's coliseum attractions chairman. He and his wife, the former Audrey Claassen, have two children: Mark (born 1951) and Jean (born 1952).

WNOX
Knoxville, Tennessee

Sign On: Went on air in 1921, first radio station in Tennessee. Purchased by Scripps-Howard in 1935 as its first broadcast facility.
Highlights: One of first ten radio stations in United States. Early broadcasts aired from locations ranging from furniture store basement to the top floor of fanciest hotel in town. Early broadcasts featured country and western music with stars like Chet Atkins, Homer and Jethro, Roy Acuff, Archie Campbell and the Carter family having first exposure on programs like Midday-Merry-Go-Round and Tennessee Barndance.

Changed from country music to contemporary in November 1963. First Knoxville station to furnish airborne traffic reports. With 10,000 watts, most powerful fulltime AM station in East Tennessee.

GENERAL MANAGER
Christopher T. Gallu

CHRIS GALLU STARTED his television career in a most unlikely place: the peanut gallery of the Howdy Doody television show, with Buffalo Bob Smith and Clarabelle the Clown. Not just once—but many, many times.

That's because his father Sam was a Howdy Doody show writer, and young Chris had no trouble being often in the audience on that early children's TV program.

The elder Gallu was solidly entrenched in show business. "My father did just about everything—from lead tenor with Fred Waring's Pennsylvanians to singing for Toscannini at the Met," Chris says.

The Howdy Doody writing followed some of Sam Gallu's singing endeavors, and after that came independent producing in Hollywood. Shows like *Navy Log, Border Patrol, Blue Angels* all were Sam Gallu productions.

Scripps-Howard Broadcasting Company

So Chris was exposed to all of this as he grew up. He was born January 18, 1944 in Queens, New York while his dad was active in New York television, then moved to the west coast, as his father moved into TV production. Chris graduated from Verde Valley School in Arizona then attended the University of California at Berkeley, graduating in 1966.

"I thought I might like to be a teacher," Chris says, "so my college degree ended up being a B.A. in history."

However, right after college, the lure of broadcasting surfaced. Chris applied for a job at the Group W outlet in San Francisco. They had no openings but were so encouraging that Chris made a major decision.

"I packed all my belongings and headed east," he says, "and my instincts were right. I landed a job with the Westinghouse station (WBZ) in Boston."

His first assignment was sales service, and then he became an account executive.

As a member of the U.S. Army Reserves, he was called to active duty in 1968 and was assigned to Germany.

There he met his future wife, Terri Purvis. "No, she wasn't German," he says. "In fact, she was from Akron!" Terri had gone to Europe to accompany her girl friend who was marrying Chris' roommate. The inevitable blind date between Chris and Terri was set up, and three months later they were married in Basel, Switzerland.

Out of service, Chris and Terri returned to the states, where he rejoined Westinghouse. Not in Boston, however, but in Baltimore, where he was an account executive with the Group W station WJZ from 1970 to 1972. Next he was national sales manager for radio station WFBR in Baltimore. After nine months he became general sales manager, including WBKZ-FM when that station was taken over.

In 1978 he joined Scripps-Howard Broadcasting as general manager of WNOX Radio.

"When Don Perris first met me his first question was: 'Are you any relation to Sam Gallu?',", Chris says. "He had bought some of dad's productions way back in the early fifties and vividly remembered him."

Chris is involved in a variety of community activities.

He and Terri have two sons, Christopher (born 1970) and Joshua (born 1973).

KMEO AM-FM
Phoenix, Arizona

Sign On: Began broadcasting February 1958 as AM station, added FM in 1964. Purchased by Scripps-Howard Broadcasting in May 1980.
Highlights: AM station, originally KUEQ, has consistently been "good music" station. FM station, originally KEPI, signed on as a classical music station, but financial difficulties caused it to go dark. It returned to air as KMEO-FM and simulcast the KUEQ-AM beautiful music format. KUEQ-AM call letters were changed to KMEO-AM. Stations' ownership included Media Horizons, Inc., and B & D Broadcasting prior to the Scripps-Howard purchase. Since Scripps-Howard took stations over combined audience ratings of both stations ahead of prime Phoenix competition for first time in years.

GENERAL MANAGER
Stephen C. Wrath

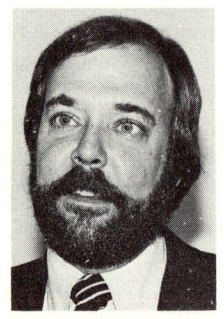

STEVE WRATH went from San Francisco to Washington, D.C. to speak and promptly wound up with a job offer in Hawaii.

That was in 1974, when Steve was general sales manager of K101, a San Francisco FM radio station. His speech was on how to sell FM radio.

"My talk was received far more enthusiastically than I could have anticipated," Steve says, "and there were a number of immediate job offers, but the one from Hawaii just jumped out at me."

So Steve packed up his wife and five children and headed for Waikikiland.

A native of Oak Park, Illinois (born April 14, 1943), Steve had come from a broadcast background. His father ran the Headley-Reed rep firm (now H-R) and during most of Steve's growing-up years, he was exposed to the life of selling and buying radio.

"Dad used to take me to the office, on sales trips with him, and he even had me listen to demo tapes of the radio stations he represented," Steve says. "That, combined with long conversations with station executives who used to stay overnight at our Oak Park home, gave me some early insight into the business."

SO IT WAS NOT entirely surprising that after a year of "digging ditches" after high school graduation, Steve decided to go to college and major in broadcasting.

"All my friends were heading for Arizona, and that seemed like an ideal complete change, so I went to Tempe and majored in broadcasting at Arizona State University," he says.

In college he had plenty of radio exposure: afternoon announcer on the school radio station, and program director. He courted and married and became a father while he was in college, as well.

After graduation in 1966, he landed a job at D'Arcy Advertising in Chicago as a media buyer. He is quick to credit his father's extensive contacts for that particular career move. "Let's face it, without my father's contacts I never would have been able to hook up with D'Arcy right out of college," Steve says. His reasoning for looking for a media buyer's position gives some sharp insight into Steve's grasp of the business: "I knew that I wanted to sell radio, but I also knew that if I was going to sell it, as my father had, and sell it well, I had to be able to know how to buy it first."

THE D'ARCY EXPERIENCE was followed by a job selling radio time ("I was ready by then," he says) at KYNO radio in Fresno, California.

Then came a crisis-style father-son conversation, after two weeks on the job, that Steve still vividly remembers.

"I was out on the street in Fresno with no list for two weeks, trying to do some selling. It was 115 degrees and I didn't like the weather or the job at that point. I called my father, who was working in San Francisco, and asked him if he could help me get out of my situation and into media buying there."

Steve's father offered his son some very specific advice.

"He told me that yes, he could help me to find a position in San Francisco, but more importantly, if I really wanted to be a success in radio, I was going to have to stick it out and learn right where I was working then. It was the best favor he could have done me."

Not only did Steve stick it out, but in three years when KYNO decided to put an FM station on the air Steve's performance had been so impressive that he was made station manager.

TWO YEARS LATER in 1971 came a move to San Francisco, as general sales manager of K101, later the speech at the NAB convention and the move to Hawaii.

In Hawaii, Steve was vice president and general manager of two radio stations, KPOI and KHSS. He stayed for three years but found that the adage "a beautiful place to live but an impossible place to make a living" was extremely applicable to Hawaii.

From the islands Steve, now divorced, moved back to Phoenix as general sales manager of KMEO-AM and KMEO-FM. That was 1977 and a year later he became vice president.

When Scripps-Howard took over the company in May 1980, he was named general manager.

Steve has a new wife, Lory, whom he met in Hawaii and they bought a new house and spend all their spare time remodeling it from top to bottom. Steve's five children are Jody (born 1965), Julie (born 1967), Steve Jr. (born 1969) and twin boys Mike and Jeff (born 1973).

WBSB-FM
Baltimore, Maryland

Sign On: Went on air on March 1, 1941.

Highlights: Purchased by Scripps-Howard Broadcasting April 25, 1980. At time of purchase, station's call letters had been WITH-FM, a virtually dormant factor in highly competitive Baltimore broadcast market.

Call letters changed to WBSB-FM and station began major Baltimore-oriented promotion, "Baltimore's Best". In this promotion, city salutes citizens for civic contribution and WBSB salutes winners on hourly basis, continuing salutes on Sunday mornings with interviews, etc.

Has given new energy to its music, personalities, news and other promotion, placing it in a highly visible position in Baltimore market.

GENERAL MANAGER
James P. Fox

ON HIS FIRST JOB Jim Fox went to work at three in the morning. He was a teenager helping his father, a produce dealer in Chicago. "I had to get to the railroad dock to unload the fruit which arrived at 3 a.m. Produce is highly perishable. I had to hustle to get the stuff ready for that day's market."

Jim, born in Chicago November 19, 1936, didn't develop any real hankering to go into the produce business. He spent only two summers on the dock.

He found his direction at the University of Illinois at Champaign. He had a fancy about being a newscaster and involved himself with the college radio station WILL. One assignment was to review on a weekly program editorials from newspapers around the country.

"I took editorials from a wide range of papers, and analyzed how they felt about a certain topic," says Jim. "It was an unusual approach and caught the attention of a radio station in Sterling, Illinois. They offered me a job as news director when I graduated."

BUT, JIM WHO had just married his college sweetheart, Roberta Goldstein, turned down the job. Instead he signed up for the Army National Guard and while waiting to begin his six months of duty, learned how to sell—Fuller brushes. He ended up as a skip tracer for a loan company.

When the Army stint was over, Jim sought a broadcast job and got on as a salesman for Chicago's WBEE, a Rollins Broadcasting radio station. He became a smooth salesman. He tackled all prospects, even the one the station had never been able to crack—Pepsi Cola.

Jim sold it. "It was a real breakthrough for the station, and for me as a salesman."

But being a salesman at a small station was no bed of roses. Jim not only had to sign up an account, he had to write the copy, and collect the money. He did that for two years.

"A friend told me I'd make a good *rep*," says Jim. "I really wasn't sure what a *rep* was." He found out, and took a job (1961) with Venard, Rintoul and McConnell, representing radio stations all over the country.

AFTER TWO YEARS he went with HR Representatives in Chicago followed by five years with Metromedia in Metro Radio Sales.

In 1970 he moved to Philadelphia to become general sales manager at radio station WIP. Four years later he went to Atlanta as vice president and district manager of another station rep group, McGavren Guild.

One station his group represented was Baltimore's WBAL, which hired him in 1975 as general sales manager. WBAL added an FM station and he served as general sales manager of both.

Jim joined Scripps-Howard in early 1980 when the organization took over WITH-FM and it became WBSB.

There are three Fox children: Michael (born in 1959), Cathi (1961) and Tracy (1966). The two older children are in college and taking radio and television courses.

Jim is a runner. He does four to six miles every day. When does he run? "Early in the morning," says Jim, "but definitely not at any 3 a.m.!"

SECTION NINE

Historical Highlights

Spotlighting Interesting,
And Often Significant,
Events From Our
Life and
Times

A Chronological Look At Scripps-Howard

With Typical Illustrations, Mostly Old, From The Archives

1878—November 2: Edward Willis Scripps, twenty-four years old, started Cleveland *Penny Press,* with $10,000 borrowed from elder brothers who owned Detroit newspaper.

1880—July 31: Branched out to St. Louis, starting *The Chronicle,* a disaster from start. He let it become a chronic invalid and drain him until it was sold in 1908.

1881—November: EWS, bothered by bronchial ailment, took sister Ellen and began year-and-a-half tour of Europe and Mediterranean.

1883—January 1: EWS acquired control of Cincinnati *Penny Post* from his brother James, who had purchased it in 1881.

June: EWS returned to United States from Europe.

1890—September 2: Changed name of *Penny Post,* to *The Cincinnatti Post.*

September 15: Started *The Kentucky Post*, across Ohio River from Cincinnati.

September-October: Created Scripps-McRae League to run his newspapers.

December: EWS visited California, bought desert acreage near San Diego and began eight-year building of Miramar ranch.

1892—June 3: EWS acquired his first paper on Pacific Coast, *The San Diego Sun.*

1895—March: Started the *Los Angeles Record.*

1896—December 23: Acquired the *Kansas City World.*

1899—February 25: Started *Seattle Star*

September 21: Started the *Akron Press.*

1900—April 11: Started the *Chicago Press.*

1902—June 2: Started NEA service.

June 7: Acquired the *Des Moines News.*

November 7: Started the *Spokane Press.*

1903—March 21: Started the *San Francisco News.*

June 8: Acquired *Toledo News-Bee.*

December 21: Started *Tacoma Times.*

1904—July 2: Acquired *Columbus Citizen.*

November 21: Started *Sacramento Star.*

1905—August 31: Started *Fresno Tribune.*

1906—April 26: Started *Denver Express.*

July 2: Started *Evansville Press.*

July 21: EWS purchased Publisher's Press; merged with Scripps-MacRae Press Association and Scripps News Associations into United Press, though this did not become effective until June 21, 1907.

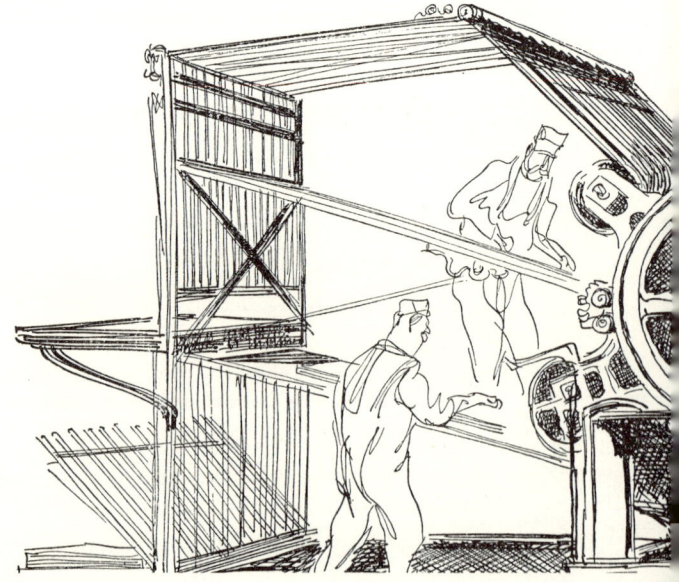

Second-hand Hoe press E. W. S

HISTORICAL HIGHLIGHTS

September 1: Started *Pueblo Sun.*

September 10: Started *Terre Haute Post.*

September 18: Started *Dallas Dispatch.*

September 29: Started *Portland News.*

October 1: Started *Oklahoma News.*

November 1: Started *Memphis Press.*

December 1: Started *Nashville Times.*

EDITOR'S NOTE—These start-ups are listed merely to give a glimpse of E. W. Scripps's vitality in launching new papers. Over the years he and his associates founded at least 32 papers and acquired fifteen. It is not possible to list them all, and their varied fates here. For an interesting roster of starts, acquisitions, kills and sales of Scripps papers see Appendix B. *I Protest, Selected Disquisitions of E. W. Scripps,* ed. Oliver Knight (University of Wisconsin Press, 1966). Another flurry similar to the 1906 expansion took place in 1921-22.

1907—June 21: EWS grouped his press services to form United Press.

August 1: Acquired *Berkeley Independent.*

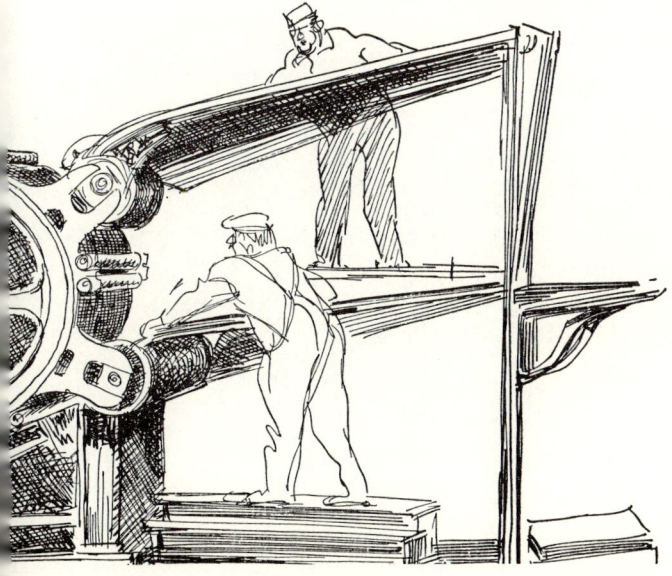

...t to launch his first newspaper

Sketch by Lou Darvas

City-copy desk of The Cincinnati Post in 1907. O. O. McI

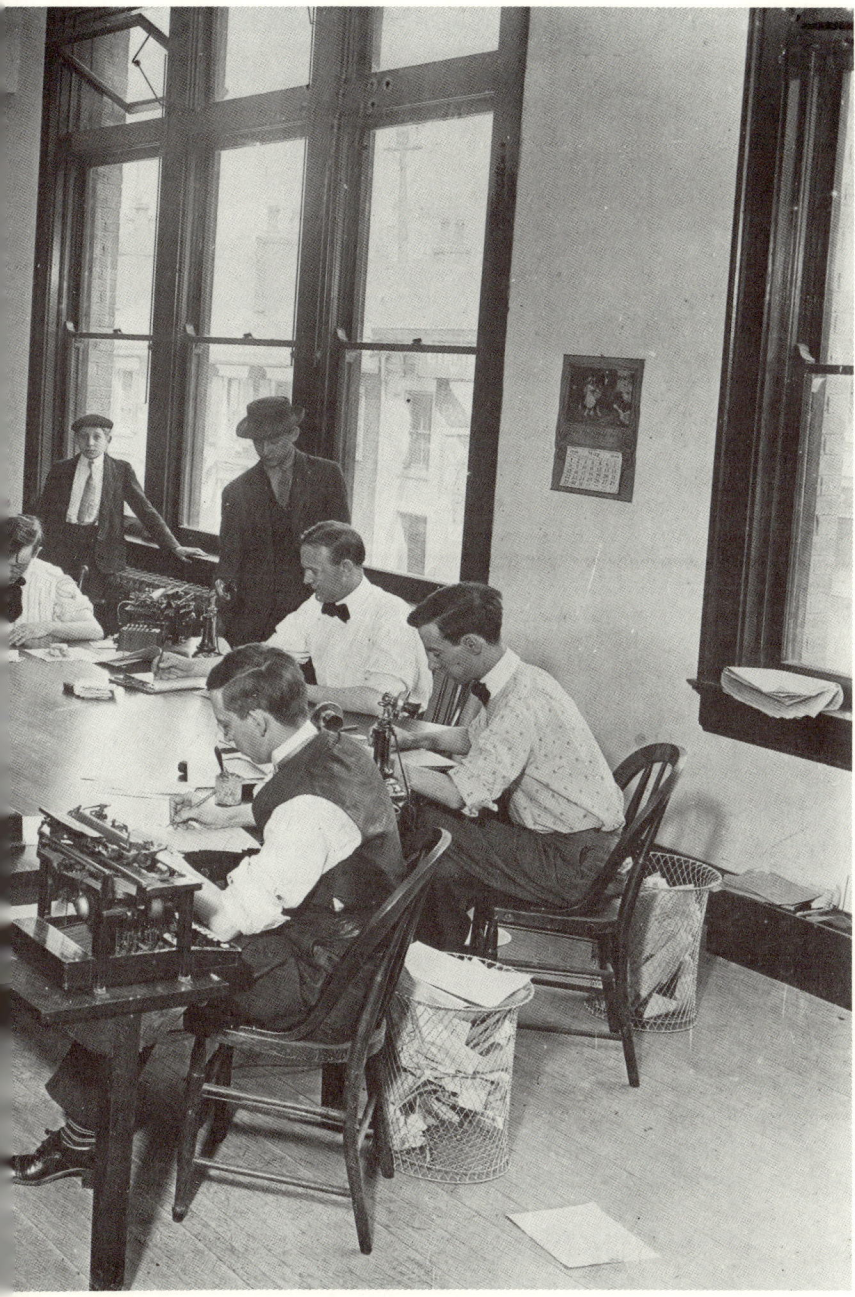

seated at 1 o'clock) was city editor, and later famous New York columnist.

1908—**February:** EWS "retired" turning over business management to son Jim, twenty-two years old, but keeping hand in with his editors.

1909—May 3: Started *Oakland Mail.*

1911—September 25: Started *Houston Press.*

September 28: Started *Chicago Daybook.*

1912—May 11: Started *Philadelphia News-Post.*

1917—EWS went to Washington to supervise coverage and editorial treatment of World War I. Jim became angry over EWS's insistence that Robert P. Scripps become editor-in-chief (and because of other business differences), broke with his father and used his and associates' stock positions to break off five West Coast papers and the *Dallas Dispatch.*

November: EWS suffered stroke and went to Florida to recuperate, learned pleasure of living on yacht, which he did most of the rest of his life.

1920—EWS withdrew from management of his many enterprises, and made Robert P. Scripps and Roy W. Howard responsible for editorial and business direction, respectively.

1921—January 21: Started *Birmingham Post.*

June 13: Started *Norfolk Post.*

October 3: Started *Fort Worth Press.*

November 8: Started *The Washington Daily News.*

November 21: Started *The Knoxville News.*

1922—United Feature Service was organized (and a year later United Newspictures, forerunner of Acme Newspictures, was started).

February 1: Acquired *Youngstown Telegram.*

May 27: Acquired *Indianapolis Times.*

August 21: Started *El Paso Post.*

June 22: Scripps-Howard motto "Give light and the people will find their own way" first used. (Lighthouse emblem added in May 1927.)

November 3: Change of name from Scripps-McRae to Scripps-Howard announced. RWH assumed joint editorial direction of papers with Robert P. Scripps.

November 22: Started *Baltimore Post.*

1923—July 27: Acquired *Pittsburgh Press.*

September 24: Acquired *New Mexico State Tribune.*

HISTORICAL HIGHLIGHTS

Ray Clapper, one of the best Washington reporters in the 30s

Ernie Pyle writing a column in his Albuquerque den

Lyndon Johnson introducing Jim Lucas to report at the White House to U.S. officials on the Vietnam war

RPS with Bob Paine on San Diego dock, 1937

Edward J. Meeman returning from 1955 NATO conference

Robert P. Scripps's 89-foot ketch "Novia del Mar"

HISTORICAL HIGHLIGHTS 387

1926—**March 12:** EWS died on his yacht *Ohio* in Monrovia Bay, Liberia, Africa and was buried at sea.

During this year: *Knoxville Sentinel* purchased and merged into *Knoxville News-Sentinel*. *Denver News and Times* purchased and consolidated with *Express* into *Rocky Mountain News*. *Memphis News-Scimitar* purchased and merged with *Press* into *Memphis Press-Scimitar*.

1927—**February 10:** Acquired *The New York Telegram*. (Bought *The World* February 27, 1931 and merged the two papers.)

1933—**February 18:** *Tribune* and *Journal* combined business operations to form Albuquerque Publishing Company.

1935—**August 24:** Scripps-Howard established Continental Radio. (Name was changed May 17, 1937 to Scripps-Howard Radio, Inc., and December 31, 1961 to Scripps-Howard Broadcasting Company.)

August 31: Acquired radio station WFBE in Cincinnati and changed call letters to WCPO.

October 11: Purchased radio WNOX, Knoxville.

1936—**August 31:** *El Paso Herald-Post* and *El Paso Times* combined business operations to form Newspaper Printing Corporation.

October 5: Acquired *The Commercial Appeal* in Memphis. Acquired radio station WMC in Memphis.

A television first—Red Barber and Van Patrick broadcast 1948 World Series over WEWS.

Washington staff in regular Friday huddle, circa early 1960s.

Editors grill Jimmy Carter in pre-election session in Washington bureau

HISTORICAL HIGHLIGHTS

1938—March 2: Robert P. Scripps died aboard his yacht off Baja California.

December 31: *Evansville Press* combined business operations with *Evansville Courier*.

1939—December 30: *Press-Scimitar* and *Commercial Appeal* merged into Memphis Publishing Company.

1947—December 17: WEWS-TV started in Cleveland, Ohio.

1948—December 11: WMC-TV went on the air in Memphis.

1949—July 26: WCPO-TV went on the air in Cincinnati.

1953—January 1: Charles E. Scripps became chairman of the board of The E. W. Scripps Company.

1957—October 1: *Knoxville News-Sentinel* and *Journal* joint operating agreement became effective.

1958—May 24: International News Service and picture service facilities joined with United Press to form United Press International.

1960—January 23: *Cleveland News* purchased and merged with *Cleveland Press*.

1961—December 27: WPTV, West Palm Beach, acquired.

1962—August 15: Scripps-Howard Foundation incorporated.

1964—November 20: Roy W. Howard died.

1965—April 12: Acquired *Stuart* (Florida) *News*.

June 4: Acquired *Hollywood* (Florida) *Sun-Tattler*.

1966—April 24: *New York World Telegram* and *Sun* merged with *Journal-American* and *Herald Tribune* to become *World Journal Tribune*. After many difficulties the new paper was suspended May 5, 1967.

1970—August 12: Acquired *San Juan Star*.

December 31: Purchased *KTEW* in Tulsa, and changed name to *KJRH* on July 14, 1980.

1972—July 12: *Washington Daily News* sold to *The Washington Star*.

1973—December 28: Purchased Fullerton Publishing Company *(Daily News Tribune)*.

1976—June 30: UPI broadcast advisory board formed.

Could Odd McIntrye and his pals from the 1907 picture have ever imagin

the modern newsroom? Shown here is part of The Commercial Appeal's.

1977—January 1: New York executive offices moved to Cincinnati.

May 10: Acquired *Grant County News* and *The Leader of Boone County*.

September 23: *Cincinnati Post* and *Enquirer* agreed on joint operating agreement. (Effective December 6, 1979.)

October 28: Scripps-Howard Broadcasting purchased KMBA, Kansas City.

1978—June 14: United Media Enterprises, consolidation of NEA and UFS, became effective.

July 1: Started *Campbell County News*.

October 1: Purchased weeklies of Southern California Publishing Company, Pico Press, Inc., and San Gabriel Valley Publications.

November 1: Purchased web press establishment in Louisville.

1979—March 1: Purchased principal weeklies in Louisville, *Jeffersonian, The Voice*, and *Reporter*. In March 1980 acquired *Southwest Advertiser* and changed name to Southwest News.

September 16: $10 million UPI Technical Systems Center opened in Dallas.

November 1: Purchased *Kentucky Standard*.

1980—February 1: Acquired Cordovan Corporation, publishers of books, magazines and business newspapers.

October 31: *The Cleveland Press,* 102 years after founding and a decade of being in serious financial straits, sold to a Cleveland industrialist.

In early Fifties, Dorothy Fuldheim begins long career as WEWS news commentator.

Early radio: WCPO d.j. Paul Dixon working from studio at home also baby-sits.

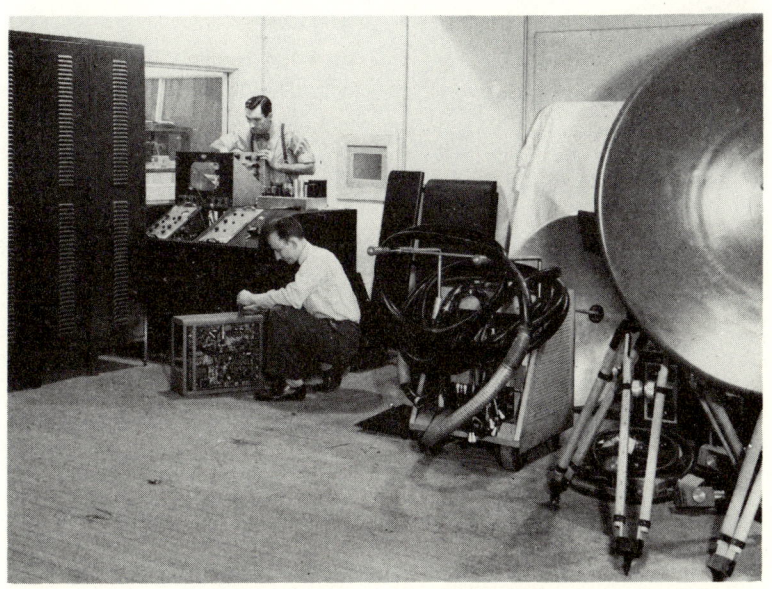

Long before era of solid state, Scripps-Howard engineers adjust broadcast gear.

An early "remote" on television:
WEWS covers Saint Patrick's Day parade in Cleveland.

Index

Acme Newspictures, 191, 197
Adams, Null, 276
Advertising, policies, standards, 41-43
Alahambra Post Advocate, 311
Alaska and Hawaii, admission of, 12
Albuquerque Tribune, 38, 144, 187, 218-220
Alsup, George, xv
Arena, Susan, 312-313, family 313
Arkansas Gazette, 141
Associated Press, 60
Aston, Frank, 208
Atlanta Business Journal, 309

Baillie, Hugh, 193
Baker & Hostetler, 162-163
Balfe, Barbara (Howard), 94
Bartholomew, Frank, 193
Baskin, John, 164, 330
Basset, Gene, 177-178, family 178
Baumgartner, Bruce O., 166
Beaton, Roderick, 193-194, family 194, 215
Beatty, Thomas, 196
Bell-McClure Syndicate, 197, 200
Bellevue *Gazette,* 346
Bennett, John K., 187
Berkley-Small, Inc., 7, 117, 206, 207
Bickel, Karl A., 92, 193, 322, 323
Birmingham Post Herald, 183, 185, 187, 222
Blabey, Eugene H., 195
Blatchford, Nick, 295
Blosser, Merrill, 201
Bloyd, James, 330, 337-339, family 338-339
Boyce, R. H., 173, 178
Braddick, Kenneth Jr., 196
Breslin, Jimmy, 201
Britten, Milton R., 276-278, family 277
Brophy, Robert E., 6, 150-152, family 151
Broun, Heywood, 199
Brown, Robert A., 207
Brucken, Robert M., 166
Brydon, Donald J., 194
Burleigh, William R., 215, 229-232, family 232, 238, 255
Burlingame, John N., 163
Burrows, Dan, 246
Butts, Hal, 204

Caldwell, Jacques, 137, 214, family 215
Callaghan, Michael W., 329, 346-347, family 347
Campbell County News, 312-313
Campbell, Richard R., 215, 240-242, family 242
Castellini, Daniel J., 6, 129-131, family 130-131, 195, 215, 330
Carmack, George, 122, 247
Carroll, Gene, 348
Catton, Bruce, 201
Central office, 101, 131
Cervenak, Edward D., 329, 330, 348-350, family 349-350
Channel 41, 363
Chicago Day Book, 208
Cincinnati Enquirer, 235, 236, 339, 340
Cincinnati *Penny Paper,* 50
Cincinnati Post, 50, 129, 147, 178, 187, 209, 228, 235, 237, 284, 323, 335
Clabes, Judith G., 258-259, family 259
Clapper, Ray, 29, award, 184, 199
Clark, Hamilton, 193
Clarvoe, Frank, 252
Cleminshaw, Charles H., 166
Cleveland *Penny Press,* 66
Cleveland Press, 9, 50, 86, 88, 103, 136, 187, 201, 220, 241, 242, 331
Clifford, Louis, 331
"Clip Tips," 40
Cochran, Negley D., 208
Cochran, Randy, xv
Code of ethics, 44
Collins, Stanley, 234
Cook, William, and Theodore Granik, 351
Columbus Citizen-Journal, 39, 187, 240, 244, 268
Commerce Tribune, 311
Commercial Appeal, The, 31, 123, 187, 223, 257, 279, 324, 327
Concern editorial policies, 13
Condo, A.D., 201
Condo, Jerry, 187
Continental Radio, 92, 93, 322, 323
Cordovan Corporation, 7, 307-310
Courier Highlights, 317
Crane, Roy, 201
Crawford, Gordon, 311-312, family 312
Crennen, Robert E., 196

395

396   INDEX

Culbertson, Ed, 102
Culbertson, Margaret (Scripps), 71
Cunningham, Morris, 187
Cutler, B.J., 6, 138-140, family 140

Daily News Tribune, Fullerton, 39, 187, 260
Daley, Roger, 273-274, family 273-274
Dallas Dispatch, 60
Dallas-Fort Worth Business, 309
Darr, James F., 195
Data Feature, 204
Data News, 204
Dataway, Inc., 157
Davis, Glenn, 326
Day, Col. William M., 147
Dembski, Gregory A., 243-244, family 244
Denny, Ludwell, 123
Denver Express, 245
Denver News, 245
Denver Post, 249
Detroit Evening News, 65
Dillman, Grant, 195
Doerr, Bob, xv
Downing, George, 166
Duke, Robert, 187
Dwyer, Vince, 175
Dye, Sherman, 126, 162-163

Eary, Ralph E., xv, 6, 146, 148-150, family 149, 158
East Los Angeles Gazette, 311
East Los Angeles/Montebello Progress, 311
East Los Angeles Tribune, 311
Eisenhower, Dwight D., 72
Elfstrom, Edgar, 260
El Paso Herald-Post, 187, 251
El Paso Times, 251
"Epitaph, An," 75
Epperson, Joseph, 325, 349
Eskey, Kenneth, 179
Estlow, Edward W., 6, 7, 113-118, family 117, 123, 128, 135, 137, 149, 152
Ethics, code of, 44
Evansville Courier, 255
Evansville Press, 95, 122, 175, 184, 187, 229, 230, 255, 258, 259, 281
Evansville *Sunday Courier and Press,* 258

Fagan, Larry, 288
Feldmann, John L., 233-235, family 233-234

Feuille, Frank III, 251
Fink, Timothy G., 207
Finnegan, Patrick, 215
Fischetti, John, 201
Fletcher, William W., 249-250, family 250
Ford, Frank R., xiv, xv, 83, 255
Fort Worth Press, 86, 104, 119, 120, 121, 208
Foster, Jack, 245
Foster, James E., 173, 179
Fox, James P., 329, 375-376, family 376
Fox Movietone, 192
Friedenberg, Walter, 173, 180
Fuldheim, Dorothy, 348

Gallu, Christopher T., 329, 370-371, family 371
General counsel, 7, 162-166
General management and staff, 113-166
"Give light and the people will find their own way," 38
Gold, Jack, xv
Goldenberg, Gene, 173, 180
Gordon, Robert, 215, 329, 330, 336, 351-353, family 352, "Mr. Clean," 352
Grant County News, 312-313
Gray, Bob, 307-310, family 310
Greene, Frederick J., 195
Grehl, Michael, 224, 255, 256, 257, 280-282, family 281
Greiner, Morris E. Jr., 215, 329, 330, 354-356, family 355-356
Groves, Ray, 195
Guidry, Annie Lou (Hanna), 121

Hailey, William, 245
Hamann, Leroy, 196
Hanna, Gordon, 6, 31, 119-125, family 123, 210, 255, 256, 281
Hanrahan, Jim, 322, 323, 325, 326
Harbrecht, Douglas, 187
Harden, Patrick, 187
Harkavy, Melvin A., 263-264, family 264
Harper, J. C., 255
Harris, Eleanor Sallee (Howard), 94
Hartmann, Robert H., 6, 134-137, family 135-136, 155, 269, 292
Haskins & Sells, 126, 130, 132, 133
Hawkins, Margaret Scripps, 85
Hawkins, W. W., 83, 84, 193
"Hawthorn," 90
Hendin, David, 202-203, 215
Hendrich, Robert C., 206-207
Herblock, 201

INDEX 397

Herzog, James P., 173, 181
Hevel, F. Ben, 329, 330, 360-362, family 362
Hewitt, Alfred E., 261-262, family 262
Highland Herald, 314
Hippeau, Claude, 195
Historical Highlights, 377-394
Hodges, Paul, 348
Hollander, Dick, 295
Hollywood Sun-Tattler, 184, 187, 265, 266, 267
Hope, Paul, 181
Horseman magazine, 307
Houston Business Journal, 308
Houston Press, 121, 122, 143, 144
Howard, Jack R., 6, 31, 83, 90-94, family 94, 117, 123, 142, 143, 321, 324, 325, 328, 329, 330
Howard, Roy W., 4, 72, 75, 77-84, 91, 92, 94, 189, 193,
  and Margaret Rohe Fund, 212, 322
Howard, Michael, 94, 248
Howard, Pamela, 94
Howard, Margaret Rohe, 94
Huey, Johnie L., 207
Hughs, Travis M., 196
Humi, Julius B., 195

Independent News Alliance, 200
Indianapolis News, 77, 78
Indianapolis Times, 79, 92, 95, 175, 177, 183, 226
In-House Awards, 40

Jacksboro *Gazette,* 120
Janssen, Richard J., 330, 344-346, family 346
Jeavons, Norman S., 164
Jeffersonian, 324
Jet Cargo News, 308
Johnson, Lyndon, 12
Jupiter Courier-Highlights, 302

Kaff, Albert E., 195
Kelly, Bob J., 195
Kentucky Post, 39, 131, 187, 233, 236
Kentucky Standard, 315, 316
Kentucky World, 233
KEMO AM-FM, 329, 346, 372, 374
KETW, 329
Kirkman, Donald G., 173, 182
KJRH, 329, 360, 362
Klingler, Ed., 230
KMBA, 329, 362, 365
Knap, Ted, 173, 182

Knoxville Journal, 274
Knoxville News-Sentinel, 153, 176, 187, 270, 284, 323
Knue, Paul F., 236-239, family 237, 239
KTEW, 362
KTUL, 252, 361

Lamb, Lawrence E., M.D., 201
Leader of Boone County, 312, 313
Lee, C. D., 193
Lee, Robert W., 252-254, family 253
Lee, William J., 6, 155-158, family 155-157
Leech, E. T., 290
LeGrand, Duard, 224
Leser, Lawrence A., 6, 125-128, family 128, 194, 215, 330
Leukart, Richard H. II, 165
Lewis, Wally, 116
Lindsay, Powell E., 176-177, family 177
Litfin, Richard A., 196
Lockhart, Jack, 31, 142
Long, Ray, 79
Looney, Ralph, 220, 246-248, family 246-247
Los Angeles business paper, 309
Lowenshon, Naoma, 215
Lucas, Jim, 90, 141, 213
Lynch, James, 200
Lyon, F. W. (Bill), 194
Lyons, Ernest E., 298-299
Lytle, J. Stewart, 173, 183

Maag-Sakai, Laurel, 39
Mack, Ray, 135, 136, 158, 269
Magee, Carl C., 38
Manis, Jimmy E. Jr., 6, 153-155, family 154
Mantle, John E., 196
Mathes, Bob, xv
Matthews, William, 312, 314, family 315
Mauldin, Bill, 199
McCall, G.W. (Bill), 265
McEachran, Angus, 222-225, family 224-225
McFarland, Kermit, 140
McFeatters, Ann Carey, 173, 184
McFeatters, Dale, 184
McGovern, Senator George, 13
McKay, Lois Ann "Beano" (Scripps), 104
McRae, Col. Milton A., 4
Meeman, Edward, award, 213, 270, 272, 276

Memphis Press-Scimitar, 40, 187, 271, 272, 275, 276, 324
Memphis Publishing Company, 146, 283
Menezes, Luis, 196
Methods and policies, xi
Metz, Robert Roy, 197-202
Metz, W.H., 226-227, family 227
Meyer, Matt, 214, 215
Meyers, Donald, 329, 366-368, family 368
Miami Business Journal, 310
Millett, Ralph L. Jr., 271-272, family 272
Millett, Ralph L. Sr., 271
Miller, Loye, 272, 277
Miramar, 70, 85, 101, 102, 107
Mirror, The, 314
"Miss Ellen's Miscellany," 65, 201
Moffett, George B., 206
Montebello News, 311
Monterey Park Californian, 311
Monterey Park Progress, 311
Mooring, Frank, 187
Morrison, Frank, 292
Murphy, Betty Southard, 164

National Spelling Bee, 144
NEA, 7, 66, 197, 201
New Deal, 12
New Mexico State Tribune, 38
News, what is, 24-25; how to write, 26-29
Newton, Bill, 90
New York World, 79
New York World-Telegram, 202, 214
Niehaus, William R., 6, 159-161, family 160
Nixon, Richard M., 12, 13
North American Newspaper Alliance, 197, 200
Novatney, John F. Jr., 164
Novia del Mar, 75

O'Connell, Robert J., 290-292, family 292
Ohio Scripps-McRae papers, 79
Ohio, EWS yacht, 61
Oklahoma News, 88, 95
Ollinger, W. James, 165
O'Rourke, John, 295
Osmundson, Dean L., 329, 368-369, family 369
Overton, Jim, 301-302, family 302, 317

Paffen, Robert P., 195

Paine, Robert F., 50, 67
Parker, George (Deac), 87, 88, 90, 103, 172
Payette, William C., 198, 199
Payne, John, 196
Pearson, Drew, 199
Pegler, Westbrook, 199
Penny Press, 50, 51
Perris, Donald L., 6, 330, 331-333, family 333, 347, 371
Peters, F.R., 255
Philadelphia Daily News, 134
Philadelphia News-Post, 70
Phipps, John H., 328
Phoenix Business Journal, 310
Pico Press, Inc., 311
Pico Rivera News, 311
Pittsburgh Post-Gazette, 154, 287
Pittsburgh Press, 39, 136, 138, 139, 141, 154, 156, 157, 184, 185, 187, 287
Port Arthur News, 121
Porter, Sue, 40, 208-210, family 209
Powelson, Richard, 187
Powers, Frank, 117, 273
Poythress, Eugene, 196
Price, Charles T., 165
Principles and policies, 13-23; government, 14, inflation, 14, taxes and fiscal policies, 15, energy, 15, conservation, 16, transportation, 16, cities, 16, crime and courts, 17, gun control, 17, education, 18, science and technology, 18, health and safety, 19, aged, the, 19, welfare, 19, illegal aliens, 20, equal rights, 20, business and labor, 20, agriculture, 21, electoral process, 21, Puerto Rico, 21, probate laws, 21, international relations, 21-22, defense, 22, Middle East, 22-23, China, 23, population control, 23, newspaper shield law, 23, right to know, 23, ethics, 44
Promotion, Good, 36-40, cheesecake, 37, public service, 37
Publisher's Press, 80
Pyle, Ernie, 199, memorial fund, 213, award, 213

Regalbuto Robert R., 329, 330, 357-359, family 359
Reporter, The, 314
Rice, Gordon, 194

Index

Richert, Earl, 6, 95-96, 122, 138, 172, 230, 255
"Ring Around the Rosie," 348
Rocky Mountain News, 94, 107, 114, 116, 141, 146, 149, 152, 157, 174, 180, 187, 245
Rosemead/South San Gabriel Californian, 311
Royhab, Ron, 178
Ruark, Robert, 90, 199
Rutman, Larry, 199

San Diego Business Journal, 310
San Francisco business paper, 309
San Francisco News, 67, 107, 186, 226, 252
San Francisco News-Call Bulletin, 253
San Gabriel Progress, 311
San Gabriel Valley Publications, 311
San Juan Star, 293, 297
San Juan World Journal, 295, 297
St. Louis Post-Dispatch, 79
Sandburg, Carl, 201
Sanford, Bruce W., 165
Sante Fe Springs News, 311
Schazin, Alberto J., 196
Scherrer, W. L., 215
Schneider, Charles, 276
Schottelkotte, Albert J., 330, 336, 339-341, family 341
Schulz, Charles, 199, award, 213
Schwartz, Berl, 185
Scripps award, 213
Scripps, Charles E., 7, 56, 102-108, family 106
Scripps, Edward Willis, 3, 5, 9, 47-63, 82, 83, 147, 172
Scripps, The E.W. Company, 5, 6, 7, 85, 94
Scripps, E.W. II (Ted), 107-110, family 108
Scripps, Edward Willis McLean, 69
Scripps, Ellen, 65-66, 200
Scripps, Robert Paine, 5, 50, 69-75, 82, 172, 215
Scripps, Robert P. Jr. (Bob), 5, 83, 99-102, family 102
Scripps, James E., 228
Scripps, James Mogg, 50
Scripps, Jim, 69, 71
Scripps, John, 69
Scripps, Julia Anne, EWS letter to, 62-63
Scripps, The Edward W. Trust, 4

Scripps Trustees, 99-110
Scripps-Howard Broadcasting Company, 7, 93, 94, 321-330, 335, 341-347, 356, 362
Scripps-Howard Foundation, 40, 90, 143, 211-215, awards, 212
Scripps-Howard News, 40, 144, 208-210
SHNA, 90, 95, 122, 172
Scripps-Howard News Service (SHNS), 137, 171, 175
Scripps-Howard Radio Company, 93, 324, 328
SHP, Inc., 314-315
Scripps-Howard Web Press Company, 314-315
Scripps-McRae, 4, 82, 245
Scripps-McRae Press Association, 67, 80
Sharp, Tom, 251
Shapiro, Joseph, 187
Shaw, Norman, 241
Slavick, Hank, 328
Smith, Dorman, 201
Smith, James E., 342-344, family 343
Smith, John P., 322, 325
Smith, O.L., 325
Sorrells, John H., iii, xx, xiv, xv, 31, 85-87, 93, letter to Ted Scripps, 167-168
Sorrels, William W., 255-258, family 258
Southern California Publishing Company, 311-312
South San Gabriel/Rosemead Progress, 311
Southwest News, 314
Steele, Jack, 139, 175
Steif, Bill, 173, 186
Stephens, J. Boyd, 208
Stevens, Will Hawley, 298
Stevenson, H.L., 194
Stokes, Tom, 199
Stolberg, David, 6, 31, 140-143, family 142, 215
Stone, Walker, 89-90, 95, 172, award, 213
Strimbu, Victor Jr., 164
Stuart News, 184, 187, 298-300, 317
Tanner, William, 219-221, family 220-221
Taylor, Homer E. Jr, 6, 145-147, family 145-146
Tele-Log, 204
Texas Fisherman, 308

Thackery, Jonathan E., 165
Thomas, John L. 164
Thomason, A. Mims, 193
Thomasson, Dan K., 171, 174-176, family 175, 177
Thompson, Alan R., 173, 186
Thompson, Berkley, 206
Thornton, Willis W., 147
Toledo News-Bee, 208
Toomajian, William M., 165
Townsend, Barney, 126
Tretter, Nancy, xv
Trimble, Vance H., xv., 239
Troan, John, 288-290, family 290
Trotter, George, 315-316, family 316
Turning on the light, 38
Turner, Harry, 187
Turney, Richard B., 165
TV Data, 204
TV Watch/Distributed Information Processing, 204-205
Tynan, Mike, 155
Typography, good, 31-35

United Feature Syndicate, 7, 197
United Media Enterprises, 7, 117, 197-205
Uncle Al Show, 336, 351
Uncle Jake's House, 348
Unifax II, 192
United Press, 4, 67, 72, 80, 92
United Press International, 7, 37, 110, 117, 188-196
UPI Data News, 173
UPITN, 192

Valley Post, 209
Van Bennekom, Pieter, 196
Vandercook, John, 67, 193
Viglucci, Andrew T., 294-295, family 295
Vincent, Margaret (Richert), 96
Virtue, John F., 196
Voice, The, 314

Wagner, James H., xv, 6, 143-144, family 144, 209, 215
Walters, Bob, and Martha Angle, 202
Washington bureau, 171, 174

Washington Calling, 185
Washington Daily News, 72, 89, 92, 94, 135, 141, 142, 172, 268, 295
Watters, Mortimer, 215, 323, 327, 330, 334-336, family 336
WBSB-FM, 329, 375, 376
WCPO, 323, 326, 327, 329, 334-336, 340, 351, 352, 362
WCUE, 343
Weaver, Don, 120
Weber, Thomas E. Jr., 299-300, family 299
Weingart, Mike, 308-310
Wentworth, Edward H., 266-267, family 267
Wessel, L. C., 127
Westergaard, Richard B., 323
Westergran, Ian, 196
Western Outfitter, 308
West Whittier Independent, 311
WEWS, 326, 332, 338, 342, 348
White, Paul D., 164
White, Ron, 149
Wilharm, John J. Jr., 165
Willenborg, Charlie, 233
Williams, J.R., 201
Williams, Joseph R. III, 282-286, family 285
Willis, Delbert, 208
Willison, Charles R., 207
WITH-FM, 329, 346
WJNO-TV, 357
WMC, 324, 328, 345, 359, 366
WMCT, 327, 328, 354, 356
WMPS, 325
WNOX, 92, 323-325, 329, 345, 370-371
Wolfzorn, E. John, 131-135, family 132
World Almanac, 197, 202, 347
World Journal Tribune, 202, 214
Wormington, Bob J., 329, 363-365, family 365
Wrath, Stephen C., 329, 372-374, family 374

Zerbe, John A. Jr., 296, 297, family 297
Ziefaing, Donald P., 164
Zorker, Donald C., 207

REF PN 4734 .S37 1981

Scripps-Howard News Service
WNOX, Knoxville
E. Paso Herald-Post
Memphis Press-Scimitar
Scripps-Howard News
KEMO-AM & FM, Phoenix
United Feature Syndicate
WBSB-FM, Baltimore
San Diego Business Journal
United Press
The Pittsburgh Press
San Francisco Business Journal
Daily News Tribune
Los Angeles Business Journal
WCPO-TV, Cincinnati
Kentucky Standard
Miami Business Journal
Columbus Citizen-Journal
The Courier-Highlights
WPTV, Palm Beach
Scripps-Howard Post-Herald
Birmingham Post-Herald
Grant
KJRH, Tulsa
The San Juan Star
Scripps-Howard Web Press Company
The Knoxville News-Sentinel
WMC/WMC-FM, Memphis
WEWS, Cleveland
Berkley-Small
NEA
VALUE QUALITY SERVICE